a dedicated follower of fashion

a
dedicated
follower
of
fashion
Holly
Brubach

Phaidon Press Limited
Regent's Wharf, All Saints Street, London N1 9PA

First published in 1999 © Phaidon Press Limited

Introduction and essays © 1999 Holly Brubach

ISBN 0 7148 3887 X

A CIP catalogue record for this book is available
from the British Library. Library of Congress Cataloging
in Publication Data available.

Design: 2x4, New York City

Printed in Hong Kong

For my mother and in memory of my father.

Introduction

One week he's in polka dots, the next week he's in stripes,
'Cause he's a dedicated follower of fashion...

Ray Davies, The Kinks, *"A Dedicated Follower of Fashion"*

ONCE THERE was a girl, growing up in a split-level house in suburban Pittsburgh, who loved clothes very much—too much, some would say. She made a deal with her mother: she would help with the grocery shopping if her mother would buy *Vogue*. She scrutinized its pages, studying the advertisements, memorizing the names of designers, acquiring a new vocabulary that featured words like "peplum" and "gazar." She planned her wardrobe with all the precision of a military campaign, saving up her allowance for months to buy an orange jersey dress from a trendy new shop called Paraphernalia. She listened to music by the Monkees, the Left Banke, and The Kinks, whose hit song lampooning an incurable clotheshorse like herself lends its title to this book.

"Don't your knees get cold?" the next-door neighbor once asked when she was wearing her perfectly cut red wool shorts with a beige cable-knit sweater and matching knee socks. "Isn't that awfully heavy?" her orthodontist remarked upon seeing her big new watch like the ones they were wearing on Carnaby Street. On these and other, similar occasions, she replied with a mumbled "no" and a withering look. Clearly, anyone who asked these kinds of questions didn't understand what clothes were for. Clothes were for announcing some inner truth to the world. Reluctantly and to her dismay, the girl came to the realization that this new language she was speaking—a visual argot, plain as day, as far as she was concerned—was to many people incomprehensible.

She learned French, in preparation for some far-off future set in Paris, the capital of fashion. Her grandmother taught her to sew, the better to approximate the clothes she saw in pictures. For the senior prom, she concocted a (to her mind) stunningly sophisticated ball gown, with a dove-gray velvet bodice, a sweeping silver moiré skirt, and a deep-plum-colored, self-fringed satin sash—

inspired by a Mainbocher dress, with its intimations of a world in which men owned their own tuxedos and women didn't do housework. Her classmates, in their white eyelet and pastel chiffon, must have been mystified. Her classmates nonetheless voted her "Most Likely to Succeed," in recognition perhaps of her dogged determination to participate in some larger world. Her aunt gave her a set of Samsonite luggage as a graduation present.

How did I get from these hometown beginnings to the front row of the fashion shows in Milan, Paris, and New York? In the retelling, stories take on an inevitability which in time supplants the state of confusion that prevailed as they unfolded. Retracing those steps in my mind, I'm reminded that the route was uncharted and indirect but highly scenic.

I arrived in fashion by way of a failed career as a dancer. As apprentice-ships go, this one proved not bad, and not unrelated. From an early age, I'd been contemplating the female body—the lines it etched as it moved through space, the gestures and positions that conveyed a certain elegance and grace, the best ways to present it, enhancing its innate beauty. Sidelined by an injury, I had taken up writing. Following the standard advice for beginners, I wrote about what I knew, which was dance. But it wasn't long before I realized that what I loved about dance was doing it, not writing about other people doing it. And so I set out in search of another subject.

I'm now persuaded that for any given writer, there are only a handful of subjects, and that they are established early on, in childhood. But at the time, the possibilities seemed endless, and not so obvious. For a while, I wrote what-ever came my way—assignments about music, art, travel, theater, sports.

And then, one day, it occurred to me: by writing about fashion, I could justify the inordinate amounts of money I spent on clothes. What I only half-jokingly referred to as "my shoe habit" would suddenly be legitimized. This was no self-indulgent whim; this was research. And so I began to set down on paper what I'd been thinking about all along—a subject I'd overlooked because, like other people, I'd presumed that it was beneath my notice. Intellectuals occasion-ally took it on when they felt like slumming. Costume historians decoded it, from the vantage point of the university. Fashion magazines addressed the con-verted. I wanted to do something else.

There is Fashion, I reasoned, and then there's fashion, and I wanted to cover them both. The former I considered to be the official version—the decrees designers and editors issued every season, emanating from the runway. The latter, to my mind, is what people actually wear, what makes them feel good about themselves. A businessman may claim to have no interest in "Fashion," but his sack suit from Brooks Brothers or his Hermès tie betrays his interest in "fashion" as it's played out in the workplace. In the clothes he wears, he declares himself, and his appearance is no less loaded with meaning than that of the most avid label queen.

I came to think of what I was doing as revolutionary and subversive, as if I were on a mission. Early feminists deplored fashion as an instrument of oppression. I saw it instead as an eloquent and delightful means of expression, and I resolved to persuade the world (especially men) of its validity.

At some point along the way, it occurred to me that fashion is in fact architecture's feminine counterpart. But whereas architecture has been revered and accorded a place in the history of art, fashion has been dismissed as inconsequential. Buildings, made of concrete and stone, are "permanent," while clothes, made of fabric, are ephemeral. Architecture's scale is public, while fashion's is intimate. Architecture is high-minded and serious; fashion, mindless and capricious.

Buildings and clothes are the primary components of our everyday landscape, and they embody the ideas and the attitudes of the time in which we live. It is, I believe, incumbent on every generation to remake the world in its own image. Alas, the courage and the effort required to invent a form for the present are so great that many designers give in to nostalgia and take refuge in the past. Over the course of the twenty years I've spent in fashion so far, every decade of this century (to say nothing of those before it) has been revived and rehashed at least twice.

One of my first jobs (appropriately enough) was at *Vogue*, where I wrote the sort of fashion captions that I had read so religiously when I was young; eventually, I graduated to feature articles. In 1983, I left to become a staff writer for *The Atlantic Monthly*. That transition taught me that the context in which an essay about fashion appeared could dramatically alter the way it was interpreted.

A "pro-fashion" statement in *Vogue* was presumed to be sheer propaganda, whereas the very same words took on credibility and weight simply by virtue of being published in a general-interest magazine. As for "anti-fashion" statements, *Vogue*, like other magazines of its kind, shrank from them, for fear of alienating advertisers. *The Atlantic*, however, having no fashion advertisers to speak of, had nothing to lose. As it turns out, writing about fashion is unlike writing about, say, film in this respect: in film, there is a tradition of serious criticism. A director may not be pleased that a critic doesn't like his movie, but he recognizes the critic's right to say so. In fashion that right is routinely called into question. Fashion is an art—and therefore deserving of museum retrospectives and thoughtful appraisals—as long as you're rhapsodizing about its sublime cut and craftsmanship, its ineffable glamour, its impeccable taste. But at the first discouraging word, fashion reverts to being a business, and the writer who doesn't promote it is castigated for her disloyalty; there is simply too much money at stake. Sure enough, I made my share of enemies along the way.

After six years at *The Atlantic*, I joined the staff of *The New Yorker* and took over the column in which Kennedy Fraser had set such a high standard. At both *The New Yorker* and *The Atlantic*, I had the good fortune to be writing about a medium that is essentially visual in a magazine that rarely, if ever, published photographs. It was up to me to paint a picture in the reader's mind, and I welcomed the chance to write descriptively.

In 1994, I took a new job as the Style Editor of *The New York Times Magazine*, where, in addition to writing a page that served as a sort of keynote address for that week's coverage of fashion (both women's and men's), architecture and design, beauty, and food, I also oversaw those pages. Such is the power of the *Times* that designers who had taken umbrage at something I had written previously and banished me from their shows for life suddenly forgave me (though I doubt that they ever forgot).

A little less than a year ago, I jumped the fence and left journalism to work for Prada, the Italian fashion company, whose enterprise I had not only greatly admired but personally supported, voting with my credit card. From my ringside seat, I had witnessed a number of valiant attempts—Prada's among them— to invent a style that would define our time. Here was my chance to pitch in and help out in some small way, and I took it. How do I know that I can do anything in fashion besides write about it? I don't. Wish me luck.

The essays collected here, though not arranged chronologically, span a period of some fifteen years, during which time much has changed: Roger Vivier's store on Madison Avenue has closed, as, incredibly, has Martha, that seemingly unshakable bastion of debutante dressing; Isaac Mizrahi has gone out of business; Hubert de Givenchy has been ousted from the house that bears his name, which was bought up when a wave of corporate acquisitions swept through the fashion business and transformed it, once and for all. In light of

Chanel's enormous success under Karl Lagerfeld's direction, my early remarks about his unsuitability for the job seem irrelevant (though I'm still not convinced that they're wrong). In some instances—and that of Lagerfeld is one— the work selected here may give a rather skewed impression of my opinions. Without the benefit of other articles that have not been included—many of them more straightforward reviews whose appeal seemed less enduring—the reader might never know the extent of my admiration for Jean Paul Gaultier, Rei Kawakubo, Yohji Yamamoto, Issey Miyake, Jil Sander, Helmut Lang, Bill Blass, Michael Kors, Thierry Mugler, and indeed, Lagerfeld, to name only a few of those designers who, season after season, produced collections that reminded me why I'd gone into fashion in the first place.

Let the punishment fit the crime: rereading one's old work is the ideal form of torture for a writer. I have resisted the temptation to retouch, correcting only those mistakes that found their way into print. Like old snapshots, the pieces that follow often strike me as embarrassing for the simple reason that they document the person I used to be. My influences are barely concealed. This is the piece I wrote while I was immersed in George Orwell, I think. Or, That was my tribute to Virginia Woolf. The former dancer teaches herself to write in full view of the audience.

For all that these essays purport to be about fashion, I now believe that fashion was merely the pretext (and a good one, at that) for writing about human nature. Clothes are a gateway to vanity, love, greed, snobbery, sex, and other fun subjects. Frankly, I can't imagine a better beat.

Holly Brubach

Serial Dresser

The French, when they can't remember something, blame it on "a hole in the memory." Through the hole in my memory have passed not only the names of people I met ten minutes ago, the combination for the lock on my suitcase, and the plots of Henry James's novels, but also some inner sense of who I was at various times in my life. Looking back over my shoulder, I regard whole chapters of my past as the misadventures of a stranger, though of course the stranger was me.

A woman I once met told me that she'd been approached at the racetrack by an attractive gentleman who looked not even vaguely familiar. "I beg your pardon," he said, "but didn't we used to be married?" She was by this time on her third husband; he had been her first, twenty years before. It was bad enough that she didn't recognize him, she later admitted, but even worse that she had such a hard time recognizing herself as his former wife. I sympathized. The older I get, the more it seems that I have been not so much one continuous person as several people, in sequence.

With some of those people I now have little or nothing in common, including our tastes in clothes. Cleaning out the back of my closet one weekend not long ago, I came across assorted evidence of my former selves: a high-school cheerleading sweatshirt worn by the pre-conscious small-town ingénue; a pair of blue denim overalls that constituted a uniform for the arty college student; a black leather jacket that served as some kind of downtown armor for a bashful newcomer to the city; a long, droopy cardigan sweater that represented a rookie writer's idea of what somebody literary might wear; a Chanel suit that, it was hoped, might confer some authority on a young woman endeavoring to live by her opinions.

Though conventional wisdom claims that everything comes back in style sooner or later, and despite a sentimental streak I've tried but never managed to eradicate, I know that I'll never wear any of these clothes again; their relationship to the person I've become is purely historical. Still, I can't bring myself to get rid of them, and in the end I left them in the closet, out of respect for those people I used to be. They meant well. Each one gave way to the next and disappeared, leaving only her clothes behind.

Life's a Beach

ONE RECENT Sunday (hazy, hot, and humid; high, 92) at Jones Beach, a state park an hour's drive from Manhattan, the people seated in ragged rows a few feet from the water's edge, all facing the same direction, like the audience in a theater, watched a steady parade of other people strolling up and down the beach, waves lapping at their ankles. "Check this out," a man said to his companion, who obligingly lifted her head from the book she was reading. If the crowds on the beaches near New York City this summer are any indication, people in bathing suits are putting more than their bodies on display. "*Unbelievable*," the man announced a few minutes later as some new specimen came into view. It is hard to get a lot of reading done under these circumstances.

There were five teen-age surfers sporting short-sleeved wetsuits and the same haircut—a shallow bowl cut of sorts, the hair shaved close around the sides, leaving a thatch on top like the roof of a hut. There was a woman in a maillot with an eye chart printed on the front, encouraging the nearsighted to come a little closer. There was a man wearing black Speedos and a yarmulke. There was one freckled family, dressed in discreet hundred-per-cent-cotton prints, who looked as if they had been airlifted in from the Hamptons. And there were three guys in bikinis batting around a black-and-fluorescent-green soccer ball. If there was a trend on the beaches this summer, it was fluorescence—fluorescent everything, from baseball caps to beach umbrellas, from boxer shorts to body boards, from bikinis to sidepieces on black sunglasses, from Frisbees to nail polish, all burning holes in the retina. The world began to take on the aspect of a bucolic nineteenth-century seascape menaced by neon signs. Stealthily but surely, it seemed, object by object, while the rest of us were asleep a band of fashion terrorists was recoloring the world fluorescent, starting with the beaches. Everywhere you looked you saw something that used to be some perfectly nice, normal color and had now turned fluorescent.

Among the people who had so far managed to escape was a little Japanese girl teaching her blond Barbie doll, dressed in a red maillot with a low-cut back, how to swim, while her brother buried their father in the sand. A long-haired Indian woman, wearing a soaking-wet printed-cotton knee-length tunic and pants, played tag with her young son in the water. A man in baggy boxer-style cotton trunks and a New York Yankees cap and a woman in a polka-dot spandex tank suit lay between the speakers of their portable cassette player and listened to Crosby, Stills, Nash & Young. A pale woman in a two-piece fuchsia-and-black checkerboard bathing suit stood facing the ocean, doing calisthenics for her upper arms.

All at once, hearing a loud drone, the people on the beach raised their gaze to the sky, where an airplane was flying low over the water, trailing a banner: "Z100/COKE ELVIS COSTELLO JONES BCH THIS FRI." Then they went back to their sports sections of the *Post*, to their children scampering in widening circles around them, to their corn on the cob.

The regulars seemed to know the territory, which divides down the middle, the middle being the beeline from the parking lot—full of Toyotas with bumper stickers, and shiny midsize sedans from Hertz, and Plymouths beginning to rust around the edges—through the low brick pavilion housing the snack bar and "comfort stations," down to the water. To the right: fluorescent bathing suits, heavyset men and women in bikinis that fit like tourniquets, raucous teenagers, couples with children, T-shirts advertising Newport cigarettes, thick-muscled men who looked as if they moved refrigerators for a living, *People* and *Cosmopolitan*, big boxy plastic-foam coolers containing cans of diet soda. To the left: khaki shorts, bathing suits in dark solid colors, couples of the same sex, fine-tuned biceps and pectorals, ACT-UP T-shirts, *Runner's World* and *Grand Street*, Poland Spring mineral water in plastic bottles, shopping bags from Balducci's. It took the appearance of a plane flying by—"CALL HAMILTON FEDERAL FOR YOUR LOW COST LOANS"—to unite these two camps, as all along the beach heads turned to read the message.

Apart from a red-white-and-blue nylon igloo on a yellow plastic frame and a respectable number of umbrellas, the beach gear was mostly makeshift—the sort of thing that people living in small apartments with insufficient closet space improvise once or twice a year. For beach bags, there were gym duffels and backpacks; for beach towels, old bedsheets in faded pastel stripes.

Another drone, another airplane: "GEORGI THE FIRST NAME IN VODKA." The people on the beach went back to looking at one another. It's amazing, I found myself thinking as I surveyed the crowd around me, how much you can tell about a person on the basis of so little clothing.

WITH ITS fantasyland mansions set back from its tree-lined streets and its lawns dotted with exotic topiaries, Deal, New Jersey, bears a closer resemblance to Bel Air, California, than to any of its neighbors along the shore. On the beach at noon on a Saturday (partly sunny, breezy; high, 83) were a woman in a mottled metallic bikini and a gold-beaded snood; a woman in a black bathing suit with big Chanel-style pearl earrings clipped to the straps; a woman in a black strapless Lycra suit with gold soutache scrollwork on the front. The bathing suits were mostly bright-colored, in shiny fabrics. There were gold necklaces and bracelets (on men and women alike), gold earrings, gold Rolexes, gold lamé beach bags. The women, in full makeup, were meticulously coiffed and manicured, many with nail polish that matched their bathing suits. The men wore mostly Speedos, with one or two or three gold chains around their necks. They left their gold-rimmed, Porsche-style aviator sunglasses on when they went in swimming, keeping their heads above the water.

Two fiftyish women—one wearing a black-and-white floral-printed Lycra tank with gold jewelry and gold-framed sunglasses, the other a poppy-printed blouson one-piece with a matching visor and a gold watch—walked into the waves and stood, knee-deep, talking.

BY THE end of the nineteen-seventies, swimsuits, like fashion, seemed to have reached a point of no return—a minimalist impasse that offered little hope and few possibilities for the future, other than occasional new variations on the standard bikini or on the maillot, which, thanks to Lycra, had become a second skin. It was during those years that Norma Kamali made a name for herself as a swimsuit designer. Now nearly twenty-five percent of Kamali's total business is in swimsuits, with the rest in clothes and accessories. Though Kamali agrees in principle with the conventional wisdom that fashion and swimsuits are for the most part unrelated—that the history of swimsuits is not so much a subdivision of the history of fashion as a tradition all its own—she admits that there are certain parallels. For one, there was for many years a prevailing style in swimsuits, which the majority of women aspired to, regardless of their body type, the way they aspired to the prevailing silhouette or skirt length in their street clothes. "There was a time—and I know that I'm to blame for it—when all you would hear people ask for was a high-cut leg," Kamali recalls. Those days of consensus, in swimsuits as in fashion, are gone. Today, all the options exist simultaneously.

In 1978, Kamali brought out a collection of long-line suits, cut to cover the upper thigh, at a time when the high-cut leg that she had unleashed on the world was still going strong. She couldn't give the suits away. In 1988, she decided to try again, with a group of swimsuits inspired by the styles that forties movie stars wore. The Hollywood glamour, she says, was something that people could relate to, and it gave them a frame of reference for the long-line suit, even though Kamali's versions were constructed differently. This time, the long-line suits walked out of the stores. Two of the styles, which Kamali has kept in production, are still among her best-sellers.

Lena Lenček and Gideon Bosker, in their book *Making Waves: Swimsuits and the Undressing of America*, call a swimsuit "a sartorial paradox: a form of undress that functioned as a symbol of dress." In a way, the long-line suit and other styles that have lately been making a comeback represent a return to a kind of modesty that's been missing in swimsuits for the past twenty-five or thirty years. By 1964, when Rudi Gernreich introduced the "monokini," a topless suit with suspender straps, soon to be followed by the thong, the history of the modern swimsuit seemed to have arrived at its inevitable destination, prompting Diana Vreeland to remark that "the bikini says to me the best things in life are free." The inexorable, protracted, slow-motion striptease that propelled not only fashion but swimsuit design for the first half of the twentieth century could only end in nakedness. Inch by inch, a woman's ankles, calves, upper arms, thighs, armpits, back, midriff, abdomen, and, finally, breasts were unveiled, offering a sexual thrill—the thrill of the forbidden made suddenly available—that, however controversial, kept the process moving forward: just as the sight of what had been concealed began to seem familiar, some new area was brought out into the open, and the thrill was revived. (For men, the progress, though made in larger stages, was no less vehemently contested: the shortening of the tunic that concealed the shape of the groin and finally, during the forties, the removal of the tunic altogether, baring the chest, were regarded in their time as threats to society's stability.) As a result, the amount of skin a swimsuit exposed was for years a gauge of its sex appeal, with each new sexy suit, considered bare and daring in its time, eventually being superseded by some newer style, even barer and more daring.

Kamali believes that that old formula—skin equals sex appeal—is now defunct. "I don't think people even look at a thong bikini as sexy anymore," she says. "It's part of a lifestyle." Sex appeal today, she contends, resides more in the construction and the cut of a swimsuit than in what it exposes. "A big impact over the last few years has been the underwire and the different types of shapings that have been introduced for breasts of different sizes," she explains. "It's the subtlety that makes it. A strap—the way a strap goes over the shoulder—can be sexy now."

Besides the sexual ennui that set in over the past twenty years, with the sight of naked flesh no longer the turn-on that it used to be, a growing disenchantment with promiscuity and recent evidence that sun exposure damages skin have conspired to cover up the body again. But, because of advances in the technology of fabrics, the suits this time around bear only a passing resemblance to the monolithic suits of the forties and fifties, which, even when hanging on a line to dry, maintained the shape of a woman's torso, as if they were worn by a ghost. To a certain extent, the history of the swimsuit is the history of the synthetic fibers and the fabric technology that were invented for it: the progress is documented by Lenček and Bosker, from Jantzen's original "elastic," or "rib," stitch, which eliminated the need for a drawstring at the waist, to Lastex, a rubber-based woven material that molded to the body, and on to the Matletex process, for gathering cotton fabric on elastic thread, and then the advent of spandex (which DuPont named Lycra), in the nineteen-sixties. The companies that eventually became Catalina and Cole of California started out as knitting mills specializing in underwear. As fabrics became capable of clinging closer to the body, the suits got scantier, culminating in the bikini consisting of three spandex fig leaves.

Kamali is continuing to work with Lycra, even though many of the suits she's designing these days are not so bare. Sometimes she uses two layers—"one doing something, and the other one flat, holding you in." A swimsuit that drapes on the body is a lot more forgiving than one that sticks to it like adhesive, and also a lot more elegant, as Louise Dahl-Wolfe's indelible images from the forties of women in lightweight wool-jersey swimsuits by Claire McCardell remind us. Kamali isn't sure what the future holds for swimwear. "But I suspect that it won't be that long before we're needing to protect ourselves with more than just sunblock," she says. "And the waters aren't exactly clean, and people are nervous about swimming pools. So if the sun isn't so great and the water isn't so great and hygiene is so important, where is swimwear going to go? It could be a whole other thing. I think we may be looking at clothes that protect us from our environment. And that to me is scary, but it's an interesting thought, and it's not one that you can just knock out of your head."

ON A Sunday afternoon (windy, warmer, partly cloudy; high, 85), the parking lot at the beach in East Hampton was full of BMWs and Mercedeses, and one of the shingle-style houses that loom in profile along the crests of the dunes was flying an American flag. In the foreground were men and women—most of them conspicuously thinner than the people at other beaches—dressed in khaki shorts or madras-plaid boxers or dark, solid-colored swimsuits in cotton-knit fabrics with a dull finish. The women wore wide stretch headbands that pulled their hair back from their foreheads; the men wore baseball caps, among them one that said "CBS News." They had left their jewelry at home. Several women were turned out in J. Crew's mix-and-match bikinis—the tops and bottoms different colors.

The best-dressed award at nearly every beach this summer goes to the surfers, in their wetsuits—the amphibious equivalent of the getups that Manhattan bike messengers wear. The new wetsuits are a big improvement on the old ones, the shiny, rubbery frogman kind. They're mostly black, contoured with insets of colors like royal blue or fluorescent green or acid yellow, and made of a foamy fabric that's absolutely matte. The best of them, cut to just above the knee, like bikers' shorts, zip up the back instead of the front. There are boards to match. At the beach in East Hampton, there were surfers attached to their boards by a cord and a Velcro band at the ankle—like fugitives from a chain gang in search of the perfect wave.

The beach bags were faded canvas totes from L. L. Bean. Scattered around the edges of the towels spread on the sand were binoculars, canvas espadrilles and Top-Siders and Keds, bottles of seltzer water and of Snapple iced tea. A half-empty bottle of Italian white wine nestled in a brass ice bucket next to a young couple in striped-canvas beach chairs. Naked children were building sandcastles. Three Labrador retrievers, a Dalmatian, and a long-haired dachshund were chasing one another in the surf. An anorexic woman in a white crocheted bikini, her skin tanned to the color and consistency of rawhide, determinedly hiked the beach on unsteady legs. A little boy buried his brother in the sand. The snack bar was selling Hotlix—clear, tequila-flavored lollipops with quick-fried worms trapped in the middle—which a poster inside billed as the new California craze.

The surfers and a young mother in a mauve straw pith helmet and a man in sun-bleached ikat-printed boxers and two topless women paging through sections of the Sunday *Times* all looked up to read the banner of an airplane flying overhead: "Your Message Here? ♥ AERO-TAG (516) 288-1873."

THE SIGHT of so many people in bathing suits brings to mind a friend's theory that most naked bodies are attractive and it's only when you start putting clothes on people—chopping up a sculptural form into shoulders, arms, midriff, hips, and legs, and exaggerating certain lines—that people begin to look awful. At a time when anything goes, on the beach as well as on the street, and in the absence of the advice that fashion magazines used to dispense about how to disguise "figure flaws," most women seem to choose swimsuits inappropriate to their bodies—suits they've seen featured in some picture or other, worn by a model they want to look like. "You want a course in psychology?" Norma Kamali says. "Sell swimsuits."

Some of the optical illusions that a bathing suit can create are unmysterious: ruffles on a bra top make a small-chested woman look bigger; ruffles on a bottom make big hips look even broader. In other cases, it helps to have a professional's eye and experience. Kamali refuses to make pronouncements about what kind of swimsuit is most compatible with what kind of figure, because bodies are so individual. "But these things I can tell you, and they're real," she says. "If the shoulder straps are set wide apart, the shoulders appear to be wider. If the shoulder straps are set in, the shoulders may appear to be smaller. If the straps are set all the way in, the shoulders appear to be wider again."

It is impossible to sit on a beach these days and not be struck by the overwhelming obesity of the American public. Granted, there are people who are conspicuously fit, who go to the gym, to aerobics class—who work on their bodies and, having invested so much time and energy in them, are willing, if not eager, to show them off—and fashion now addresses itself to these people. And then there are the overweight by more than just a few pounds, the people neglected by designers and the editors of fashion magazines, who imagine that fashion can provide women with an incentive to lose weight. There are, apparently—astonishingly—very few people in between, few "normal" people, for whom eating and exercising are natural functions rather than conscious decisions.

We hear it said again and again what a crime it is that our society makes people who are overweight feel ashamed of their bodies, and yet, judging by the way the population on the beaches this summer was dressed, what's remarkable is how many fat people seem completely lacking in self-consciousness. Many fat women seem to think that simply by wearing a bikini they look sexy, the way that a man wearing a leather jacket looks tough. Clothes in this case cease being themselves and become signs of some personality trait that the wearer wants to advertise or acquire.

At Softwear Sportswear, a shop in Greenwich, Connecticut, Meg Felton advises women who need some camouflage to opt for prints in choosing a bathing suit, because they're more distracting than solid colors. "Solids show every bump and ripple," she explains, "whereas if you have a print, people look at the print." A twenty-seven-year-old alumna of Macy's Executive Training Program, Felton opened her own store last November to sell bathing suits custom-made with the aid of computer graphics—a licensed idea that originated in California. Hers is the only store on the East Coast to offer the service. The advantage of doing custom work, she says, is that she can produce, for instance, a size-8 suit with extra length in the torso for a woman who is long-waisted, or a suit cut high on the leg but wide enough in the seat so that it won't ride up.

A customer comes in, tries on a few different styles from a range of proto-types, and models them for a video camera. Felton freezes the image on a computer screen, then begins to show the customer what could be done to modify the suit: cutting the leg a little higher or carving away at the armholes or narrowing the straps; adding a band at the waist for a belt; adding slashes of contrasting color, which she calls splices, at the hips, to make a more slender line; splitting a V-neck tank down the middle to create a bicolored suit. She can play with stripes, making them go up and down or across or at an angle, meeting at the center seam in a chevron pattern. Her designs break no new ground; they are, depending on your point of view, either basic or classic. And her fabrics, all of them American, reflect the dearth of beautiful materials. Still, she has a good eye, and she knows how to make a suit fit a body's peculiarities. She will also do

maternity suits, including one ingenious style gathered into a band of elastic down the center, which enables the suit to "grow."

THE PEOPLE on the beach at Ocean Grove, New Jersey, one Saturday morning (hotter, periods of sun; high, 98) were neatly grouped in families, wearing bathing suits that were modest and athletic-looking, in routine colors and un-remarkable prints. Founded in the summer of 1869 by ten Methodist families that had come together for rest and fellowship, Ocean Grove was for years so devoutly religious that until 1977 no cars were permitted on the streets on Sundays. Today, the peaked roofs of its Victorian houses, with their lacy woodwork trim, are visible from the water's edge.

One woman wading out into the surf was dressed in a blue-and-white striped tank suit that might have been left over from her high-school swim team. The men wore boxer-style suits with a tiny pocket, for change, or with a webbed belt. Two women wearing one-piece suits straight out of the Land's End catalogue—full cut, the necks scooped not too low—sat playing gin rummy with a little girl and drinking diet Sprite, which they poured from cans into paper cups. Among the beach bags were a few straw totes embroidered with raffia flowers—souvenirs, perhaps, of vacations in the Caribbean. An occa-sional pair of earrings—small studs or gold hoops—was the only jewelry. There were teenage girls in bikini tops and cutoffs that were turned up and sewn instead of frayed.

On a bulletin board beside the boardwalk, handbills had been posted: a notice of a kite contest, the schedule of concerts at the Ocean Grove Audito-rium (Patti Page, the Tommy Dorsey Orchestra, the Drifters and the Coasters), open invitations to a Surfside Song & Testimony Service and to sermons ("Learning to Love All Over Again" and "Giving Away What You Cannot Keep") by Dr. Anthony Campolo. One flyer announced the appearance of the gospel magician Dave Siefert—"Presenting Jesus Christ Through Magic"—and featured a picture of a man pulling a rabbit out of a hat.

ON A Tuesday afternoon (sunny skies, humid, chance of showers toward evening; high, 88) on the beach at Coney Island, there were strollers and bicycles parked in the sand. Just behind the boardwalk, where the corrugated-metal fronts of boarded-up stores are covered with graffiti, the Wonder Wheel turned listlessly; the rattle of the Cyclone could be heard down by the water. The people on the beach turned their backs on the high-rise housing projects towering over the shoreline and stared out to sea. An airplane flew into their field of vision: "TRY TEEN SPIRIT ANTI-PERSPIRANT."

Not far from a white-haired man who looked like a Giacometti sculpture with a bath towel for a base and a woman in a purple lamé bikini reading a discount-mail-order catalogue, six elderly women and two elderly men had gathered. The backs and seats of their beach chairs were made of plastic webbing, basketwoven. Wet swimsuits had been hung to dry from the spokes of their two beach umbrellas. A young mother in a white bikini, with a little boy on a telephone-cord leash attached to his wrist, was saying her goodbyes. "Who loves you? Who loves you?" one woman called after them insistently as they started across the sand toward the boardwalk, looking back over their shoulders and waving. A thickset woman in a skirted bathing suit printed with lilacs and a matching purple bathing cap returned from a swim, dripping wet. Her shoulder straps were tied together in back with a shoelace, to keep them from slipping. Another woman, wearing a full-cut bathing suit printed with palm fronds and orchids, asked her neighbor, a gray-haired man with a concave chest, a question that began in Sicilian dialect and ended "and how would you know?" A collapsible luggage cart stood off to one side of their beach towels.

Three women speaking Russian, one of them wearing a turquoise Lycra bikini with silver Lurex trim, sat watching a little boy molding the turrets of a sandcastle with a Dixie cup. The landscape was scattered with cans of Sunkist orange soda and gallon bottles of diet Pepsi and packages of Dipsy Doodles. The beach bags were from Key Food and Payless. "Cold beer! *Cerveza!*" a bare-chested man with tattoos on his arms called, weaving through the crowd and pulling behind him a cart that held a battered plastic-foam ice chest. A woman in a T-shirt and shorts knelt in the sand beside a cooler and shouted through a battery-powered megaphone, "Ice cream! Two for a dollar!" Radios were tuned to stations playing salsa music.

A father, dressed in a gray-and-white striped shirt, stiff jeans, and Adidas, held on tight to the hands of his two little girls as they cut a straight path from the boardwalk to the water. His daughters, their hair in neat cornrows, wore black-and-white gingham sundresses with fluorescent pink and green piping. At the water's edge, each little girl removed her white sandals with one hand, never letting go of her father with the other. At the point where the waves played themselves out, he lifted his toes and rocked back on his heels at their approach.

The girls, their sandals dangling from their hands, solemnly stamped their feet, making little slapping noises.

A woman dressed in a black cotton shirt and shorts, Birkenstock sandals, and a big straw sun hat sat in the lotus position with her eyes closed. Six children buried a friend in the sand, shovelling furiously. A man and a woman in matching Tarzan-and-Jane leopard-patterned bikinis lay face down on a sheet printed with the "Star Wars" logo. The woman with the megaphone planted herself in the sand nearby and shouted "Ice cream! Half price! Two for a dollar!" in a belligerent tone. A man with a ponytail and a gold earring, wearing black Bermuda-length boxers with the Spalding logo across the seat, stood talking to a friend in Spanish. The woman who had been meditating opened her eyes, reached into an embroidered cotton bag, and pulled out an eyedropper, which she used to put a few drops of something on her tongue. A man in a fluorescent-green toy scuba mask snorkelled around one of the rock jetties, seemingly looking for something he'd lost. Two small girls etched a hopscotch game in the wet sand. A photographer in a yellow baseball cap strolled the beach, offering to take people's pictures with his sidekick, a green plush Ninja Turtle whose costume looked homemade.

ON THE racks at Sunsation, a swimsuit boutique in Belmar, New Jersey, there were bikinis of all descriptions, including one with two gilded lavender plastic scallop shells held on by a nylon cord, for a bra, and a skimpy gauze diaper bottom; a black Lycra flapper style, with matching fringed elbow-length mitts; a skimpy Pebbles Flintstone model, in Ultrasuede, with jagged edges. Sherry Michaels, the store's owner, says that at the height of the season Sunsation sells an average of one hundred and fifty bikinis a weekend. By the beginning of August, the men's department, just beyond the tanning machine, was all out of G-strings with detachable loincloths.

A few towns farther down the coast, at Point Pleasant, on a Saturday (hazy sun, sultry, turning windy; high, 96), the parking area for the beach looked like a Chevrolet dealer's used-car lot, full of Camaros. "Wanted, Dead or Alive," by Bon Jovi—a local hero—came blasting from one of a row of weathered houses fronting directly onto the boardwalk, their decks, like grandstands, crowded with rowdy, beer-drinking young men who were already, by five in the afternoon, well on their way to getting totally trashed. After sundown, the beach at Point Pleasant is for making out, and is only slightly less crowded than it is by day.

Men with tattoos and women with long striped fingernails roamed the boardwalk, two by two, holding hands, buying ice-cream cones, playing shooting-gallery games for Fred Flintstone and Barney Rubble dolls. The Frog Bog, where contestants catapult green rubber frogs onto rotating lily pads, was doing a brisk business. There were no more seats on the little train running on rails set in the sand. An inflated statue of Bud Man presided over the pier.

The women were aggressively tanned, wearing tiny bikinis in colors with the volume turned up all the way. With their drop earrings, their gold ankle bracelets, their eyeshadow and lip gloss, their full hairdos with lots of body, they looked as painstakingly turned out as socialites in evening gowns. The men wore fluorescent Bermuda-length boxers, with religious medallions and pendants that said "100%" (proclaiming their purebred Italian bloodlines) hanging from gold chains around their necks.

A doubles volleyball tournament was in progress: two Amazonian women, one of them in a royal-blue maillot and the other in a minuscule bikini, versus two slightly smaller women, in slightly larger bikinis. A crowd of spectators had gathered at the boardwalk railing. A woman with decals on her fingernails, which were lacquered fluorescent orange, tapped another woman, a blonde with long hair in spiral waves, on the shoulder. "Excuse me," she said. "Is that a perm or is that your natural?" It was a perm. The first woman had tried something similar, she said, but it hadn't worked. In a voice that drifted upward at the end of every statement, the blonde told her what to ask for at the beauty salon: "Tell them to use the white-on-black rods? Because if you get them a little too big? Because of the length of the hair? It'll pull it out."

The roar of an airplane engine diverted the attention of the crowd from the volleyball tournament (3–0, Amazons) to the sky. The message moved across the field of blue from right to left and continued on up the coast, toward the beaches in Belmar and Ocean Grove and Deal: "JERSEY SHORE THIS BUD'S FOR YOU."

The Eye of
the Beholder

IN THE video for George Michael's "Freedom," released last November, Michael himself is nowhere to be seen, but his voice carries us along as the camera cuts from one girl to the next in a glamorous relay, with five unofficial members of an international modelling cartel mouthing in succession the words to his latest hit song. Linda Evangelista sits huddled inside a big cowl-neck sweater, waiting for a kettle to boil; her hair, which started a trend when she cropped it nearly three years ago, is now platinum blond. Cindy Crawford, the Revlon girl, with her trademark mole above her lip, soaks in a bathtub. Tatjana Patitz, a voluptuous German blonde, with narrow, almond eyes, lies in bed, staring at the ceiling and smoking a cigarette. Naomi Campbell, a black soubrette with a penchant for wigs, and Christy Turlington, a radiant, pixie-faced ingénue, her full lower lip in a natural pout, complete the cast (along with a few forgettable men). They move through rooms that are very sparsely furnished, like a gang of beautiful girls squatting in an abandoned sorority house. These are the girls who all posed together for the cover of the January 1990 issue of British *Vogue*—the faces for a new decade. Someday, we'll see a rerun of this video and think, That was the year of those girls—the way we look at old photographs and magazines and think, Those were the days when Earth shoes were all the rage, or That was the year of the Dorothy Hamill haircut.

Now that movie stars, baring their battered souls to Barbara Walters or writing memoirs of their stay at the Betty Ford Center, have succeeded in convincing us that they're no better than the rest of us, the glamour surrounding fashion models is greater than any Hollywood starlet's. Now that men and women who forty years ago could have blithely gone about their careers as sex symbols have taken to wearing horn-rimmed glasses and attending poetry readings and lobbying on behalf of the rain forest, fashion models seem to be

Valentino and Givenchy; Helena Christensen, the dark-haired Danish model, a relatively recent arrival who is rapidly closing in on the big stars, has modified her walk to make it a bit more flat-footed than usual. For the penultimate passage—a group of floating ball gowns, their skirts quilted and padded and painted like wedding kimonos with traditional Japanese motifs (a crane or cedar trees or Mt. Fuji) in red, gold, black, and white—the music switches from Euro rock to the "Blue Danube" waltz.

A notorious perfectionist, Kawakubo insists on at least one fitting and two rehearsals in the days leading up to her show; most other designers require one or two fittings and no rehearsals. At the end of the rehearsal, she gathers her assistants around her in a circle on the floor backstage and reviews her notes. The assistants get busy, making last-minute adjustments. The models change back into their own clothes for the time being—Kristen into a black cashmere cardigan sweater, vintage nineteen fifty-something, which she wears tied at the waist to expose a black lace-trimmed bra; pumpkin-colored stretch shorts; and two pairs of tights, black fishnet over black opaque. Helena asks Kristen where she got her bra. "J. C. Penney's," Kristen tells her.

Kristen sits on top of a table, her legs folded under her, waiting her turn in the makeup assembly line, and rehearsing dialogue from a dog-eared movie script in preparation for a screen test she has scheduled for later that afternoon. Bruno Nuytten, the French director who made *Camille Claudel*, is considering her for his next movie, in the role of an American model in her mid-twenties living in Paris. Except that the character commits suicide at the end, Kristen says, the part is her all over. As she practices her lines aloud, one of the makeup artists, a curly-haired Frenchman, listens and corrects her pronunciation. She has lived in Paris for five years all told, but her command of the French language is still tentative, her pronunciation approximate. (She calls the *haute couture* the "hot couture.") "*Si tu te sens capable de porter tous les deuils,*" she reads. The makeup artist corrects her on the word *deuils*. "DIE" she writes next to it in the script, and tries it again. "That's good?" she asks.

"*Ça va,*" he replies.

The press attaché, standing nearby, tells her about Jean Seberg's accent in *Breathless*, and she seems reassured.

A woman in black jeans and a gray sweatshirt, with a sweater knotted around her waist, silences Kristen long enough to trace the outline of her lips with a brown pencil, then says, "Open."

Kristen describes her face as a blank, her features as plain, without definition, when she's wearing no makeup—an assessment that is, to be honest, fairly accurate. Her skin is astonishingly white, like a painter's canvas; her eyebrows are rather vague; her eyes are a pale quartz blue but not especially large or striking; her mouth is quite wide, with two possible lip lines—one the boundary of her lips' natural color, the other the outer edge of their contour. "Makeup artists love my face, because they can draw on it," she says. The woman in the gray sweatshirt applies a patch of deep-purple lipstick to the back of her left hand, which she uses as a palette, and, cradling Kristen's jaw to steady it, transfers the color to Kristen's lips with a brush. "Oh, you got Wet 'n' Wild!" Kristen says, recognizing the tube. "Ninety-nine cents at Woolworth's! Looks like black, but it's a little plum. It's dry, but . . ."

"All dark colors are very drying," the makeup artist says, shrugging. She paints Kristen's nails with a coat of black polish, followed by one of red. "So, you are learning French now?" she asks.

"*Un peu,*" Kristen answers, making little waving motions with her hands to dry her nails.

The girls stare off into space as the makeup artists work on their faces. At a table in one corner, a Japanese man in a shirt and tie steams a gray silk shantung jacket trimmed with transparent vinyl; another man, with a tape measure draped around his neck, sits bent over a long red vinyl skirt, stitching up the slit at the back.

The woman who books the models for both the women's and the men's shows for Comme des Garçons tells me, as we stand off to one side, surveying the action, that the male models are a completely different breed. For them, modelling is a job, she explains—it's something they do for the money. And the girls? I ask. For the girls, she says, it's *them*—the way they look is who they are. (Later in the day, during one of the early passages in Yohji Yamamoto's show, the photographers—ready to riot over the places they've been assigned—suddenly break into a raucous chorus of boos and hissing. Ariane, who was on the runway when the commotion started, comes running to her rack, which is next to Kristen's, in tears. Sobbing, she changes into her next outfit. The models nearby gather around her, trying to comfort her. "Ariane," Kristen insists, "it isn't *you!*")

At ten-ten, six seamstresses crouch around one of the ball gowns, spread out on brown paper on the floor—three of them guiding the fabric into place, the three others sewing furiously. Most of the models are doing the things that people do when they have time on their hands: listening to a Walkman, rereading a letter, copying names and telephone numbers from torn scraps of the paper tablecloth at last night's bistro dinner into an address book. No one is reading a newspaper. But then there is no real incentive for most of these girls to take an interest in the outside world. A reporter spending a week in the *cabine* comes reluctantly to the conclusion that the cliché about models being superficial is not without some basis.

Kristen watches Yasmeen, a Canadian model, applying eyeshadow and brow pencil from a kit of her own, in defiance of the makeup artists' specifications. "The tramp!" she mutters, with an indignation that is only partly feigned. In fact, many of the girls make a practice of adapting the designer's vision to the way they prefer to see themselves. Kristen and two other models who have left their faces exactly as the makeup artists did them complain that alongside these girls who have added extra makeup to emphasize their eyes they're going to look dead on the runway. "It's not fair to the designer, it's not fair to the makeup artist," Kristen says, shaking her head.

At ten-thirty, Kawakubo and six of her assistants are wrapping a length of indigo tulle around a blond model, who stands rooted, like a maypole, as they bustle around her. Through the walls comes music from Daniel Hechter's show, going on in the tent next door: "You're sixteen, you're beautiful, and you're mine!"

"Wow," Kristen says. "They're really hip over there."

"O.K., excuse me, girls!" the director calls out. "*Attention, s'il vous plaît!* Just two or three things. Most are very good. I need more power—more powerful. So I change some part of the music. And one thing: Don't open your mouth. I mean, this makeup, when you open your mouth it looks awful. So be careful." He claps his hands. "O.K.! Thank you for your cooperation."

At ten-fifty, one of the fitters is polishing a black vinyl duckbill cap with a tissue; a waiter in a white apron is standing at a table, arranging plastic cups on a tray. Kristen fidgets. "I thought I could study my script, but I can't," she says. At eleven, the fitters, most of them Japanese students, are positioned beside the racks, holding stockings already gathered and waiting to be stepped into. "Stand by," the director calls. The models go to their racks to dress. Kristen climbs into a pair of pale sheer pantyhose followed by black opaque tights; a fitter holds a shoehorn as she slides into square-toed black flats. Her first outfit is a long black gabardine skirt overlaid in front with a clear vinyl panel. The fitter sprays an anti-static aerosol up the inside of her skirt. "We're all going to be sterile," Kristen laments. A hairdresser makes the rounds, removing clips.

A German model has got her houndstooth dress on wrong. "No? *Mein Gott!*" she cries. Five Japanese women come to her rescue, twisting the top sections, pulling one arm through. Ariane wonders aloud whether the dress she's wearing, a stretchy black-and-white lumberjack-plaid tube, makes her hips look wider. A champagne cork pops, and the tray of plastic cups is passed. "Good luck, everyone!" Kristen calls out. "Be strong, and no open mouths! *Salute!*"

The girls are herded into a line that begins in the wings and trails down the stairs leading to the *cabine*. Cordula smokes a cigarette. Most stand impassively, as if they were queued up at a cash machine. The music starts; the line advances. Kawakubo is stationed at the top step, arranging the way the clothes fall before each model goes onstage. The soundtrack, overhauled since the rehearsal, is now mostly acid rock. Between forays down the runway and back, Kristen rushes from the exit to her rack; steps out of her clothes, leaving them in puddles on the floor for the fitters to pick up later; and, putting a white silk pillow slip over her head, so as not to leave any makeup smudges on the clothes, wriggles into her next outfit. She steps into black flat-heeled go-go boots; the fitter kneels behind her and zips them up the back. When a silver lamé dress gets stuck on her head, she squeals in panic. One model, already dressed and with time to kill in her gabardine suit for the finale, stands off to one side eating a brioche. In a black shirt with red vinyl sleeves, Kristen watches the girls wearing ball gowns take their places. "Oh, why couldn't I have had a ball gown?" she wails, to no one in particular. The "Blue Danube" waltz begins. "Well," she reasons, "I do have a ball gown at Yohji Yamamoto." She pauses, still thinking, looking not quite consoled. "It's wood," she explains. For Yamamoto's Constructivist finale, she has been assigned a dress of wooden slats which fastens with nuts and bolts.

There is applause backstage as the last group, a series of suits, is sent out. Kawakubo is gently prodded onto the runway for a hasty, modest half bow. Kristen returns, shedding her outfit. "Total success," she announces, climbing into her own clothes for the frantic dash to the tent next door, where Angelo Tarlazzi's show is scheduled to start in twenty minutes.

IN AN article in the March issue of French *Vogue*, Gérard Miller, a psychoanalyst and author sent by the magazine's editors to cover the spring haute-couture collections, writes of the sexual standoff between the models and the photographers which occurs in fashion shows: there is, he claims, no more terrifying representation of woman than these women—the purer the face, the more streamlined the body, the more one discovers the threat that every woman engenders in the unconscious mind. Inaccessible women, he calls them, who transform these impotent men, hunched over their cameras, into pillars of salt: "*La beauté absolue et l'horreur de la castration!* " But where do these women come from, he wonders, and who made them?

Kristen McMenamy comes from Easton, Pennsylvania, where, as a teenager, she pored over fashion magazines, studying the girls pictured in them, looking into their faces, as if in their expressions she might find some hidden message addressed to her—some words of encouragement, some advice about what to do or where to go. Mostly, she sat around wishing that she looked like Cindy Boucher, a girl who went to her high school—a blond cheerleader with the perfect body, perfect teeth, perfect smile. "She never talked to me," McMenamy recalls.

All the girls in her neighborhood had the same haircut. McMenamy was as tall at thirteen as she is now; her classmates nicknamed her Skeleton. She would lighten her hair, lie out in the sun for hours, burning her fair skin, and spend all her money on the makeup featured in the magazines she studied. "There was a list of things you were supposed to be: blond, tan, pretty," she recalls. "I'd like to know who made that list." McMenamy's most vivid memories of her years at Notre Dame High School are of eating lunch alone in the cafeteria, because she had no friends. "I forget everyone's name—that's how bad my childhood was," she says. "I've blocked it out." She didn't save her yearbook or buy a class ring, because she was "so ashamed" of that chapter in her life. Not only was she never asked for a date, she was laughed at for being freckled and red-haired. So it seems some roundabout sort of justice that a few years back she caused a minor sensation by appearing on French television in a commercial for George Killian beer, an Irish red ale, or *bière rousse*, and delivering one of those lines that, for no good reason, like "Because I'm worth it" or "Where's the beef?," become etched in the popular memory: "*Je suis rousse, et alors?*" I'm a redhead. So?

McMenamy was a straight-A student until, at sixteen, she started hanging out in local nightclubs. She sent some pictures to *Cosmopolitan's* cover-girl contest. The winner was a blonde from California. McMenamy combed the list of semifinalists for her name: not there. In Allentown, she went to modelling school. In three weeks, for five hundred dollars, she was taught how to smile, how to walk, how to put her hands on her hips. None of her teachers believed she had a future. "I was even a reject there," she says. When she was seventeen, she went to New York to make the rounds of the big agencies with her portfolio—an album of party snapshots and out-of-focus studio pictures taken by local wedding photographers. Together with a friend, who had come along for moral support, she went from Wilhelmina to Zoli and on to Elite, and, finally, to Ford, growing more and more discouraged. At the end of the day, Eileen Ford herself came out to look at her book. "I wanted her to be my savior," McMenamy says. Ford suggested that she go back to Easton, go to college, get married, have a family, and forget about modelling. She also told Kristen's friend, who had no interest in such a career, that she had potential. Kristen cried the whole bus ride home.

About a year and a half later, she got a call from the head of a small agency called Legends, in New York, who had seen the pictures she'd submitted to *Cosmopolitan*. For the first time, she went to the appointment wearing no makeup, as she'd always been instructed to do. The agent made her no promises but took her on, and sent her straight to a hair colorist, who turned her from a bleached blonde back into a redhead. She was, by her own description, overweight, pigeon-toed, and shy, with her hair in her face. No bookings followed, but she did a lot of test photographs; after a few months, the agency sent her to Paris on a one-way ticket and told her to get some tear sheets—a common strategy for models who are just starting out and don't fit the glorified-girl-next-door description of beauty which still prevails in America. In Europe, the notions of what's attractive aren't so narrow. The model who returns to New York, which is where the money is, on the strength of a reputation abroad often finds that clients who weren't willing to take a chance on someone so unconventional before—or perhaps weren't able to see her appeal—suddenly come around.

In Paris, after a year of demoralizing go-sees for yogurt ads, McMenamy at last came to the attention of Peter Lindbergh, a much admired German fashion photographer, who works in a dramatic, darkly original style, and it was he who saw in her something that the others had overlooked and brought it out into broad daylight. From then on, she was overwhelmed with work. By the time she made the decision to come back to New York, three years ago, she was known within the industry as one of the most successful models in Europe.

But in New York her career began to falter. It was, she says, a matter of the way she was used. "I would be booked for sportswear catalogues and put in a pink jumpsuit," she recalls. Tessa Jowers, the director of model management at Elite, which now represents McMenamy in New York, says that to a large extent it's the nature of the work in America. A lot of the bookings here are for ads for some department store's Mother's Day sale or for Cover Girl or Maybelline or J. Crew—"the kinds of things that are appealing to white-bread America, the one-hundred-per-cent-cotton kind of crowd," she explains. "A lot of fashion here seems to be aimed at the masses. People worry about pleasing Middle America—you've got to sell to those people to stay in business. Whereas in Paris they'll bank everything on the artistic value, and then, by doing that, they make something chic and it sells."

McMenamy admits to being choosy about the jobs she accepted. "I wouldn't fly to Chicago to do a sweater for Macy's," she says.

Jowers thinks she was justified. "There are some girls who are only going to go so far, and they should take whatever comes along and get what they can out of it," she says. "But Kristen is going for a high-profile, top-model career—editorial with the top photographers, advertising under contract to a designer or a fragrance—and it's by holding out for the important jobs in periods when she wasn't busy that she has got to this level."

After two years in New York, McMenamy says, she felt as if she were back in high school, trying to conform. In the spring of last year, she packed her bags and returned to Paris, and has been there ever since. The work that comes her way there is more interesting, she says, and she's appreciated for her idiosyncrasies. She is still choosy. She routinely refuses to go to Germany to do catalogues, though they pay very well. "I don't think about the money I'm making," she insists. In fact, she says, she would do the jobs she loves for practically nothing. When she works with a photographer like Peter Lindbergh, for instance, she wants every picture "to make history." On the days when she knows she hasn't worked well, she says, she feels like giving the money back. She is not, Lindbergh agrees, a commercial model. "She has always that artistic side, which is very strong," he explains. "You can put her nowhere and say 'Do something,' and you get the most incredible pictures."

Martine Sitbon, the designer, and Marc Ascoli, the art director responsible for both the line Sitbon designs under her own name and the line she designs for Chloé, call themselves members of Kristen McMenamy's fan club.

They tell the story of the time last season when she came for a preliminary fitting for the benefit of the executives at Chloé. Not having been forewarned that their tastes ran to the more conventional, she acted out what Ascoli calls *"une vision de la couture complétement phantasmagorique, extraterrestre"*—advancing, striking a haughty pose, giving the president a pointed look, retreating, every movement at a pace that was unbelievably, inhumanly slow. She heard "Chloé," Ascoli explains, and thought "Couture!" The executives, fascinated and appalled, could not be persuaded to hire her for the show. This season, Ascoli and Sitbon advised McMenamy to present herself in a manner that was a little more "standard," and there was no problem. Even so, what's "standard" for McMenamy would be quirky for anyone else. At her most conventional, she has the unmistakable air of an oddball. This is not an impression created by her physical proportions or by the geometry of her features. Unlike the models Jean Paul Gaultier promotes—girls who look peculiar but carry themselves with all the grace and poise of a legendary beauty—McMenamy looks lovely, if not quite usual; her eccentricities spring from something inside, which occasionally contorts her features and makes her movements slightly convoluted.

"Personality" is the word that comes up time and again when people talk about McMenamy. Lindbergh says it's what he looks for in a model and what he saw in her. "First, personality. And then what people call 'beauty,' but I think you can't detach one from the other," he explains. "When you see her face, it's like the interior is outside. Many of the other girls, they have more of a facade, but she looks the way she is inside—the inside is on the face, and it's very touching. That's what I think is beautiful. Otherwise, what could be beautiful, I have no idea. It's not a question of no wrinkles, or something like that."

EVERY FEW years or so, a model or a fashion-magazine editor or somebody else in a position to talk about what women look like issues a statement to the effect that when it comes to our standards of beauty we're making progress. Mostly, such remarks serve as the occasion for us to congratulate not the women we find beautiful but ourselves—for being so highly evolved, so humane and sophisticated and open-minded, that we're able to recognize their beauty. Cindy Crawford has been known to flatter her constituency with the remark that only fifteen or twenty years ago a girl like her could not have had a successful career as a model without first having her mole removed—the most recent installment of the agitprop that in the seventies seized on the space between

Lauren Hutton's front teeth as a sign of how far the world had come. The desire to think that human nature is getting better, that we're more enlightened than the people who came before us, is not new, nor is it confined to our perceptions of fashion, though fashion tends to play on it. Lois W. Banner, in her book *American Beauty*, a social history of American ideals of beauty, recapitulates the theories of various nineteenth-century optimists who hypothesized that America was becoming "an amalgamation of racial types," and that out of that mixture would come "a higher kind of beauty"; similarly, she notes, certain Darwinians were convinced that the human race would become progressively more beautiful, since beautiful men and women chose each other as mates and passed their beauty on to their children, "while ugly people, unchosen, had no progeny." We see the folly of ideas like these quite clearly, and find the notion that people should be getting better-looking with each successive generation quaint and amusing. The sorts of looks that people in the nineteenth century considered ravishing (Lillian Russell's, Lillie Langtry's) for the most part leave us indifferent today. That our taste in faces and bodies changes from one era to the next is clear; that it changes for the better, however, is not. Still, we pride ourselves on being able to appreciate beauty that one hundred years ago would have gone unremarked, as if we were right and the people back then were wrong.

Our notions of what's beautiful are still fairly narrow, particularly in America, where generations of immigrants eager to fit in aspired to a homogenized ideal, without prominent features of the sort that could be construed as "ethnic," or lower-class. The reversal in fashion which came about in the sixties, with new ideas being launched in what the ancien-régime haute-couture houses grandly referred to as "the street," revised our standards of beauty as well. The aristocrat, which had been the predominant type, was joined by two others: the moppet and the earth mother.

It is tempting to view Kristen McMenamy as the harbinger of a new era, or a new set of standards, but—for the time being, at least—she seems more an exception to the rule. The path of her career has been uphill; her success is within limits that don't seem to apply to the big stars. "I'm a cult model," she explains. I ask her if the stardom that girls like Evangelista and Turlington and Campbell have attained is within her reach. "No, never," she replies. Why not? What do they have that she doesn't? "Natural beauty." McMenamy says that she always longed to be the kind of girl who wakes up in the morning looking beautiful, and that she has finally got around to accepting the fact that she's not. Even Tessa Jowers acknowledges that the so-called natural beauty isn't McMenamy's type. "You don't want to see Kristen in her bathrobe," she says. "You want to see her in a beaded miniskirt."

Marc Ascoli says that there are certain "divas" on the runway who are truly beautiful, incommensurably beautiful—it is, he remarks, almost a kind of magic to be as beautiful as that—and they also have personality, but they don't push it, because it's enough to be beautiful. He calls McMenamy a model with the ability to please or disturb—even, he says, to embarrass, to inspire in her audience anxiety that at the slightest mishap she might go to pieces. (Indeed, when at Gaultier's show this season McMenamy slipped on the synthetic-ice floor—laid for the benefit of skaters who were part of the entertainment—and nearly fell, there was a heart-stopping moment of panic which, it occurred to me, wouldn't have been nearly so acute if Evangelista or Turlington, who carry themselves with such aplomb, had stumbled.) It is this bizarre, slightly precarious quality that comes across on the runway and in photographs—that comes crashing through high fashion's decorum and veneer—and Ascoli says that because of this quality McMenamy is in fact more important than the superstar models, "*les grandes poupées belles, avec la beauté impeccable, plastique.*" McMenamy is, in his words, "*étrangement belle*"—strangely beautiful. There are, he acknowledges, people who even find her ugly.

"Yes, I think she's beautiful," David Seidner, who photographed her for Claude Montana's current ad campaign, says. "But it's certainly not a classic beauty—it's a kind of awkward, esoteric beauty. And also very contemporary. I don't think she looks like a beauty from another time. She has a kind of decadent look about her, because of the color of her hair and the color of her eyes and the way her mouth scowls slightly." He calls her a cross between Lucille Ball and Sandra Bernhard.

I asked a makeup artist who has worked with McMenamy if he thought she was beautiful.

"What is beautiful?" he replied rhetorically.

I asked him if he thought Christy Turlington was beautiful.

"Yes," he said.

THE DAY after the Comme des Garçons show, McMenamy is at her boyfriend's house, a whitewashed villa surrounded by a lawn and high walls in Paris's Sixteenth Arrondissement, for a shooting for the French edition of *Glamour*.

The photographer is Manuela Pavesi, a fashion editor for Italian *Vogue* who has recently taken the camera into her own hands. Since the story is about McMenamy's distinctive sense of style, Kristen is wearing clothes from her own wardrobe: a burnt-orange acrylic bodysuit, black fishnet tights, and—a souvenir of the last Chanel haute-couture collection—black satin high-heeled shoes with bows at the instep. Her hair, shoulder-length, has been teased and combed over a fall; the makeup artist has not stinted on the eyeshadow. McMenamy sits on the floor as Pavesi, standing on a chair, registers her approval by clicking the shutter. Changing position, McMenamy moves her legs, establishing a rhythm.

She moves. The shutter whirrs. Move. Whirr. Move. Whirr, whirr, whirr. Move. Silence. She moves again. Whirr.

Back and forth, McMenamy and Pavesi carry on this wordless conversation. Occasionally, Pavesi will interrupt. "I prefer—" she begins.

"You like it the other way?" McMenamy asks, resuming an earlier pose.

"That's great," Pavesi says, and then the words subside and the exchange between McMenamy and the camera resumes. The longer you look at McMenamy, Pavesi says, the more interesting she becomes. "She has this ability to be very concentrated, but in a natural way—a way of being naive and sophisticated together," she explains. "She's like an actress to me." Pavesi says she has watched McMenamy work with other photographers, "sometimes not very important photographers—and she always made the picture look good."

For the next shot, McMenamy pulls her bodysuit down over her seat, so that the sleeves are hanging, and knots a black cashmere cardigan over her black lace bra. The crew moves to the terrace. McMenamy leans against a wall lit by the late-afternoon sun. Pavesi positions herself about ten feet away, and stations her assistant in between, to hold down the fronds of a potted palm, which is too heavy to move, so that they don't jut into the bottom of the picture. McMenamy folds her arms in front of her waist; Pavesi responds with the camera. "What happens now if you are trying to hold the sweater, almost to keep it closed with your hands?" she asks. "Is a Marilyn Monroe shot." McMenamy tries it. "That's nice," Pavesi says. Whirr, whirr. McMenamy makes small adjustments in the position of her jaw. She looks deep into the camera and, changing the message in her eyes, runs through a series of expressions: dreamy, provocative, direct, accusatory, questioning. Is this the way you want me to look? she seems to be asking. She moves her lips, pursing them almost imperceptibly. "I really like it now because you are so vulnerable, you know?" Pavesi says. "And it's really you." The light is nearly gone. McMenamy lowers her eyes, then quickly looks up into the camera again. "That's great, Kristen," Pavesi says. "Thank you."

Taxis are called, and McMenamy takes hers directly to a photographer's studio, near République, where Helmut Lang, the Austrian designer, is fitting his collection, scheduled for presentation the following afternoon. He and Michèle Montagne, who organizes his show, greet McMenamy warmly. "What do you want to wear?" he asks her.

"The sexy things," she replies.

The three of them reminisce about Lang's show in Japan. "Not even *Tokyo*," McMenamy complains, rolling her eyes.

"Kobe," Montagne explains.

"We're on a plane for eleven hours," McMenamy continues, "then spend three hours on a train, and then we get to this place where you couldn't even shop."

McMenamy tries on her first outfit, a perforated tunic in cocoa-brown synthetic suede over a gold knit minidress, with brown suede boots; an assistant takes a Polaroid of her in it. She changes into a dress like a giant pom-pom, covered with long brown fabric fringe, and walks the length of the studio for Lang, parting the fringe at her stomach to reveal a plain sheath underneath. He tells her not to do that, to leave what's underneath a mystery, and trims the top layer so that the shape isn't quite so bushy. Next, she tries on a sheer silver organza shift with angel wings outlined in silver sequins on the back. "We try something under it," he tells her. "If it would be less nude, it would be greater."

"Yeah, really," Kristen says. "What happened to the mystery?"

"I think for us she is bringing something really special to the clothes— a kind of sickness," Montagne says. "But a nice sickness. If you have a quite elegant outfit and you put it on a classical, elegant girl, it becomes really boring, somehow, but if you put it on Kristen it becomes modern. Plus, we like her. We have really a kind of family. We are not rethinking our casting every season. Sometimes the agency calls and says 'This girl put on weight,' or 'This girl cut the hair,' or 'This girl is pregnant.' We say, 'Well, we don't care.' Normally, when we like somebody we like them for what they are."

THE FASHION-show-as-theatrical-production, which we now take for granted, is in fact a fairly recent development. Before the ready-to-wear raised the stakes—back in the days when fashion's precincts were no bigger than the salons of the haute couture—new collections were presented in the houses themselves, with no music and, often, no bravado. Each model carried a card displaying the number of the outfit; the audience was seated on narrow gilt chairs, two or three rows deep. A veteran fashion editor recalls that when she arrived in Paris in the late forties the models at most houses were an assortment of body types—some short, some tall. At that time, fashion still considered itself a service industry: designers conceived their collections for different kinds of women, and the clothes were presented on the body types for which they were conceived. At the show, a short, small-boned client would pay special attention to the outfits worn by the models who were short and small-boned: those were the ones that would suit her best. It wasn't until sometime in the seventies that the current standard came to be the rule, and the tall girls prevailed. Not surprisingly, the change came at the time when fashion shows were moving out of the salon and into larger arenas—a convention center in Milan, hotel ballrooms in New York, the tents in Paris. Seen from these longer distances, the tall girls commanded the stage. Today, most runway models start at one hundred and seventy-eight centimeters, or five feet ten, and the manner in which the shows are presented has come to influence the design of the clothes. Martine Sitbon concedes that from time to time she scraps an idea because it's not something that would look good worn by a tall girl on the runway. Only Sybilla and Romeo Gigli defy the norm, setting one hundred and seventy-eight centimeters as a maximum. Gigli says that on a taller girl the proportions of the jackets he designs get distorted.

It was the Japanese—Rei Kawakubo, Yohji Yamamoto—who first booked photography models for their runway shows, when they brought their collections to Paris in the early eighties. Until then, there had been runway models, girls trained to parade the clothes, who had perfect bodies but not necessarily beautiful faces, and photography models, beautiful girls who, in the language of the business, "didn't know how to walk." Soon the models who dominated the pages of fashion magazines took over the runways as well, and now girls like Evangelista and Turlington seem to be everywhere, conferring their glamour on the collections of the major-league and the would-be-major-league designers so liberally that a big show without them by this time looks a little second-rate, as if the house couldn't afford them.

The lights go down, the music starts, and the excitement sets in: something is about to happen. But, for all the showmanship, the choreography, and the special effects, the experience inevitably feels empty. This is not a ballet or an opera or a play. What we see is not a meditation on the nature of human experience but a fantasy that is sometimes hard to decipher. Instead of being transported to some imaginary setting, outside time, we enter a world in which the here and now is made to seem more urgent than ever. Instead of the technique required to present the choreographer's or the composer's or the playwright's intentions, we get the technique required to present the designer's. Mostly, this consists of walking. Most people, until they've seen a fashion show, never realize that walking could be so complicated. Whether to step with the toes first or with the heel, how to put one foot directly in front of the other, as on a tightrope, so that the hips sway more than usual from side to side, what to do with the arms—these are the technical questions that models confront in the course of their work, and though their "roles" in most cases consist of nothing more than navigating the runway, there's no denying that the way they walk amounts to a performance.

At Jil Sander's show in Milan this season, a burst of applause greets Linda Evangelista's every entrance. Cool, self-possessed, chin down, eyes level, her platinum hair like some Hollywood movie star's halo in a portrait by George Hurrell, she steps out onto the runway as if she owned it, swinging one leg around the other. This season, there seems to be something new in her gaze, something bored or vaguely hostile. "Lin-da! Lin-da!" the photographers call after her as she pivots at the end of the runway and begins the journey upstage. She turns, not immediately but a few seconds later, to let them know that she has thought it over and decided to turn, that she's honoring their request this time but doesn't do everything they ask.

Helena Christensen walks with a rolling, seamless gait, her hips twisting slightly; she gives the photographers a lingering look over her shoulder as she turns. Gisèle, a short-haired Brazilian model with a prominent nose, adjusts her back heel slightly inward with every step forward. The photographers call her name; she smiles in reply. But their favorite by far is Marpessa, with her foxy stride. At the end of the runway she poses—arms akimbo, hips jutting way out to one side, torso at an angle—and basks in their hungry attention.

There is Naomi Campbell's giddy half trot, as if she were ready to dance and were obliged to walk instead, with the sort of sexy syncopation that Tennessee Ernie Ford used to call "a hitch in her git-along." There is Yasmin LeBon's cautious advance, a worried look on her face until she reaches the end of the runway, where her brow clears and she breaks into a small, wry smile, as if to let us know that she is above these clothes she's wearing and this job she's doing. There is Christy Turlington's indolent glide, her arms quiet. Claudia Schiffer, the Brigitte Bardot look-alike with a slight case of piano legs, stumps down the runway—appallingly clumsy. Kirsten Owen, a Canadian girl with short-cropped blond hair, makes her way gravely, chin level, shoulders pinned back, eyes straight forward or down, with a little bounce at the bottom of each step, as if she were sinking into the spongy turf of a putting green after a rainstorm.

In the midst of this company comes McMenamy, with her jangly gait, energetically awkward, almost goony at times but touching somehow—her arms swinging in a rhythm not quite synchronized with her legs, her legs frisky and not quite under control, as if they might run off with her at any moment. The impression she leaves is one of knees and elbows. She travels the route down the runway and back with an air of preoccupation, as if her mind were at work on a difficult problem or were constructing some elaborate fantasy from which she can't afford to be distracted. Gérard Miller, the psychoanalyst who was French *Vogue's* emissary to the haute couture, describes the mannequins' attitude as *au-delà*—their attention is focussed elsewhere, somewhere beyond the room where the show is taking place. They do not play to the audience. Neither does McMenamy. Her manner is equally remote, but, unlike the rest of the girls, who seem to have gone outside themselves as a means of transcending the scrutinizing stares, she seems to have travelled inward, where nobody can follow her.

BEHIND THE scenes at Chanel, the supernumeraries are all wearing Chanel jackets and lots of jewelry. One of the hairdressers wears a printed silk Chanel vest over a white T-shirt. Even the reporters—and the *cabine* is crawling with them, all scrounging for some human-interest detail that will make their stories come poignantly to life—are turned out in what looks to be all the Chanel they could muster. Some have assembled entire outfits, head to toe; others sport a token pair of earrings or a quilted leather bag, worn as a badge, in tribute to, or perhaps as a subtle means of ingratiating themselves with, Karl Lagerfeld, the line's designer.

Yasmin LeBon, who is English and is married to Simon LeBon, the lead singer of Duran Duran, has reported for work this morning with her baby daughter in a carriage. As the TV crews swarm around LeBon, who is sitting still for one of the makeup artists while her daughter plays with a blusher brush, and

Evangelista, who is wearing a pink tweed Chanel jacket and jeans, McMenamy tells one of the hairdressers about her screen test. It went well, she says. The director has decided to use subtitles—in French—during her French speeches.

Lagerfeld, sporting his signature ponytail and sunglasses, is sipping a Diet Coke with ice and answering one reporter's questions as others crowd around, waiting their turn. He interrupts the interview to get a fan, which he opens and flicks as he talks. A blond American woman with a TV crew in tow asks him about hemlines. He tells her that any horizontal line cuts a woman, and that he prefers to think vertically, to concentrate on the long, tight line of the arms and legs.

"Some people would say that's a cop-out," she replies. "Where do you see hemlines now, Karl Lagerfeld?"

"I don't see the hemlines anymore," he insists, evidently impatient with her line of questioning.

"You know," she persists, "these American women are *fixated* on hemlines."

He changes the subject, and talks about makeup.

On the outer fringe of the group of journalists clustered around Lagerfeld are two reporters trading information. One has just finished interviewing Christy Turlington. "She's twenty-two, she's engaged, and she's quit smoking," she tells the other.

The blonde interviewing Lagerfeld fires her last question: "Have you gone too funky this time, funky Karl?"

Gilles Dufour, Lagerfeld's right hand at Chanel, says that McMenamy, who modelled for the pictures in this season's press kit, has "a fantastic way of posing for photographs, a new way of acting with her hands, her face, her legs." He goes on to say, "Every two or three years, there's a new person to come along, and she's the new girl now. We go in her direction."

Lagerfeld calls her "a chameleon, an actress." She is not, he says, "a robo-model." He chose her not only for Chanel but for the publicity photographs for the line he designs under his own name and for the Fendi collection, which he also designs, because, he explains, she's the only model who could look so different, who could give each line a distinct identity. "She is ready to do anything," he says. "For her, the most important thing is the next photo." He flicks his fan. "Also," he adds, "there is something very touching, very vulnerable about her."

In the next room, sitting at one of the tables as a makeup artist puts the finishing touches on her eyes, which are shaded with brown and outlined in

black, McMenamy says of Lagerfeld, "He's given me back my pride after I lost it in New York." A hairdresser fits a short black wig over a blue nylon cap covering her hair.

"*Vous allez chercher vos mannequins, s'il vous plaît!*" Dufour calls out, like a town crier, circulating through the crowd. "*On va commencer!*"

McMenamy moves next door and locates her rack, with its poster-board chart listing every outfit: there are separate columns for stockings, scarves, bags, belts, gloves, hats, shoes, and jewelry, and a row of earrings is clipped to the right side. She puts on her first number: a double-breasted black coat, slit to the thigh, lined in red, with an Astrakhan collar, and red snakeskin platform ankle boots, capped, Chanel style, in black at the toe and the heel. A quilted gold leather dog collar is too big and slips down her neck; an assistant pinches it in back and staples it tighter.

"Christy! Helena!" calls a woman clutching a list of the girls in sequence. "Kristen! Gisèle!"

McMenamy falls in line, holding the end of a "leash" attached to the dog collar—a gold chain threaded with black leather—in one hand, like a poodle taking herself for a walk.

"Lisa! Lisa! Karen! Emma! Nadège!"

Gisèle opens her black ciré raincoat like a flasher to reveal a black fishnet body stocking with two black silk camellias—Chanel's signature flower— as pasties.

"Stephanie! Yasmeen!"

This season, Lagerfeld has found his inspiration in the street: in the B-boy style worn by the guys who sell fake-Chanel sweatshirts on the sidewalks in New York; in bikers; in club kids dressed in early-seventies, late-hippie clothes that they bought at the flea market. There are silver quilted-leather duckbill caps; black leather motorcycle boots with double-C medallions connecting the ankle straps; rectangular "CHANEL" plates like ID bracelets, the letters cut out, dangling from gold chains; denim suits; bluejeans with the side seams traced in the gold chain that Coco Chanel used to weight the bottom of her classic jacket; chunky gold cuff bracelets in pairs, connected, like handcuffs, by a long chain draping across the back; platform shoes in tweeds that match the suits.

"Jennifer! Kristen! Yasmin LeBon!"

The girls run from the exit to their racks, ripping off earrings, bracelets, necklaces as they go. Chain belts fall to the floor with a clank. Kristen lies down on the floor, and the fitter takes hold of the jeans she's wearing, studded all over with Chanel buttons, and yanks them off with one mighty tug.

"Gisèle! Christy! Helena!"

Victoire de Castellane, one of Lagerfeld's assistants, who often models in the show, stands waiting her turn, wearing a black satin cocktail dress over a black fishnet body stocking, with big earrings clipped to the lobes of black satin Mickey Mouse ears on a headband.

"Gisèle! Gisèle! Gisèle! Gisèle!"

The final passage is a group of full-skirted evening gowns worn with motorcycle boots and quilted-leather bomber jackets.

"Karen! Linda!"

Lagerfeld turns up the collar on Evangelista's white leather jacket, banded in black.

"Karen! Karen!"

"*Oui!*" Karen shrieks.

Yasmin LeBon scoops up her daughter, who has been dressed in a pink jumpsuit banded with black satin and fastened with Chanel buttons, and carries her down the runway, to cheers and applause that combine to make what from backstage sounds like one big, undifferentiated din. Lagerfeld follows. Moments later, a horde from out front surges backstage to congratulate him. André Leon Talley, the creative director of American *Vogue*, arrives, escorting Sylvester Stallone, whose girlfriend modelled in the show.

FASHION MODELS are professionally silent. In photographs and on the runway, they never speak, and so do nothing to contradict the benefit of the doubt we give them on the basis of their looks. We are slow to believe that anyone as beautiful as, say, Helena Christensen or Christy Turlington could be ruthless or stupid or cruel—though we're perfectly prepared to accuse the people we meet as we go about our everyday lives of being all these things. The equation of beauty with virtue is sooner or later, for all of us, disproved by experience, but the idea lingers in some corner of our minds beyond the reach of logic— a remnant of the stories we were told as children, in which we could always count on the witches to be ugly and the good fairies beautiful. In real life, there is no such justice, but there is, in America, at any rate, a long-standing faith that the practice of virtue produces beauty in those who weren't born with it—that, as the saying goes, people by the time they're fifty have the face they deserve.

Writing about the early part of this century, Banner says in *American Beauty*, "Both feminists and beauty experts argued that spiritual qualities were more important to creating and maintaining the appearance of beauty than were physical attributes. Both argued that beauty was potentially available to any woman, if she followed the proper ethical path."

In a turn-of-the-century beauty manual, which Banner quotes, Ella Adelia Fletcher wrote that a girl's "very earliest observations and intuitions teach her this fact, that Beauty's path through life is a sort of rose-bordered one, a royal progress; for to Beauty the world, big and little, high and low, pays homage." These days, Beauty's path is a narrow catwalk, built several feet above the ground and bordered not by roses but by photographers, and the homage takes the form of fame, movie-star boyfriends, and fees that can range as high as the fifty thousand dollars Turlington reportedly received for Gianni Versace's show this season. "As the girl ripens into the woman," Fletcher continued, "every experience in life teaches her that her share of its successes and pleasures will be in proportion to her own ability to win favor, to please, and that the first and most potent influence is physical beauty." For all the apparent headway that has been made in women's lives in the past century, this much remains unchanged: beauty is still a crucial issue, dividing girls early on into haves and have-nots, and, to the extent that some girls' personalities are shaped by their beauty, other girls' personalities are shaped by their lack of it.

Until the world came around and reversed its verdict on her looks, McMenamy was one of the have-nots. Though she has been vindicated, she still carries with her the memory of childhood slights and insults. In fact, it's only lately that she has come to think of herself as "beautiful" at all, and one senses that it's a notion that hasn't entirely sunk in. To all appearances, she has ascended into the ranks of the great beauties of our time, but not without some misgivings, some reluctance to lay claim to the privileges that come with this prime territory. She tries constantly to come up with new poses. Lindbergh says that at a shooting "she's very nervous always that she will not be good enough, that the picture will not be perfect enough." She has, he says, somehow managed to keep a level head, as most successful girls in this business do not; she is not conceited. "She has always doubts about everything," he explains. She has worked hard to justify herself as a model. Contemplating the behavior of some of her colleagues at a shooting, she says, "How dare they just stand there and look beautiful?" Many, if not most, of them are girls who grew up beautiful, girls whose entrance into a room was consistently greeted with smiles. Strangers offered to carry their suitcases. Men wrote them letters and sent them flowers and begged to be allowed to spend the rest of their lives with them, so that over time these girls came to expect the attention, the kindness, the favors that the rest of us, as we grew up, experienced so rarely, so gratefully. Even now, presiding over the runway at Chanel, decked out in the height of the haute couture, at the center of attention, McMenamy seems to find something vaguely amiss in the world's reflex response to a beautiful girl. While the other models greet the crowd's approval as nothing more than they deserve, she seems slightly dazed by it.

Even if she were inclined to take it for granted, though, the fact is that she's never allowed to get used to it for long. Off the runway, she says, she is never noticed. The discrepancy between who McMenamy is in her photographs and who she is in her life is wider for her than it is for most models. "Linda's Linda," she observes. "She looks the same in the street as she does in the picture." The discrepancy may be one of the reasons that McMenamy isn't more widely known as a model. She looks so different from one picture to the next that sometimes her own mother doesn't recognize her.

It often happens that men ask to be introduced to McMenamy on the basis of how she looks in one of her pictures, and when they finally meet her they're disappointed. "They come up to me and say, 'In that beer ad, you were my dream,'" she says. "*Were.* I walk down the street with no makeup on, and people don't look at me twice. And yet when they see me in magazines they think, Hey, I'd really like to get to know *her.* I'm very photogenic, I know, and I look sexy in front of the camera. I'm an exhibitionist. And I love playing." It's easier, she acknowledges, to play at being somebody else in front of the camera than to do it in real life. "What I do in my profession is a little bit wrong, because I'm selling things you don't really need," she says, but without the ring of conviction, as if this were something that someone once accused her of at a dinner party. "If you've got big boobs, it sells bathing suits," she explains. "If you've got a nice face, it sells magazines." But here she becomes more animated, and the words again sound like her own. "I'm selling unreality," she continues matter-of-factly. "But I don't think about that. It's fun for me, because I can be anything. Because it's an illusion. *I'm* an illusion."

Visionaries

A SULTRY afternoon in L.A., sanctuary of the sun god, capital of the movie industry, playground of rock stars—New York may have lost its glamour, but L.A.'s is intact: this is a city built on attitude. A young man strides purposefully into L.A. Eyeworks, an optical shop on Melrose Avenue, and comes to an abrupt halt in front of a display along the left-hand wall. A striking woman with long black hair and black-framed glasses approaches him. "Is there something I can help you with?" she asks. "Yeah," he answers. "I need some shades."

AT 10 A.M. on the Sunday after a party for which Tony Gross crossed the Channel, he comes down the stairs of his two-star Paris hotel wearing a three-piece, red-and-black pinstripe suit, a big gold watch, a massive diamond pinkie ring, and sunglasses. Gross is the creative half of Cutler & Gross, London opticians, which has been in business for eighteen years now. A few years ago, the firm started producing a wholesale line of sunglasses; while Graham Cutler minds the store, in Knightsbridge, Gross designs the frames, which are sold all over Europe, America, Japan, and Australia. The sunglasses he is wearing—slightly mean-looking, he hopes, with small, rimless, oblong dark-green lenses suspended from a narrow gold bar—are vintage 1962, not of his own design. He never wears glasses from his line. "All the people who make glasses wearing their own glasses—it's so corny," he says. Gross, who is bald, heavyset, and what the English call shortsighted, explains, "I'm trying to do a look. I'd like to be Jean Gabin. I've got the build, I've got the suit—and, well, that's about it. Everything else is lacking."

A man with a mission, Gross is out to move sunglasses away from the bookish, Brideshead look and toward something sexy. The period he worships, he says, is the fifties and early sixties. "I would personally rather look like a

Greek shipping magnate than like a successful Wall Street banker. Or, if I were a girl, I'd rather look like Audrey Hepburn than like some bluestocking who has just got her degree at Oxford." He talks about the similarities between wearing glasses and wearing a mask—the element of fantasy, the precedents in primitive cultures. "There's a lot of literature about psychology and eyes," he says. "Eye contact is, of course, the first sexual contact we ever have. And then there are all those expressions, like 'giving people the eye'—we don't give them the nose or the mouth—and all those aggressive things, like wanting to poke somebody in the eye or wanting to tear his eyes out, which, of course, Freud said means wanting to castrate somebody. I don't want to go overboard about this, but you can see the sexual connotations."

Gross describes the glasses he designs as being at the same time "retro" and "cutting edge." He says that he looks backward for inspiration, that he never tries to be "clever." In an attempt to revive the wide-eyed sort of sunglasses that became famous as Jackie Onassis's shield against the paparazzi, he has designed several models reminiscent of the sixties, including a group of figure-eight-shaped plastic frames with "clashing," rather than matching, lenses (red with fuchsia, yellow with red, clear with blue); many of these have wide sidepieces, so that they can be worn, sixties style, on the top of the head. There are narrow, white plastic frames with red or green lenses, pink marbleized plastic frames with pink mirrored lenses, and "cowboy glasses"—gold frames, tooled at the bridge and the corners, with mirrored silver lenses.

In 1985, the laws in England changed, and opticians were suddenly allowed to advertise. Now when a pair of Cutler & Gross sunglasses appears in a magazine the firm is credited. This change, as Gross sees it, conveniently coincides with a shift in thinking that has been taking place, with people coming to regard glasses less as a medical necessity and more as a fashion accessory. In England, he admits, the battle has been uphill all the way, given the national suspicion of fashion. "And the climate doesn't help," he says. Gross has a joke about English sunglasses—that they have clear lenses. Other countries have been quicker to come around, but only partway. Gross is glad to see sunglasses being sold in department stores, but he laments the conditions. "As the big designers are going into glasses, theirs are often put with their clothes. And mine end up at a counter somewhere near the perfume department, where they're appallingly displayed, all crammed together. They lie there—well, I think of them as dead, really."

In Paris, on the Rue Saint-Martin, one Sunday afternoon in February: A crowd of fashion journalists, retailers, and would-be designers stands in front of the entrance to Yohji Yamamoto's showroom, spilling over into the street, and waits for the doors to open for the showing of his spring collection for men. "Fashion's got so *boring*," a man with a British accent complains to his companion. "Don't you agree?" The companion does. "Really," the man goes on, "there is nothing to get excited about, nothing that makes you sit up in your chair and think, I simply must have that." The companion nods sadly.

"I didn't know you wore glasses," one woman says to another, who is sporting rectangular pistachio-colored frosted-plastic frames, with clear lenses.

"I used to wear contact lenses," the other says, "but I stopped."

"I know," the first woman says. "Contacts are such a nuisance."

"No, it wasn't that," the second woman explains. "I just all of a sudden started seeing all these glasses I had to have. First it was sunglasses, then I had some sunglass frames made for my prescription. And I liked the way I looked in them so much that I wore them to work. Then I ordered some more. Now I have fourteen pairs. I only wear my contacts if it's raining."

At a party last spring in Washington, guests watch the Academy Awards on television: Geena Davis and Jeff Goldblum arrive on camera to present the award for documentary short subject. Davis is wearing an off-the-shoulder sea-foam-green satin dress with a long skirt and a bustle. She and Goldblum read the nominations on the teleprompter. Davis tears open the envelope, puts on her glasses—pretty, upswept tartan frames—and, looking the camera squarely in the eye, announces the winner. "Huh," one of the party guests, a film critic, says in amazement. "What?" asks a woman in his vicinity. "Look," he says, nodding toward the TV set. "There's Geena Davis in an evening gown, wearing *glasses*."

Christian Roth, a tall, affable young man with twenty-twenty vision, works out of a suite of rooms in New York's garment district, designing a line of glasses for his company, Optical Affairs, and marketing frames designed by Jean Paul Gaultier. Roth was born in Germany and first visited the United States fifteen years ago, as a teen-ager; from then on, he says, his dream was to return. In 1982, after working for six months at an optical shop in Berlin, he began designing his own line, came to New York, and founded his company. The market in high-quality, innovative eyewear—what is described on Seventh Avenue as "fashion-forward"—was wide open, he says. The only problem was price. "Because at that time the market wasn't really ready for a hundred-and-fifty- or two-hundred-dollar retail price. But there was hardly anybody else, and there was a big market, so the business worked well from Day One. Since then, so many new companies have been started—every designer name you can imagine has turned up with an eyewear license. And existing companies from the sixties and seventies have upgraded a lot—they can't offer regular merchandise anymore, they have to offer something a little bit interesting. So I would say five years ago the buyer picked from ten lines and today he picks from two or three hundred."

Roth's biggest seller this summer has been a pair of rimless sunglasses that opticians are encouraged to cut to suit the customer's face, using diagrams that match frame shape to face shape. He also makes frames covered in lizard or in "fur" (a leopard-spotted calf); "antique" silver frames that "age," or oxidize, with wear; tricolor sunglasses (like trifocals in color); and a wooden parquet frame. In Gaultier's collection, there are metal frames with magnetic clip-on sun lenses, glasses with spring-hinged sidepieces, frames embellished with nuts and bolts and other assorted hardware. The customers for these are, Roth admits, mostly men.

Not surprisingly, Roth thinks that the recent trend toward having more than one pair of glasses is a healthy one. "For example, an elegant lady used to have twenty pairs of shoes and only one pair of glasses," he says. "Today, she has thirty pairs of shoes and ten or twelve pairs of glasses, fitting with particular things in her wardrobe. Most people say shoes are so important, but if you look at somebody the first thing that hits your eye is the frame, and not the shoe." In the campaign to promote the notion of eyewear as fashion, Roth says, *Elle* has led the way, as the first fashion magazine to put a model wearing sunglasses on the cover—defying the prevailing opinion that eye contact is what sells magazines at the newsstand.

IN THE early nineteen-thirties, the United States Army Air Corps asked Bausch & Lomb to develop eyewear that would protect against the sun's rays, in response to complaints from pilots, who were experiencing eyestrain, headaches, and nausea. The result was the first lens that could block ultraviolet and infrared light, check glare, and still accurately convey the colors of the spectrum. Anti-glare goggle-shaped glasses were issued to the military in 1932, and four years later Bausch & Lomb introduced a civilian version of these aviator sunglasses (eventually trademarked Ray-Ban). Norman Salik, the company's vice-president in charge of promotion and publicity, calls this "MacArthur look"—the leather flight jacket, the aviator sunglasses—"the start of the Ray-Ban tradition." Six years ago, he says, Bausch & Lomb undertook marketing surveys in four different countries, and in every case the results came back the same: among the words people used most often to describe Ray-Ban aviator glasses were "American" and "macho."

Bausch & Lomb now sells Ray-Bans in some sixty different shapes and in dozens of materials; there are over one hundred versions of the aviator alone. Salik attributes the recent surge in the optical business to the use of sunglasses in fashion magazines and in the movies. In May 1982, *GQ* featured in its fashion pages a pair of Ray-Ban Wayfarer sunglasses, a style first introduced thirty years before, and over the course of that year sales of the Wayfarer climbed to more than eight times what they had been. When Tom Cruise appeared in *Risky Business* wearing Wayfarers and in *Top Gun* wearing Ray-Ban aviators, sales of those models went through the roof. As proof of how much the industry has grown, Salik cites the sunglasses boutiques and kiosks that started in California, Texas, and Florida and are now turning up all over the country; the Sunglass Hut, in the Danbury Fair Mall, in Connecticut, did five hundred thousand dollars' worth of business last year.

AT A BUS stop on Fifth Avenue: An elderly woman with swollen ankles turns to a man who is tuned into his Walkman and asks, "Does this bus go to Thirty-fourth Street?" He continues moving his head in a turtle-like motion and tapping his thigh, in time to his private music. "Excuse me." She tries again, a little louder. "Do you known if this bus goes to Thirty-fourth Street?" He turns his face to her but says nothing. In his mirrored aviator sunglasses she can see herself—the picture of frustration. "Hey," she says, giving him a good shove on the shoulder. "Is anybody home?"

THE NAME that arises most often in conversations with people in the fashion industry about eyewear is Alain Mikli. It is Mikli, they say, who made everyone sit up and take notice of glasses in their own right, as something more than an adjunct to clothes. It is Mikli who has pushed back the frontiers, and if the glasses he's designed haven't always been wearable, at least they've made their point; glasses that would have qualified as outrageous ten years ago are merely unusual today, now that Mikli has gone such a long way beyond them. In person, Mikli has the appearance and demeanor of a café intellectual. He wears a white shirt, blue jeans, and glasses from his own collection—stern-looking oval lenses rimmed in matte-black wire, with a bar of clear plastic crosshatched in blue, green, and purple across the top. Tall and serious, with long, dark hair and a low, quiet voice, he talks about his work in eloquent, often philosophical terms.

Glasses, to his way of thinking, are *"pour s'habiller le regard"*—to clothe "the gaze"; he calls himself a *"couturier pour les yeux"*—a dressmaker for the eyes. To dress *le regard*, he says, is much more important than to dress the body. One can conceal a physical flaw with clothing, but one can't hide anything in *le regard*. It is *le regard* that is for him the most important thing about a person—the thing that is the strongest, the most subtle, the most intimate. It is *le regard*, he explains, that enables us to communicate with the outside world, to see what's happening around us, to perceive danger; it is thanks to *le regard* that two people who don't speak the same language can understand each other. It is in *le regard* that we recognize each other, that we express everything—grief, delight, unhappiness, contentment, affection, disapproval. Mikli says he finds it fascinating to play with all this in the glasses he designs.

What, then, about sunglasses and the way they mask the eyes? Mikli says yes, there are sunglasses—Ray-Ban Wayfarers, for instance—that hide the eyes, that are a uniform of sorts. Wayfarers, he finds, give everyone—men and woman alike—the same aggressive expression, the same androgynous face; the individual puts them on and becomes the stereotype. Mikli has just finished designing a collection for Ray-Ban's international division—five sunglasses frames intended as a feminine alternative to the macho classics. The shapes are upswept and less severe, suggestive of the way the eyes turn up at the corners when a person smiles; the lines are curved rather than straight; and the contours are sculptural, not flat like those of the Wayfarer. Mikli says it's possible to use sunglasses to change *le regard* altogether, to give a face an entirely different expression—an expression of violence, of sensuality, of sweetness, or whatever one chooses. So that, even though the eyes are hidden, by the act of reproducing the shape of the eye in some exaggerated form sunglasses can reconstitute *le regard* and remodel the face.

Mikli grew up in Grenoble, where his mother owned a clothing store, and in Paris. He began wearing glasses at sixteen, choosing classic, rather commonplace metal frames, he recalls, in the hope that nobody would notice. He says the experience was traumatic, though probably not unlike what many people have gone through on being told that they need glasses—feeling that their appearance has been somehow disfigured, that their image of themselves has been violated, that their glasses come between them and others. In one of Mikli's ads from last year, a young man wears the model that Mikli calls his self-portrait—frames of shiny gold metal with a beak over the nose, like Cubist Groucho glasses. The profile matches Mikli's. "*N'avez-vous pas honte de rire d'un myope?*" the caption says. Aren't you afraid to laugh at someone nearsighted?

Mikli says that he went to the Lycée Fresnel, an opticians' training school, because it was the closest school to his house in Paris. After graduation, he worked for a while in an optical shop, fitting customers for run-of-the-mill glasses that he didn't like and that the people buying them didn't seem to like, either. In time, he came to wonder where it was written that glasses had to make the people who wore them look and feel so miserable, and, in an attempt to right just one of the things wrong with the world, he began designing frames. In the eleven years since, he has worked with a number of French, British, and American fashion designers, concocting special glasses for their runway shows and, in the cases of Claude Montana and Maud Frizon, devising collections to be sold under their names.

Mikli's headquarters are on a small street in Paris's Thirteenth Arrondissement, a part of town that fashion has not yet overrun. Behind the reception desk is an enormous black-and-white photo of a jovial, mustachioed, rotund, hairy-chested man—a friend of Mikli's—wearing a sun monocle. Upstairs, in the showroom, are flat metal sculptures, like cookie cutters, of a man's face in profile, with a notch at the bridge of the nose for displaying glasses. The current collection encompasses frames in every imaginable shape and material—in plastic tortoiseshell with infusions of red, green, and black; in clear plastic containing chips of color, like a terrazzo ice rink; in plastic striped with tiny slats that are one color seen from one side, another color seen from the other. There are (for Montana) black glasses set with rhinestones, with long narrow lengths of black Lycra at the temples, to wrap and tie like a scarf or a turban around the head.

For his own amusement, Mikli has over the years been experimenting with the classic round shape, the simplest and most traditional, as a way of extending the genre—as a game. The results range from round sun lenses in a ferocious-looking thick matte perforated-steel frame, for Montana's men's collection;

a sinister strip of white plastic, no wider than a Band-Aid, with tiny, dark, binocular-like lenses set in it; delicate, circular steel frames with spirals at the bridge and the temples, for Maud Frizon; and round lenses whose upper half is bordered with an arc of red enameled aluminum—Mikli describes these as "*anti-mode.*"

Up the street is the workshop where Mikli's prototypes are made and his archives are stored. His dog, a rambunctious black briard named Coquine, conducts him and a visitor on a tour, pausing every now and then for them to catch up. There are dozens of what Mikli calls *études*, undertaken out of sheer curiosity and never produced for sale—like the pair of black-velvet-covered frames that were part of one season's research for Montana's collection. Delving into drawers marked " '79–'80" and " '82," Mikli pulls out a phantasmagorical bright-blue plastic frame studded with rhinestones, and a pair of asymmetrical sunglasses with a rectangular lens framed in black and a triangular one framed in white—relics from what he calls the era when he was in the clouds.

Mikli talks about glasses with a vocabulary borrowed from the couture. He talks about being inspired by plastics and metals the way a designer is inspired by fabrics; he talks about using a smooth, shiny plastic, like a lining, on the inside of a pair of matte-plastic frames—something warm and *agréable* for the side that comes in contact with the skin.

Though he speaks with great respect of *créateurs* like Montana, Gaultier, and Azzedine Alaïa, he finds most fashion now rather blasé. We've seen so much, he says, and we're so critical. The tendency always is to compare what's new with what has already been done. So most designers, consciously or not, reproduce the images that are familiar to us, playing on the silhouettes and styles that have entered our common language and, in some cases, have become clichés. Mikli believes it's the past that hinders fashion today. But designing glasses is a different story. The tradition in which he works is comparatively shallow, with no counterpart of the illustrious era of the haute couture, dominated by Chanel, Dior, Balenciaga. As a result, it's easier to be innovative.

When Mikli was in school, he was given precepts—"the shape of the glasses must follow the line of the eyebrows," for instance—and for a time he followed them. Little by little, he came to realize that the rules had been deduced from what people were accustomed to seeing, that they were nothing more than formulas for the conventions. But if one wants to break the conventions, he says, there are no rules, and then everything is possible.

Mikli's ads rely on so-called real people, not actresses or rock stars or fashion models. Most of these real people are his friends; some are his employees. In a "catalogue" of black-and-white portraits by Nigel Scott, they look thoughtful, complex, peculiar, not fashionable but urbane, in a perpetual state of forward motion; these people are where it's happening, whatever it is. The idiosyncratic cast of characters is elevated by means of these pictures to a level of scrutiny usually reserved for fashion models and movie stars: this is the apotheosis of the oddball, and the by-product is another kind of glamour— the glamour of being not beautiful or famous but interesting. In these instances, the glasses serve to complicate the faces.

A WOMAN, a journalist assigned to interview a Nobel Prize-winning author, is standing in front of her closet in her bathrobe—her contact lenses in, her makeup on—frantically searching for something to wear. The phone rings. It's her boyfriend. "Wear your red suit," he says.

"Too bright," she answers.

"Well, then, your navy-blue jumpsuit."

"Not dressy enough."

"How about that black knit skirt?"

"Too sexy."

"Well," he says, and she can hear in his voice the effort it's taking him not to lose his patience, "how do you want to look?"

"Intelligent," she answers.

"Wear your glasses," he tells her.

DENNIS LEIGHT calls Oliver Peoples "a family business," "a corner store." Three years ago, he and his brother Larry, and Larry's wife, Cindy, and a friend from childhood, Kenneth Schwartz, decided to start an optical shop on Sunset Boulevard, in Los Angeles. About four months before the store opened, Dennis Leight got a call from a friend in New York, an antique dealer: the entire inventory of an eyeglasses distributor, which had been in storage since his death, in the thirties, had just surfaced, and the friend had bought it. Were the Leights interested? Larry Leight went to New York, took a look at the contents of a few of the dozen or so enormous cartons, and bought them all. Inside were unassembled fifty-year-old frames made of hand-tooled gold or silver, in their original wrapping. Unpacking the boxes, Dennis Leight found an old receipt made out to one "Oliver Peoples," and the four partners liked the name so much that they adopted it for their business.

The shop still has some of those old frames tucked away, but mostly Oliver Peoples sells glasses of its own design, many of them inspired by vintage models. Dennis Leight prides himself on the details: engraved patterns across the bridge and around the rim, and other old-fashioned touches, which make the glasses precious-looking, like a watch or jewelry—something to be worn with pride. There is nothing innovative or even unfamiliar here, unless it's the way materials are sometimes combined—a tortoiseshell frontpiece, for instance, with matte-black metal arms. People who want to look like movie stars will have to go elsewhere; movie stars who want to look like intellectuals go to Oliver Peoples.

After ten years in the optical business (seven of them at L.A. Eyeworks), Dennis Leight says, "I never hear people buying glasses say anymore what I used to hear them say all the time: 'Oh, these are just for the daytime: around the house or at work—I wear my *contacts* at night.' Now we get people in here who don't even need a prescription, ordering glasses with clear lenses. Sometimes they'll tell us that they're trying to look a little older for their job, or that they want to look as if they read more books, but what it usually comes down to is that they just want glasses to wear as a part of their outfit." The kid who walked around with a naked face and made fun of his four-eyed classmates has grown up to want to look like them. The revenge of the nerds.

ON A recent trip to the West Coast, shopping for sunglasses at L.A. Eyeworks with a friend: An agreeable young woman is helping us. My friend tries on one pair—black, in a cynical, squinty shape—and consults the mirror. Silence as he studies himself. The young woman leans across the counter and asks him, in a low, confidential tone, "What's going through your mind?"

LUNCH ON a weekday at the Bistro Garden, in Beverly Hills: A woman dressed in the latest fashions that Rodeo Drive has to offer is waiting for her date, and he turns up at last—a man wearing a band-collared shirt, a sand-colored linen jacket, and sunglasses with reflective lenses. They order.

"Do I have to sit here and watch myself eat?" she asks.

"I'd rather leave them on," he says, and, by way of explanation, lowers his sunglasses, so that she can see his eyes. The expression on his face is pained.

"Rough night?" She says.

When they've finished their cappuccino, she reaches over and draws his face close to hers. He looks surprised, then expectant, like somebody about to be kissed. She takes out her lipstick and, holding his face steady with her left hand, reapplies her red-orange mouth with her right, using his sunglasses for a mirror.

A WOMAN waiting to meet some friends at a restaurant in lower Manhattan takes a seat at the bar and orders a drink. A man wearing an Armani suit comes in and takes the seat next to her. "What's that you're reading?" he asks.

"A letter," she answers, in a tone intended to discourage further conversation.

"A love letter?" he persists.

"No," she says sourly.

"So tell me," he continues, "what do you do?"

"I'm a police officer," she replies, not entirely convincingly.

"No kidding," he says, looking at her legs.

"No kidding," she says, looking around for someplace else to wait. She consults her watch. Where are her friends? It's already fifteen minutes past their reservation. People are standing two deep at the bar.

"There's nowhere else to go," the man beside her says triumphantly.

"No, I guess there isn't," she replies, and, reaching into her bag, she pulls out her sunglasses and puts them on.

A TRAVELLER with some time on his hands at the San Francisco airport this past spring might have browsed through an exhibition on the departures level of the international terminal called "The Eyes Have It: A History of Eyewear from the 1700s to the Present Day" and sponsored by the San Francisco Airports Commission, and seen these things:

A pair of round iron spectacles with bottle-green lenses, American, circa 1750.

A pair of tiny oval tortoiseshell frames, the kind currently popular with people in the forefront of the fashion business—dated 1790.

Very funky looking spectacles made of tortoiseshell, brass, and glass, with a high-arched bridge and low sidepieces, from China, circa 1800.

Early Eskimo snow goggles of whalebone and sinew.

Wire-rimmed figure-eight-shaped glasses with cobalt-blue lenses, mid-nineteenth century.

Photographs of Cary Grant as Barnaby Fulton in *Monkey Business*, 1952, wearing thick lenses that look like the optical equivalent of orthopedic shoes, and of Marilyn Monroe as Pola in *How to Marry a Millionaire*, a year later, wearing rhinestone-studded cat's-eye glasses, a hat with a veil, and a mink collar.

A chart used to test the vision of children who don't yet know the alphabet. Twenty-twenty: green star, yellow plus sign, red circle, blue heart, green flag.

Various glasses from the L.A. Eyeworks museum collection, including a pair of black plastic frames in the shape of two sixteenth notes, and a rhinestone-encrusted pair, in the shape of a butterfly, with two jewelled antennae extending upward from the bridge—both pairs made in France, sometime in the late forties.

A brief introduction to two displays of recent, one-of-a-kind glasses, reading, "UNIQUE DESIGN EYEWEAR presents a further departure from the conventions of eyewear to eyewear as sculpture. Embellishing on blank frames, designers have created narrative, figurative, architectural and decorative works in mixed media, and have established an iconography of eyewear." The items on display were identified in museum-style captions, such as

LINDA HESH
Dinner Time, 1988
Frame: Goa by l.a.Eyeworks
Engraved spring steel,
sterling silver spoon
and fork, grey sun lenses

and

THOMAS MANN
Untitled, 1987
Frame: Gigantor by l.a.Eyeworks
Sandblasted carved black plastic,
powder painted black chassis,
hand laminated plastic, zinc screws,
brass washers, prismatic plastic
lenses

THE OPENING-night party for *Dirty Dancing* in New York, two summers ago: After the screening, the guests proceed to Roseland, where a crowd has gathered on the sidewalk to watch them make their way to the door. The director—not yet famous—gets out of his limo in the company of three not even potentially famous friends, one of whom is wearing sunglasses. "Is that somebody?" a woman standing at the curb asks her friend.

WHEN GAI GHERARDI and Barbara McReynolds founded L.A. Eyeworks, in 1979, they presented it in their ads as an optical shop selling eyeglasses from the fifties, sixties, and eighties. "We didn't even *acknowledge* the seventies," McReynolds says. The seventies, in their opinion, was when the theretofore distinguished history of eyewear design took a nosedive. Although they confess to having participated wholeheartedly for a time in the seventies look, by 1979 they were finding it ugly, if not ridiculous—an opinion from which they have not wavered.

One summer afternoon, they are in the office, the back room at the store—McReynolds, who has shoulder-length gray hair, wearing a black knit dress, a black-and-white striped jacket, and matte-black eyeglasses, and Gherardi, plump, wearing a black-on-beige tattersall dress and yellow tartan frames. Amid the clutter on the desk are: Polaroids of the store's ads; a miniature green felt sombrero trimmed with silver sequins; a red plastic yoyo; a goldfish bowl filled with big white shooter marbles commemorating the store's tenth anniversary ("l.a.Eyeworks," the marbles say. "Est. 1979"); a silver bowl, like a shipwrecked serving dish, with little plastic people hanging over the sides; and an arch made of a hollowed-out half of a tree trunk, under which five small frogs huddle in a pyramid, breathing in unison. At night, Gherardi says, when all the people are gone, the frogs come out and jump around the office.

Gherardi and McReynolds were friends in high school, in Huntington Beach, California (McReynolds played guitar with Gherardi's boyfriend), but then went their separate ways until 1968, when Gherardi was between jobs, thinking about becoming an architect, she says, and McReynolds asked her to come help out in the optical shop where she was working, at the University of California at Irvine. Gherardi was soon converted to optometry, but they also used the shop for draft dodgers' meetings and other political activities. Gherardi says that for both of them the optical business has been a vehicle for expressing themselves. The places they worked were not your standard, neighborhood opticians.

"No," McReynolds says. "There was always rebel work going on."

By 1979, McReynolds and Gherardi had had enough of the big white Emmanuelle Khanh sunglasses that covered the face like a windshield, enough of glasses that were jewelled or monogrammed or emblazoned with the wearer's sign of the zodiac—although, Gherardi says now, all those things were necessary at the time, to get people to stop thinking about glasses as a prosthesis and start thinking about them as fashion. During the formative stages of L.A. Eyeworks, at the height of the signature-eyewear boom, McReynolds and Gherardi laid down a few rules for themselves: no names and no logos on the outside of the frames; no "faceted-glass" lenses (the rimless, beveled look); no Optyl, the injection-molded plastic that had been so rapturously received by the optical industry; no sidepieces coming from the bottom of the rims; no Porsche Carrera sunglasses, even though they were then one of the best-selling sunglasses in the country. "That left us with not a whole lot to choose from, one would think," Gherardi says. "Obviously, we couldn't just go and buy from our local salesman." They went to Europe and brought back frames from Alain Mikli and other designers they found there. They made the rounds of manufacturers, saying, McReynolds recalls, "'Show us your worst-seller.' What everybody else was buying we didn't want. What we were looking for no one else wanted."

"So we put together a very generic kind of statement," Gherardi continues. "We took those kinds of frames, and we dyed them, we sandblasted them, we mirrored their lenses—we did all sorts of things to them. We also left them as themselves. And we presented them in a whole new context."

"We took the frame your grandfather wore, with a gold or silver chassis," McReynolds says, "but instead of presenting it on a sixty-five-year-old man we presented it on a beautiful twenty-two-year-old model."

Gherardi adds, "We took a pair of glasses you'd seen on Henry Kissinger for twenty years and put them on a great-looking guy, and all of a sudden they looked really nice, really appealing. Also, the time was pretty exciting: 1980 was dawning, clothing was looking interesting. The face was much more in celebration than it had been before—it wasn't covered with miles of hair. Off went the sideburns, out came the cheekbones—and there was this mass of face."

From the outset, L.A. Eyeworks offered a range of colors (twenty-two in the first collection alone) in addition to the ubiquitous black and tortoiseshell. The frames have mostly been small. "We put glasses back on the face," McReynolds says. "We wanted them to be able to accentuate, and not take away from, what a person is." The result may be most apparent in the store's ad campaign, which over the past eight years has featured a series of high-contrast black-and-white portraits of celebrities like Andy Warhol, Jody Watley, Eric Roberts, Chaka Khan, Pee-wee Herman, Vanessa Williams, David Hockney, Grace Jones, Bryan Ferry, Jodie Foster, Divine, Greg Louganis, and the Kipper Kids, all wearing L.A. Eyeworks glasses, always with the same tag line: "A face is like a work of art. It deserves a great frame." The frames in these pictures are an integral part of the faces: the glasses aren't barriers between the people wearing them and the world. This is a long way from the seventies ad campaign that also featured famous people wearing sunglasses, and asked, "Isn't that you behind those Foster Grants?" The people in the L.A. Eyeworks ads, though most of them are wearing sunglasses, aren't wearing them as something to hide behind, as a disguise. The old notion of glasses as sexual camouflage is finally obsolete: a woman no longer needs to wait for the man who realizes that underneath her glasses is a stunning creature just longing to get out. Yet there's still something sexy about glasses: like clothes, they're there to be taken off.

I ask Gherardi and McReynolds whether they believe that it is possible for a frame to bring out a face's good features, and, if so, whether some people might not actually look better with glasses than without them. "That's so loaded," Gherardi answers. "That's such a loaded question. Yes."

McReynolds explains, "See, we see it the same way as clothes. It's a look, it's a feel for the moment, it's not permanent. It's like when you go to your closet in the morning: Am I going to wear black today? Should I wear a color? What color lipstick? Should I wear jewelry today? Am I in my gold mood? My silver mood? Should I wear my green glasses? It's the same thing, and it can change, like your eye makeup, your clothes, your shoes. For us, the essence of it always is that we just want people to feel *good* in their glasses."

"When I say that's a loaded question," Gherardi goes on, "I mean, who wants to kiss with glasses on? There are times when it's just nicer to see a face as it came on the earth. But then there are all those other times—you're wearing this or that, doing something, you need to see. And then, yes, you really can accentuate a feature—you really can shorten a nose, or give someone a browline, or make a face with a very square jawline look longer."

The notion of wearing glasses with fashionable clothes—a notion that designers like Christian Lacroix and Giorgio Armani promoted even before they had eyewear collections in their own names—is, McReynolds and Gherardi say, what they've been advocating all along. The glasses contradict the vanity that the clothes imply. The clothes may elevate the person wearing them to a dazzling level of sophistication and style; the glasses bring that person back down to the realm of human imperfections. The glasses are worn ironically. They are the wearer's way of telling the world, "I'm not just your average pretty person, not a fashion victim or a fashion plate—I'm doing all this intentionally." Gherardi says, "I can walk around in plaid glasses—and I am a *huge* girl—because that's how I make the point that I'm not some housewife from Ohio, that there's a little edge to me, somehow. And I don't even care if anybody else notices—it's just my own edge, that I need to put on for myself."

FOUR YEARS ago, on one of those intoxicating early-spring days that look and feel like summer, at L.A. Eyeworks: Some twelve customers are stationed in front of the mirrors, trying on one pair of sunglasses after another, engrossed in new permutations of their own faces. The door opens, and a young man wearing jeans and a T-shirt with the call letters of a radio station printed across the chest enters and announces to whom it may concern, "Hey, Bruce Springsteen, headed this way!" The customers leave their mirrors and crowd close to the window. Moments later, sure enough, Springsteen strolls into view. In front of the store, he slows his pace and turns his head to look in the window, and there he sees, behind the display, a chorus of a dozen people, all wearing sunglasses, staring back at him.

✳ ✳ ✳

Witness for the Defense

In Paris in January, Rei Kawakubo presented her Comme des Garçons men's collection for fall, entitled "Sleep." An assortment of striped pajamas worn with sweaters, jackets, and bathrobe coats, it was, she said, her attempt to revive lounge wear, which had once been an important category in the gentleman's wardrobe. The date assigned to Kawakubo for her show was, as it happened, the fiftieth anniversary of the liberation of Auschwitz, and two critics saw in the striped pajamas a reminder of the Nazi death camps. Their outraged reviews, in *Le Figaro* and *The International Herald Tribune*, prompted a visit to the Comme des Garçons showroom by members of the European Jewish Congress and a spate of articles denouncing Kawakubo as, at best, an unwitting anti-Semite. As a gesture of conciliation, she withdrew the pajamas from the line. Other items in the collection had been stenciled with numerals, randomly scattered, and with footprints. As the scandal escalated, the pajamas came to be described as stamped with "identification numbers"; the models, as "emaciated," with "shaved heads"; and the footprints, as made by military boots trampling the Jews underfoot. (In fact, no numbers appeared on any of the striped garments; many of the models had long hair; and the tread had been made by a basketball sneaker.) Last month, the mayor of the Third

Arrondissement refused to rent Kawakubo her usual, city-owned space, for her women's show—for fear of losing the Jewish vote in the coming elections.

For those of us in the audience that evening in January, the Holocaust connection was one of many possible interpretations, and a highly subjective one, at that. Some spectators saw the show as a late-night get-together at a boys' dormitory. Others were dismayed by the overtones of emergency, as if the models had been wakened in the middle of the night. To my mind, they looked like insomniac patients roaming a hospital ward. "There is no meaning," Kawakubo insisted, and, indeed, the body of her work has been abstract—a formal exercise.

Some of the most irate objections have been lodged by people who have never seen the clothes. Suspicious of fashion, they've been quick to charge it with crimes they're sure it must be capable of committing. But more striking than the accusations against Kawakubo is the recklessness behind them. In what amounts to an act of aggression in and of itself, righteous indignation strangles all opinion and hijacks any discourse that the clothes might have inspired.

* * *

The Religion
of Woman

AMONG THE people who work in the fashion business, it is almost unanimously assumed that skirts will soon be getting longer, if only because they've been short for a while now and people—particularly the ones who work in the fashion business—are ready for a change. "Short looks so démodé and Out," Karl Lagerfeld declared on the front page of *Women's Wear Daily* in March, at the start of the fall ready-to-wear shows. The fashion press seems to have appointed Lagerfeld its new oracle, and he obliges to the hilt, handing down pronouncements as if the cure for what ails fashion were a few sweeping statements from a designer with strong convictions. In Milan, the first stop on the four-city semiannual circuit, the small talk between shows revolved around hemlines and their impending drop: the eventual consensus was that skirts, if they came down, would fall precipitously, to mid-calf or lower, instead of inching their way kneeward. But what seemed to me more interesting than the details of the discussion was the fact that it was happening at all. This season, for the first time in ages, the people in the business seemed to assume that there would be some sort of agreement reached on hemlines—if not this time around, then the next—and that women would follow the designers' lead. For those of us cursed with a long memory, the tone of this debate was reminiscent of the way things used to be, before women gained what was regarded on both sides as the upper hand.

Probably no other issue in fashion is as charged with feminist rancor as the question of hemlines, which during the early seventies came to stand for women's craven subjugation to a cartel of designers—who, for convenience's sake, were depicted as exclusively male and of one mind. The idea of women rushing, lemming-like, in search of a dress in the latest color, or raising or lowering their skirts to the most recent requisite length, now seemed downright ridiculous. What could they have been *thinking* all those years? Clearly, feminists concluded, they hadn't been thinking at all. Or else they'd been playing along with their oppressors until the moment was right for revolt. When, in 1970, having finally chopped off their wardrobes to the mini level, women refused to adopt the new midiskirt that designers were proposing, their uprising was hailed as a great and decisive victory.

Designers kept right on presenting their collections as if they mattered. The press, which had portrayed itself as the messenger of the gods until all of a sudden women started taking potshots at the messenger, recast itself in the role of go-between. Fashion magazines continued to dispense advice, but they changed their tone from breathless to reasonable, justifying the most expensive items as "investments," and, in an effort to demonstrate their solidarity with the women who were their readers, advocating comfort and "ease." The clothes that designers paraded on the runways were now characterized as mere suggestions, meant to help women as they got on with their busy lives. As for hemlines, they drifted downward at first and then, in the early eighties, settled somewhere in the neighborhood of the knee until a few years ago, when the miniskirt made a comeback, swept in on a tide of sixties nostalgia. But even then the fashion press refrained from announcing the fact, except to remark that if miniskirts were once again ubiquitous it must be because women wanted them, not because designers had decreed them.

As I listened to all the talk about hemlines this season, I kept thinking that surely women were past the point of being dictated to, and I said so one morn-ing in Milan to the woman on my left, an executive from a large American department store. "You're wrong about that," she told me, and went on to explain that the women who are her customers—intelligent women, she added, accustomed to thinking for themselves—are again looking to designers and fashion magazines for guidance. The logic, as she explained it, is along the same lines as the reasoning behind what has lately been called the backlash against feminism: instead of allowing women to relax and worry less about their clothes, all the recent freedom in fashion has brought on a case of anxiety. The choices are overwhelming. After two decades of unprecedented free reign, she said, women once again want to be told what to wear.

The discussion surrounding the fall collections did include a few dissent-ing voices, declaring that women ought to be able to wear whatever skirt length they pleased—which ten years ago would have gone without saying. But for the most part the people in the fashion business, including many designers, seem to feel that the balance of power has finally shifted back in their favor. This perception may be based more on the current emotional climate and a strong dose of wishful thinking than on statistics: retail sales are still dismal (blame the economy), and fashion-magazine circulation is still flat (although insiders take heart at the scramble that has *Vogue* and *Harper's Bazaar* rushing to buy up editors and photographers, now that Liz Tilberis, the former editor-in-chief of British *Vogue*, has been brought in to head the *Bazaar*).

There is, one senses after running for a few seasons with the fashion pack, a palpable longing to get back to the way things were in the fifties, when fashion was at the height of its power, when women gave it their allegiance and took the sort of passionate interest in clothes that these days is found almost exclusively among professionals. Many of the people who work in fashion now are too young to have been working in it then, but in their conversation and in their minds they often find themselves referring to those better days, as if the fifties were the norm rather than an aberration brought on by a unique set of circumstances. Two great designers, Christian Dior and Balenciaga, ruled. Two great photographers, Avedon and Penn, articulated the glamour of the era. The success of Dior's New Look, launched in 1947, had brought women back to the stores in droves, as they hurried to put difficult times behind them, abandoning their skimpy wartime suits, made in compliance with the fabric rations, for voluminous skirts and all the trappings of the new silhouette. Retailers then set out to induce the same sort of shopping frenzy on a regular basis. The public-relations and advertising machinery was cranked up and began issuing seasonal pronouncements, which were taken to heart by a whole generation of women who had come of age in the Depression and, in many cases, had never had a store-bought dress. Shopping became their recreation. Women embraced fashion as they embraced the future, for the hope it offered. The future hasn't looked so promising since.

THAT FEMINISM, one of the chief preoccupations of the nineteen-seventies, should be on the wane in fashion at this moment is particularly ironic given the clothes that designers showed for fall, which often looked like the seventies reincarnate. Seventies nostalgia was probably inevitable, and it arrived right on schedule, just as the sixties revival was running out of steam. Menswear—for women—made a comeback, looking quite dandified: a chalk-striped jacket and matching vest worn with leggings, at Ralph Lauren; pleated flannel trousers worn with crisp white shirt collars, and neckties tucked into black long-line bras, at Dolce & Gabbana; jackets made from panels of pinstripe flannel sewn into geometric patterns, at Christian Francis Roth; a Prince of Wales plaid vest with bra cups built in, at Byron Lars. The tuxedo, calling to mind Yves Saint Laurent's seventies variations on *le smoking*, made a stronger showing than it has in years. There were handkerchief skirts, a late-hippie favorite, and black leather bell-bottoms, at Perry Ellis. Vivienne Westwood and Karl Lagerfeld have been relentlessly promoting platform shoes, which were standard in the early seventies, for some time now; this season, there were platforms in other designers' collections as well. The Wild West has returned, with prairie skirts and fringed suede jackets and cowboy boots. Jeans are the uniform, as they were in the seventies, for day and evening: in white leather, at Versace; in quilted pink velvet, at Dior; in denim printed with a gigantic photo of Marlene Dietrich's face, at Westwood. Ellis Flyte and Richard Ostell, two English designers working in tandem, had a sudden success with a collection of clothes that owe a lot to Zoran, the high priest of seventies minimalism. The midiskirt, which, after women's initial rejection of it, took hold and held sway for most of the seventies, was everywhere. Even Joni Mitchell and Herb Alpert and the Tijuana Brass came in for revival on fashion-show soundtracks this season.

With the return of the seventies, fashion comes full circle. Some twenty years ago, when designers first went retro on us, it was the thirties they were resurrecting; now it's the thirties as seen through the eyes of the seventies—twice removed. By the end of the seventies, we had worked our way into the forties, with shoulder pads and aggressive-looking suits. Then, in the mid-eighties, with Christian Lacroix's pouf-skirted party dresses, came the return to the New Look of the fifties—tight, strapless bodices and bouffant skirts. After that, fashion moved on to the sixties. We've been consuming the past at an accelerated rate: it takes us only five years or so to go through a decade.

For fashion purposes, everything that happened before the nineteen-twenties, when women took off their corsets, hiked up their skirts, and began to live and dress in a way that we can identify with, is prehistory. When designers reach back to a more distant past, it is not a whole image they conjure up but details of it. We know the fashions of other centuries through paintings and, later, photographs, but from the nineteen-thirties on, the clothes people wore are familiar to us mainly through movies and television. They exist in a kind of continuous present, on late-night cable TV, on video, in revival cinemas—an endless loop of the past six decades, all available simultaneously. That designers return to this material again and again is not as surprising as the fact that their fascination with it runs in cycles that seem to be sequential.

Watching designers exhume the seventies, I began to wonder whether we're doomed to relive the same few decades over and over forever. Since the recycling began, even designers on the cutting edge have seemed to take it for granted that the future would be simply another chapter of the past: while mainstream designers recapitulated one decade, the avant-garde would move on to the next. Those of us whose job it is to keep track of fashion witnessed these proceedings with a certain resignation, hoping (some of us) that if we let the cycle run its course it would stop with the sixties. That hope was shot down this season.

Designers twenty years ago, surveying the rubble of all the social conventions demolished during the sixties, can perhaps be excused for fleeing their own moment and taking refuge in the past. But the retro cycle in fashion has continued—not, I think, for any lack of imagination but because the mood for the last decade or so has been so bleak. Despite the hype—the celebrity designers, the supermodels, the rock stars in the front row—there is a certain sense of futility undermining fashion these days.

The resemblances between the early seventies and our own moment are not entirely superficial: the economy is in a slump, as it was then; the collective impulse is once again back to nature, in the food we eat and the shampoo we buy, in front-page alarm about the future of the planet; disillusionment with the government is epidemic. And yet there are, you would think, enough differences to give the nineteen-nineties a character and a style of their own. Nevertheless, many of the longer skirts that designers showed this season were exact replicas of the ones we wore in the seventies: skinny columns, slashed along one side seam to the thigh or up the center of the back; wrap versions falling straight and flapping open with every stride; narrow, fitted styles released in a flurry of kick pleats at the knees; and a few full swirling circles. All of which are fairly standard solutions, some more graceful than others, to the engineering problem that the midiskirt poses—how to give the knee enough range of motion for walking. The last time we wore midiskirts, it was before the advent of stretch fabrics. This season, the only new design was a result of that innovation: a long stretch tube. Frozen in a pose, it looked great—hugging the contours of the thighs, clinging to the knees. The silhouette was spindly. The minute the model started to walk, however, the glitches became apparent and the glamour collapsed. In some cases, the skirt crept upward, obliging her to stop and shimmy it back down again. In others, it was so tight that her gait was severely hobbled. In the collection that Lagerfeld designs under his own name, he presented ankle-length narrow skirts in stretch tulle, like a veil drawn taut, over opaque tights—an idea that came off as cluttered and less attractive than the leggings we already own. Virtually none of the longer skirts that designers proposed this season struck me as plausible alternatives to the short skirts women have been wearing, but not even the sight of Christy Turlington stumbling down the catwalk at Fendi in a long, tight tube skirt and platform shoes could slow the bandwagon. By the time buyers and the press pulled into New York for the start of the American collections, in early April, the feeling was that the mini length might be credible for another season or two but then the future would be upon us, and, like it or not, skirts would be long.

Geoffrey Beene tells a story of being on a plane not long ago and being asked by one of the flight attendants for his advice about hemlines. "I can't believe you are asking me such a question," he answered. "That goes against everything that women's liberation stands for."

"But, sir," she replied, "I was never a part of that."

It is tempting to see this season's hemline controversy as yet another instance of women losing ground that they had fought so hard to win. Here, at first glance, is one more way in which the so-called post-feminist era bears considerable and disconcerting resemblance to the pre-feminist era, as if feminism were finally nothing more than a blip on the screen. "Post-feminism," like "postmodernism," is a label for an era with no identity of its own—an era invented in reaction to the one that came before it. Both movements were founded on the conviction that the previous generation's revolution was a failure, and both disdained the idealism that had prompted feminists and modernists alike to believe that they had come up with the solution to what's wrong with the world. Like postmodern architecture, post-feminism seeks refuge in historicisms, invoking a time when women, like buildings, were more decorative, more intent on pleasing the eye of the beholder.

Feminist dogma has always been hostile to fashion, on the ground that it is nothing more than an instrument of oppression—that it coerces women into squandering their money, their time, and their energies in a desperate and ultimately futile attempt to assuage their insecurities, which have been exacerbated, if not inflicted, by (what else?) fashion. This attitude is, remarkably, still alive and well, and it continues to obscure the real issues, which have more to do with how women use clothes to help them consolidate their identity and with how they choose to present themselves to the world.

Susan Faludi, in her book *Backlash: The Undeclared War Against American Women*, depicts women in the eighties fleeing stores because they couldn't find clothes appropriate to their lives. Like the dogmatists of twenty years ago Faludi views fashion as something foisted on women. The sensuous pleasure to be found in the slide of fabric along the skin or in the line of a seam drawn along the body's contour seems to be lost on her. If she makes backhanded acknowledgment of the way in which women look to fashion as a mirror, it is only to condemn it. "Personal insecurity is the great motivator to shop," she insists, and in support she cites a survey by the ad agency Wells Rich Greene. "The more confident and independent women become, the less they liked to shop; and the more they enjoyed their work, the less they cared about their clothes," she says. "The agency could find only three groups of women who were loyal followers of fashion: the very young, the very social, and the very anxious."

As attacks on fashion go, this one is not particularly new or original—part reverse snobbery, part puritanism repackaged in the wrapping of women's rights. What strikes me as more outrageous and, finally, more pernicious than accusations of this kind is the compulsion—particularly surprising on the part of feminists—to dismiss fashion, one of women's longstanding pastimes, as beneath the serious consideration of intelligent people. "It is the masculine values that prevail," Virginia Woolf remarked. "Speaking crudely, football and sport are 'important'; the worship of fashion, the buying of clothes 'trivial.' . . . This is an important book, the critic assumes, because it deals with war. This is an insignificant book because it deals with the feelings of women in a drawing-room. A scene in a battlefield is more important than a scene in a shop—everywhere and much more subtly the difference of value persists." The shift that occurred in the feminist movement in the late seventies—the realization that the goal was not for women to succeed in "a man's world" but for both sexes to come around to a greater appreciation of women's experience—seems not to apply where fashion is concerned.

For those of us who love clothes and subscribe to feminism, the problem has been as much practical as philosophical. What to wear? If fashion, like art, had traditionally been made for what feminist art historians call "the male gaze," could we somehow devise a style of dress that wouldn't look to men for their approval? Was there some other way for a woman to express her sexuality in the clothes she wore—as a statement instead of as an invitation? If tight clothes and high heels seemed to us out of the question, it was because they had no dignity: they announced a woman's eagerness to please men, on men's own terms, while who she was got lost in a blur of breasts and hips and legs. We have not been alone in our attempts to sort out these issues. During the seventies, *Vogue*, under Grace Mirabella's leadership, took up the feminist cause (which *Mirabella* has since continued). Several designers joined in. Giorgio Armani brought his expertise in men's wear to bear and came up with women's tailoring that looked intelligent and poised. Donna Karan took her own, personal style and elaborated on it for the benefit of other women. Rei Kawakubo introduced clothes, for Comme des Garçons, that made their appeal on a cerebral level, investigating the principles of construction and dressmaking, ignoring a woman's duty to look attractive. The irony of all this, of course, is that the great feminist designer of our century preceded the seventies wave of women's liberation by some fifty years. Coco Chanel devised a formula for women that was the equivalent of the suit for men—founded on comfort and common sense and self-assurance. If there has been a backlash in fashion during the past ten years, it has been led not by Lacroix, as the feminists contend, but by Lagerfeld, who, in the collections he has designed for the house of Chanel, has little by little obliterated Chanel's message.

A lot of long-standing feminist anger toward fashion, it now appears, turns out to be misplaced—to be anger toward men, some of whom interpreted women's refusal to wear clothes that divulged their bodies as an affront, or, at the very least, as a sign of sexual recalcitrance. In retrospect, it seems that most feminists, dressing in such a way as to stipulate that men take an interest in us as people before they take an interest in us sexually, underestimated the degree to which sexual desire in men, however enlightened and well-meaning they may be, is in the end fetishistic, focussed on body parts rather than on the whole. To what extent are we willing to make ourselves into the images men need to get sexually aroused? Here is where the puritanism of American feminism comes into play. In America, where fashion, always burdened with the weight of moral implications, has lately been staggering under the added freight of sexual politics, complicity has become a dirty word, and what goes on between men and women is now too loaded to qualify as a sport. On the runways of Paris and Milan, however, designers continue to present clothes with a forthright sex appeal that is not, to their way of thinking, at odds with women's progress. While some American feminists have founded their polemics on the notion that what's wrong with the world is masculinity, their European counterparts have never lost sight of the male point of view.

Male fantasies persist in fashion, in collections by designers like Thierry Mugler and Gianni Versace. In the video for George Michael's "Too Funky," featuring a Mugler fashion show, one model wears a strapless leather bodysuit with motorcycle handlebars and rearview mirrors projecting from the sides of the waist. For fall, Versace presented a hybrid collection—country and Western crossed with S&M—that included evening gowns with bodices like harnesses, jeans with suede fringe outlining the contours of the buttocks, and a cowboy shirt in black leather. In interviews, Versace has consistently justified his clothes by arguing that feminism has given women the right to be sexually aggressive. Like Madonna, the new sexpot puts herself at the service of men's fantasies because she chooses to: she's in control. (This season, women of two minds about this issue can have it both ways: at Moschino, there is a bolero jacket with a photograph of bare breasts printed on the front.)

I'm willing to bet that many women, watching a show like Versace's this season, end up feeling as confused and uncomfortable as I did, and yet how dull fashion would be if men's fantasies, even the inhospitable ones, went unrepresented. But where, I wonder, are women's fantasies? Armani and Karan and other designers who have furnished women with the clothes they need for the new responsibilities in their lives are realists, rarely straying very far from the facts. Oddly enough, the leading proponent of female fantasy for the past few years has been a man—Romeo Gigli, whose rhapsodic designs in rare fabrics hold out the hope of romantic individualism.

It is the worship of Woman that fashion and feminism have in common. For all their differences, they are branches of the same religion. If fashion in its mysticism is like the Catholic Church, then feminism has been like the Reformation. For some time now, their followers have been dwindling—the result, perhaps, of widespread disenchantment with the rites of fashion or with the rigors of feminist dogma. Women are going their own ways, in the absence of any organized attempt to address the dilemmas in their lives. Meanwhile, at the Vatican of fashion, the debate about hemlines continues.

✳ ✳ ✳

Quoting Chanel

EVERY ERA has an ideal image to which women aspire. The late sixties was the height of our love affair with youth. Movies, magazines, pop music, and advertising extolled the life and the looks of the teenage girl—the prototype was a long-haired, blank-faced, disco-dancing adolescent, thin as a stick, dressed in go-go boots and a mini-skirt by Courrèges or Mary Quant. Today, most women no longer want to look like teenagers. The ideal is the woman with both a career and a family. She's older, in her thirties or forties; she has come into her own. She has character—you can see it in her face. She looks womanly now. She is wearing a Chanel suit.

The current resurgence of interest in the clothes Coco Chanel designed is not nostalgia, because they can't transport a woman backward, the way a dress by Poiret or Vionnet can. Her designs are not so much of their time as outside time. Chanel steered clear of fashion, which comes and goes, and formulated a style instead. The virtues of that style are, at the moment, at a premium.

"Classic" is the adjective routinely called on to describe Chanel clothes, and now that most women are no longer willing or able to buy a new wardrobe for the sake of a change, classic clothes have the moral advantage. But besides that, today's woman wears Chanel because it's dignified, unspectacular, elegant. It's both proper and sexy, but the sex appeal is that of a woman who's competent, who knows her way around. The schoolgirlish side of Chanel dresses and blouses with soft bow ties at the neck is deceptive. The woman who wears them would look like a good girl, as if she played by the rules, if it weren't for the costume jewelry—fake pearls, cut-glass cabochon necklaces, giant-sized earrings—piled on, gypsy-style. It's the jewelry that gives the Chanel look a faintly naughty edge, that makes it ambiguous and interesting in a way the clothes by themselves are not. The woman the Chanel style conjures up is self-possessed, wise, and mature—of a certain age, or at least of a certain experience.

The clothes in the Chanel fall/winter couture collection, designed by Karl Lagerfeld, one of the most important designers in fashion today, are along the lines Chanel herself drew up and stuck with until her death, in 1971. Chanel has gone down in history as the originator of costume jewelry, the little black dress, Chanel No. 5, pleated skirts, trousers for women, fur-lined coats, and sunbathing, but she has gone down in memory as the designer of the famous Chanel suit, a style so widely copied, even in her lifetime, that it's practically in the public domain.

There are plenty of suits in this season's couture. At the show I attended in Paris, Lagerfeld offered them in striking color combinations, like fuchsia and yellow or pink and pearl gray, as well as in more standard ones, like black and white or navy and white, in fabrics such as basketweave woolens and jersey ribbed to look like corduroy, set off by silk crepe or mousseline. The jackets are single-breasted or narrowly double-breasted, edged in braid, with or without collars. The skirts are straight and narrow, slit or kick-pleated. But regardless of its distinguishing features, nearly every suit is according to the time-honored Chanel formula: a cardigan jacket, with pockets at the waist (for cigarettes), and a matching skirt and contrasting blouse. In the ready-to-wear for this spring, the lines of the suits are elongated but not distorted: the jackets are mostly to the hip, the skirts to mid-calf. Several suits look the same as ever from the waist up but with pants instead of skirts below. The colors are mostly pastels and navy blue, and there are a lot of stripes. In both couture and ready-to-wear, the spirit of Chanel is intact, even if the letter at times seems slightly skewed.

THERE IS no separating the Chanel style from Coco Chanel's life. What she sold was the way she dressed. It seems safe to say that under Chanel's direction her house never produced anything that she herself wouldn't have worn. Her taste was wholly subjective, and for that reason her designs had the ring of conviction missing from clothes by designers who try to satisfy a variety of women.

The illegitimate daughter of a peddler, Gabrielle Chanel was born in the Auvergne in 1883, and was soon after consigned to an orphanage run by nuns. Other than that, the facts are hazy, because later in life Chanel did all she could to obfuscate her past and frustrate anyone trying to write about it. Some of her biographers, for instance, go along with the story that her father nicknamed her

"Coco." Another contends that Chanel came by the name during a brief stint as a cabaret singer, with a repertoire of only two numbers: "Ko ko ri ko" and "Qui qu'a vu Coco?" Chanel's explanation was that it was nothing more than a shortened version of *cocotte*, the French word for "kept woman."

Indeed, Chanel had been taken in at twenty-five by a cavalry officer named Etienne Balsan. But she refused to dress her part, and instead wore plain, dark-colored dresses that put the other *cocottes*, in all their satin upholstery, to shame. Balsan set her up as a milliner, with her own boutique in Deauville and later in Paris. As her business grew, she began making dresses.

Chanel apparently loved wearing men's clothes, which she freely borrowed from her lovers' closets. Menswear gave her inspiration—for trench coats, sweaters, blazers, and for new uses of materials, like wool jersey, that had never been employed in women's clothes. There is a photograph of Chanel setting out to go fishing in Scotland with the Duke of Westminister, wearing his tweeds. The boots she has on are his clodhoppers. His blazer is too big for her. Looking at this picture, you can't help but be struck by how impudent and chic Chanel looks, and by the pride she takes in wearing her boyfriend's clothes.

Chanel cast herself as an arbiter of taste, a role that would take her higher and further than that of dressmaker. She made friends with Picasso, Stravinsky, Misia Sert—the artsy "in" crowd of Paris in the nineteen-twenties—and designed costumes for Diaghilev and Cocteau. When Diaghilev died in debt, in Venice, it was Chanel who paid for his funeral.

Already, Chanel's life has provided material for a Broadway musical, *Coco* (with Katharine Hepburn), and a movie, *Chanel Solitaire* (with Marie-France Pisier). The myth that surrounds her life is a fairy tale for our time about a plucky girl who goes to work and earns herself a fortune, who refuses to be tied down to one man in marriage and sails instead from one glamorous affair to the next, who keeps an exotically furnished apartment above her workrooms on the rue Cambon and a bedroom across the street at the Ritz.

The facts are right, but the aggrandizement does Chanel a disservice: her independence seems to have been difficult and complicated in real life. An orphan and a loner, she learned early on, by necessity, how to take care of herself, and then apparently longed the rest of her life for someone to take care of her. Her series of love affairs was not a systematic quest for experience but a string of high hopes and increasingly bitter disappointments. As for her career, she found work that she did well and took relentless pride in doing it. There, if anywhere, lies Chanel's example. She chose to do something when she might easily have done nothing.

In 1954, at age seventy, Chanel reopened her house, after fifteen years in retirement, with a collection that reiterated what she'd been saying all along. The message was too low-key for the fashion press, which had been expecting something more sensational. But women, especially in America, got the point and overruled the press by buying the clothes. Chanel was a popular success; the critics changed their minds.

From then on, she worked to consolidate her style. She settled on the most flattering proportions for a suit—the jacket to the hipbone, the skirt to the knee. She perfected the suit's construction: the back panel of a jersey skirt was lined so that a woman couldn't "sit out" the seat; jackets were weighted to hang properly, with a gold chain sewn into the hem; the armholes were cut high, so that a woman could swing her arms full circle and the body of the jacket would stay in place. Chanel designed chain belts as jewelry, to drape across the belly rather than to cinch the waist. Buttons were jewelry, too—big brass lion's heads (because Chanel was a Leo) that decorated the front of the jacket. The clothes, even for evening, became simple and concise, the background for lavish accessories.

As a young woman, Chanel had founded her style on her instincts. As time went on, she brought logic to bear on it and refined it to a science. There was nothing mysterious about Chanel's formula, which was anyone's for the taking. Adolfo has built an entire career on it. Yves Saint Laurent works his own variations on it and frankly acknowledges his debt. Adele Simpson, Evan-Picone, and other middle-priced American lines borrow heavily and regularly from Chanel.

With so many designers paying tributes to Chanel—tributes selling for a lot of money—it was just a matter of time before the people at Chanel would decide to cash in and turn out the real thing. The couture had coasted along after Chanel's death under the guidance of her assistants. Then, in 1977, it was announced that Chanel would begin producing ready-to-wear. Frances Stein, a former editor at American *Vogue* and for several years Calvin Klein's right hand, was hired to supervise the Chanel accessories line, which includes jewelry, bags, shoes, and knits. One year ago, Karl Lagerfeld was brought in to design the couture.

So far, this new regime's policy has been to authenticate each collection by reprising in it some of Chanel's designs. In this season's couture, there was a strapless black velvet evening dress, with a black chiffon mantle to veil the shoulders, much like a Chanel dress from 1956. A sleeveless black crepe dress with a heavy white lace bolero overtop in this year's ready-to-wear cruise collection is a direct quotation from a 1937 design.

Of course, a big-name designer like Lagerfeld hasn't been brought in just to reissue another batch of golden oldies every year. His task—and Frances Stein's—is to take the Chanel style and extrapolate from it. Stein does this skillfully, picking up where Chanel herself left off and, by some sort of creative empathy, turning out clothes that look like what Chanel would produce if she were alive today. This winter, Stein brought out the basic Chanel suit in black-and-white cashmere sweatering—an ingenious crossbreed of the tailoring that Chanel was famous for and the soft comfort that makes knits so popular now. The pastel-tinted pearls that Stein is introducing for spring, in pale pink, green, coral, yellow, and gray, look like a good, inevitable idea Chanel never got around to. Stein reaffirms Chanel's principles; her new accessories line is a clear vote of confidence in all Chanel stood for. Lagerfeld, however, seems to be hedging.

It's no wonder. His attitude toward fashion is one that probably can't be reconciled to Chanel's, if the past is any indication. Fashion in Paris during the nineteen-thirties was an ongoing clash between Chanel, the friend of the Cubists, and Schiaparelli, who was a Surrealist at heart. With her "chest of drawers" suit and her necklace of aspirin, Schiaparelli made news while Chanel made clothes.

But the difference between Schiaparelli and Chanel wasn't merely the difference between humor and the lack of it. There's a whimsical aspect to Chanel's designs, too, at least to many from the twenties and thirties. The Costume Institute at the Metropolitan Museum of Art has in its collection two surprising Chanels: one, a black-and-beige day dress from the twenties, has clouds and rain embroidered on the skirt; the other, a long black tulle-over-crepe evening dress from 1938, is patterned with bright-colored sequin fireworks. A twenties black chiffon chemise, in a sale last month at Sotheby's, is appliquéd with 3-D fabric pinwheels. Each of these is a one-shot dress, but taken together they are evidence of a lightheartedness that is surprising in the sober, upstanding woman who masterminded the suit. So Chanel was no stiff, but unlike Schiaparelli, whose clothes today look like little more than a series of one-liners, she always subordinated the idea of a dress to the image of the woman wearing it.

Chanel and Schiaparelli, or at least the positions they took, still exist in fashion today: Chanel is Yves Saint Laurent and Schiaparelli is, oddly enough, Lagerfeld. In his recent collections for Chloé, there are echoes of her jokey sensibility—evening gowns decorated with *trompe l'oeil* rhinestone showerheads, brooches as spigots, dresses in the shape of electric guitars, and piano-keyboard bracelets. You get the idea that Lagerfeld can't quite bring himself to take fashion seriously. Neither, for that matter, could Coco Chanel, but at least she chose to design clothes instead of facetious commentaries on the changing state of fashion. Lagerfeld seems contemptuous of clothes. In the furs he designs for Fendi, and even in his more wearable numbers for Chloé, he makes "fashion statements," and often important ones. Chanel's clothes, however, were understatements.

You can't help but wonder whether the people at Chanel got the wrong man for the job. In this season's ready-to-wear, which takes its cue directly from Lagerfeld's couture, there's a white satin evening gown with a *trompe l'oeil* Chanel suit outlined in sequins on the front, a blouse made of fabric patterned with bottles of Chanel No. 5, and big rhinestone 5s to be worn as earrings. I've got nothing against irony, and I can see it in the fact that the style invented by Chanel, who eschewed fashion, has now become all the rage. But I'm not sure that an evening gown or a blouse or even an earring is the right place for another designer to remark on that turn of events. In the collections he has designed for Chanel, it's as if Lagerfeld can't make up his mind whether to carry on the tradition or send it up.

Lagerfeld's position at Chanel is unprecedented and ultimately, I think, unenviable. No other house in the history of fashion has, on the death of its founder, brought in another designer with a large reputation and a distinctive style and expected him to work within the confines of its own well-established tradition. Whether or not this is possible is a good question; why Lagerfeld would want to do it is another. The style Chanel set down is so narrowly defined that, if his new designs are going to be in keeping with it, Lagerfeld's hands are tied. After two collections, he still hasn't figured out how to make his mark on the Chanel style without in some way defacing it.

The hoped-for meeting of the minds has turned out to be a polite exchange of views, with Lagerfeld and Chanel taking turns. The most successful numbers in this season's couture were those in which he put his own ideas aside and paraphrased hers: an ivory-and-white wool bouclé suit edged in red, white, blue, and beige; a lapis-blue tweed suit with a long jacket, with closings like brooches and gold chains draped like watch fobs across the front; a fuchsia chiffon evening gown with a train that flows like liquid. Lagerfeld's two cents came in a group of overkilling evening jackets inspired by eighteenth-century furniture and Meissen snuffboxes, festooned with cherubs, gold-encrusted scrollwork, marquetry, and sable. At these prices—$15,000 to $50,000 for the evening clothes, $5,000 to $15,000 for the day wear—most women would expect to get something that would last them the rest of their lives.

Women who bought a suit designed by Chanel had the assurance that it would be timeless, but today's suits look timely instead. The models for the collection wore three-inch-high heels and skirts cut narrow enough to hug their rumps. Presumably, Lagerfeld thinks that touch-ups like these will make the Chanel style look young and racy without drastically altering it. In the end, though, they undermine it. Chanel didn't make clothes to fit snugly or to show a lot of skin. There's a staunch sense of propriety to everything she designed, even her evening gowns, and faith that what is most attractive about a woman is not the motion of her hips. Lagerfeld has taken the Chanel standard and souped it up. He recognizes the style's integrity, but he doesn't seem to trust it or to think that it's enough. From the looks of this collection, he believes that, in however small a way, a woman has to endear herself to the world.

A Model Bride

Two days after the end of the spring 1998 European fashion shows (many of them delayed by the late arrival of Demi Moore), some forty editors, designers, photographers, and models travelled to London for Kristen McMenamy's wedding.

The invitation said four o'clock, but at five minutes past a late-comer rushed in to find only the groom, four other guests, a gaggle of photographers, and sixty gilt chairs arranged in rows, with names on the seats: Boy George, David Bailey, Rupert Everett. Already, this was shaping up to be more like a fashion show than a wedding. It was a brisk Tuesday in October, and Kristen McMenamy, the self-proclaimed ugly duckling whose success as a model has been her revenge on all the cool kids in junior high who wouldn't let her sit at their table in the cafeteria, was marrying, in London, Miles Aldridge, a young English photographer she had met in Karl Lagerfeld's car.

True to fashion protocol, the rest of the guests straggled in over the course of the next hour, greeted at the door by the cameras. Manolo Blahnik, straight from root-canal surgery, worried that his face would look puffy in pictures. Vivienne Westwood arrived with her husband, Andreas, who was wearing a kilt, knee socks, and ghillies with a two-inch heel. Oblivious of etiquette, nearly everyone was in black. At five-ten, Blahnik pointed to an empty seat in the front row: "We're waiting for Demi Moore," he joked. Finally, at five-thirty, the bride appeared, preceded down the aisle by four flower girls (one, her daughter, Lily) and two bridesmaids: Saffron Aldridge (the groom's sister) and Naomi Campbell—both models and both wearing . . . black. McMenamy was in a ravishing one-shoulder draped chiffon dress Lagerfeld had designed for her (in a fabric dyed to match her pale skin) and a feather headdress by Philip Treacy.

Lagerfeld gave the bride away. When the registrar announced, "If any person present knows of any lawful impediment to this marriage, . . . " McMenamy looked back over her shoulder to see if there were any takers. During the vows, the couple turned to face each other, affording a view of the bride's five-months'-pregnant profile. The groom got the giggles. At last, they were pronounced husband and wife, and friends cheered and flashbulbs popped. The paparazzi took pictures of Lagerfeld taking pictures of the bride and groom. Rifat Ozbek noted that Kristen and Miles resemble each other, and that couples who stay together often do. "So that's what you should do," he advised Naomi Campbell. "Find someone who looks like you."

July 1989

For Better or for Worse?

FOR MANY of us who stood on the beach in the nineteen-seventies and looked on while the maid of honor sang "Both Sides Now" and the barefoot couple plighted its troth with excerpts from Khalil Gibran's *The Prophet*, the news that in the eighties weddings seemed to be taking a turn for the more traditional came as a relief. Who could have foreseen that the results would often be, in their way, no less preposterous? Here we are, in an era when etiquette has gone the way of hats and gloves—when no one writes a thank-you note anymore, much less wears black to a funeral—and yet people planning weddings turn to the "experts" and slavishly follow their every instruction.

An entire industry stands at the ready. "From the moment you announce your engagement, life becomes a matter of questions, choices, decisions, an exciting whirl of plans and preparations," begins a promotion for Liberty of London in a recent issue of the English magazine *Brides and Setting Up Home*. "Your dress. Your shoes. Your bridesmaids. The cake. The flowers. And your first home. Colours, fabrics, patterns, plates, your china and glass, your table linen, pretty sheets for your bedroom, rugs for your floor." *Brides*, in America; *Sposabella*, in Italy; *Mariages*, in France, strike a similar tone—friendly, experienced, breathless. To my mind, which is perhaps slightly cynical but not entirely lacking in the capacity for romance, the anxiety and fatigue brought on by leafing through these magazines, full of ads for video cameramen, makeup artists, and rental limousines, would be reason enough to elope.

Over the past few years, I've watched maybe a dozen friends, not all of them with an active interest in fashion but most with a distinct sense of style, step into bridal gowns and become icons—virtually anonymous, life-size versions of those dolls perched on the top tier of wedding cakes that look like Busby Berkeley sets in buttercream frosting. The dresses my friends wore were not all the same, of course—some had bouffant sleeves, some had straight sleeves, some had jewel necklines, some had scoop necklines, some had trains, some didn't—but the effect was similar, and it was straitjacketing. Another friend, who recently managed to find a bridal gown that didn't compromise her image of herself, proudly announced, "I don't look a bride in it—I look like me." Now, why is it that the idea of being a bride has come to be so narrowly proscribed? Why is it that bridal gowns seem to exist in some freeze-dried never-never land—outside time, outside fashion—that bears no relation whatsoever to the style of the decade we're living in? Why is it that we expect the image of a bride to remain constant when the way women see themselves—and the way our society sees women—is changing all the time? Why is it that we turn to the realm of fashion for so many of our fantasies but that when it comes to getting married—the subject of some of the most important fantasies in life—we turn our back on fashion? And this is the big mystery: Why is that so many bridal gowns, however pretty, however ornate, and even grandiose, look so spectacularly bland?

The tradition that brides are now busy harking back to is in fact relatively brief and highly revisionist. Anne Schirrmeister, an art and costume historian and a former assistant curator at the Metropolitan Museum of Art's Costume Institute, says, "It's not until the late nineteen-thirties or early forties that the wedding gown that's a one-shot deal comes along—the special dress that you put in a box so it can rot in the closet. That's also the point at which wedding dresses start to move away from what's in style and into their own peculiar tradition. Before that, wedding dresses were always worn again. Middle-class people often got married in their best clothes—not white but whatever color was chic at the time. In the eighteen-sixties, there were brides dressed in pastels, and a little later, with the introduction of aniline dyes, there were brides in shades of bronze and turquoise—bright, rich colors." In both France and England, for most of the nineteenth century the poor and the lower middle class got married in black silk. Schirrmeister has done research in Paris, going through middle- and lower-class death inventories. "You always find one black silk dress," she explains. "That is the person's best dress, and it had none of the connotations of mourning. Black meant formal, respectable—for important occasions. That's the dress the person got married in and attended her child's christening in and died in."

Schirrmeister says that when Queen Victoria married, in 1840, she wore white, breaking with royal tradition. Before that, royal brides had worn dresses made from cloth of silver. Victoria was seen in her own time as a modern bride, advocating a return to simplicity—which is, of course, not at all in keeping with the way we now think of her. "Victoria's wedding wasn't photographed," Schirrmeister adds, "and drawings of her dress weren't sent around, so she really had no influence in particular on wedding dress, but the clothes her children wore for their weddings were photographed, and the designs were circulated. Theirs was the first royal influence on wedding dresses outside court circles. Throughout the Victorian era and on into the twentieth century, brides who were socially ambitious imitated royalty by wearing white. There's a really interesting eyewitness account by Gertrude Jekyll, who talks about how pathetic it is that the laborers in the next village wear white and have pages, just like the royals, and don't realize how stupid they look. In general, white wedding dresses throughout the nineteenth century follow the fashionable look of the day. Basically, they look just like an evening dress, because white was often worn in the evening. Or, for weddings in the morning, the bridal gowns looked like white street dresses, made of the best cloth that the bride could afford."

Today, when women think of a "traditional" bridal gown, the dress they have in mind is usually a pastiche of elements from Dior's New Look and Victorian fashion: his off-the-shoulder necklines and full skirts; the mutton sleeves of the eighteen-thirties; the V-shaped waist, which was popular in the eighteen-forties and continued, on and off, throughout the nineteenth century (it's now standard attire for the fairy-tale heroines as seen by Walt Disney); the long train and big bows, like bustles, reminiscent of the eighteen-eighties; and, God forbid, lace mitts. "I can't tell you how many otherwise sensible women want to wear mitts," Schirrmeister says. "Mitts *were* Victorian, but the Victorians would never have worn them to get married in."

THE BRIDAL realm, as anyone who shops for a dress soon learns, is a world apart, off to one side of the world where the rest of life takes place, and its architects are designers—"specialists"—who mostly do nothing but bridal wear. For an industry founded on what it maintains is the most important event in a woman's life, its standards are, for the most part, appallingly low. In a recent edition of *Woman's Day's* "101 Wedding Ideas for Brides," ads for San-Martin International Bridals, photographed at the Beverly Hills Hotel and other California vacation spots, show Mariska Hargitay, then of "Falcon Crest," Lauralee Bell, of "The Young and the Restless," and other TV actresses in effusive dresses of polyester satin, peekaboo lace, and frothy ruffled tulle, that look like a cross between antebellum prom gowns and Hollywood negligees. At the top of the market is Pat Kerr, who draws on an extensive collection of antique fabrics and laces for the one-of-a-kind bridal gowns she designs. She recalls that when she got into the bridal business, nine years ago, the tulle veils were cheaply finished by machine with an overlock stitch; she introduced ribbon edging.

Kerr lays the credit for the resurgence of storybook weddings at the doorstep of Buckingham Palace. A generation of girls who watched the televised weddings of Prince Charles and Prince Andrew are now preparing to get married themselves, and she provides them with all the trappings: dresses for brides, bridesmaids, maids of honor, flower girls; she does antique-lace garters, which many brides later frame, and small silk satin cushions for bearing the rings, embroidered with slogans like "On This, Our Wedding Day." In New York, her collection is sold at Martha, where the service is specialized, too. Lynn Manulis, who, with her mother, owns and manages Martha, says, "We have meetings with our clients about their photography sessions, to decide how they should wear their hair and makeup. Then we send one of the fitters to the wedding, to look after all the last-minute alterations, to see that every hook is in place."

Manulis talks about the importance of "participating in the dream" when it comes to selling wedding dresses. "These young women change right in front of your eyes," she says. "The first thing is to take away all the trappings they come in with. I like to put them into a beautiful robe and talk to them, and then we go on from there. Really, you have to take each woman and separate her from all the others—it's like being a portrait painter. Most of them have fantasized about their wedding. And when they express themselves it requires a good listener."

Oscar de la Renta, who occasionally makes a wedding dress as a favor to a client, goes about it in much the same way. "I suppose that bridal gowns are for first weddings," he says, "and when you get married for the first time you have been thinking about it for twelve or twenty years, so every girl knows what she wants. I always ask to talk to the girl alone, without her mother. After all, it's the bride's day."

"If you ever want to get to know a woman, do her wedding dress," says the Broadway costume designer William Ivey Long, who from time to time designs bridal gowns for friends and private clients. "I always tell my friends who are getting married, 'If you have the nerve to do this in your life, I certainly have the nerve to go through it with you. You deserve all the support you can get.' It's a very bold thing, getting married. Women step into their bridal shoes, and the cold sweat of the ages comes over them. There's a lot of fear. And whatever I can do to assuage that fear, I do. That's what design is: preparing people to meet the twentieth century. It's a hard job."

Here on the verge of the nineteen-nineties, however, most women, when it comes to facing their wedding day, take refuge in the styles of the past. "The girl who comes in in a Chanel suit can become the most fragile flower in the right gown," Manulis says. "Then she sees herself not as the successful young executive woman, as she presented herself half an hour before, but as an extraordinary eighteenth-century beauty. She has found another part of her personality."

"They come in with their marvelous suits and their silk blouses, straight from the office," Carolina Herrera says. "The first thing they'll say to me is 'I dress very simply.' More often than not, the girl who comes in with that attitude and sees the transformation that takes place when she puts on a dress with a long train and a headpiece with flowers and lots of tulle decides in the end that that's all she wants."

WHAT IS this atavistic Cinderella streak lurking deep in the heart of career girls? We're all shopping for the chance to try on some new identity, beyond the slightly frayed one we wear every day, but evening clothes afford us that opportunity—and not for one time only but on a fairly regular basis. In fact, the exercise of projecting oneself into a new character is more appropriate to an evening's diversion than to one's wedding day. A bride, to my mind, should be dressed not as someone she has never been before and will never be again but in keeping with the woman she has been and is and will continue to be, and, as it turns out, this requires a lot more imagination.

Most fashion designers observe the haute-couture custom of closing a show with a bridal gown, but usually it's a finale piece, not a dress to be made and sold, and often it's not so much a dress to be married in as a comment on marriage. Robert Molnar, a young American designer with a strong political bent, ended his collection of sexy, camouflage-printed sportswear for spring, 1983, with a bride in a minidress who had an MX missile chained to her ankle. As part of a Madeleine Vionnet exhibition two years ago, the Fashion Institute of Technology displayed her austere ivory silk-crêpe bridal gown from the late thirties, which, upon closer inspection, bears a remarkable resemblance to a nun's habit.

A handful of fashion designers have launched their own bridal lines. Scaasi's, for Eva Forsyth, and Carolina Herrera's are perfectly consistent with the styles of the other clothes they design—his are festive, souped-up, sometimes graceful, and hers are restrained, detailed, expensive-looking—but the appeal of their bridal collections extends beyond their regular customers to women who for their weddings aspire to be dressed by "society" designers. Herrera's wedding dress for Caroline Kennedy established her reputation as a bridal designer, the way the Emanuels' dress for Princess Diana established theirs. "I think brides are all the same," Herrera says. "They want to look pure and innocent, and very romantic at the same time."

This is not an outlook that accounts for the women—among them the models Elle MacPherson and Gail Elliott—who have chosen to get married in dresses by Azzedine Alaïa. His retail bridal collection, commissioned last year by Pronuptia, the largest manufacturer of mass-market bridal gowns in France, includes dresses made of stretch rayon, rubberized silk organza, or waterproof taffeta ("very sexy," Alaïa says, "for jumping in the swimming pool"), with full organza capuchins and white stretch wimples for the ceremony at the church. For the bride who is pregnant, Alaïa designs a dress that is tight and revealing, so as not to hide what he calls "the beautiful gift" that she brings to the wedding. In one photograph in the catalogue, the bride, in a siren white stretch sheath that hugs her every contour, is smoking a cigarette.

Pronuptia inaugurated the "Pronuptia vu par ..." series two years ago, with a suite of bridal gowns by Jean Paul Gaultier—among them a two-piece affair with a zip-front midriff top and a mid-calf silk-taffeta skirt, pouffed and hobbled at the knees (and shown with white fish-net stockings worn *over* flat shoes), and a white jersey sheath with sleeves that end in gloves and with a deep V neck, cut to slide off the shoulder, exposing a white ruffled tulle-and-stretch-satin bustier underneath. This season, Thierry Mugler has designed four bridal outfits for Pronuptia—among them a white hooded, wide-leg jumpsuit, and a strapless white cotton-piqué dress with wings appliquéd on the bodice and with a short full-circle skirt supported by tulle underskirts (this last shown with white stockings, seamed up the front).

It is said that all brides, regardless of their looks, are beautiful, because nothing becomes a woman more than the knowledge that she is loved and because that knowledge is never more certain than on her wedding day. (The personification of Estée Lauder's Beautiful, a fragrance, is the famous model

Paulina Porizkova dressed as a bride: "This is your moment to be beautiful," the caption in the ad says.) A bride is also supposed to be young, demure, graceful, happy, and serene. But what a bride is *not* supposed to be is in some ways more telling. She is not sexy. The so-called illusion neckline, a deep décolletage veiled with a sheer lace turtleneck, is as close to racy as most brides are permitted to come. She is not skeptical or ironic, since these are qualities one comes by through experience. Nor is she funny—humor runs the danger of putting things into perspective. She is not worldly wise. The bride is a symbol, and in symbolic terms she is blank; the story of her life is yet to be written.

In an era when most women married young, leaving the shelter of their parents to embark on a family of their own, when few middle-class women worked, when childhood and adolescence flowed directly into marriage, and womanhood arrived a little later, these notions may have been closer to experience. But despite all the things that haven't changed for women in the past fifteen or twenty years, this much is different: a woman's future is no longer sealed on her wedding day. Weddings pick up where fairy tales leave off. Somewhere between the spun-sugar vision of the Sleeping Beauty awakened by the Prince's kiss and the fact of the matter—which is that, married or single, a woman is responsible for herself—lies a narrow aisle that is difficult to negotiate. Today, when many women bring to married life a truckload of furniture and a backlog of memories—to say nothing of children by a previous husband—the image of the traditional bride seems downright disingenuous.

The most recent bridal gown Long made, for a friend in her thirties, was a deliberate departure from the Cinderella tradition. "I knew what I didn't want," he says. "No ruffles, no lace, and no goddam seed pearls. So I opted for a Charles Jamesian ball gown." The result was a severe bodice, fitted and boned, with sculptural panels of fabric that fly around the shoulders, echoing their shape, and a skirt with a train that could be drawn up asymmetrically, for dancing. "Only the bride's grandmother was on to what I was doing," Long says. "At one point, she said to the bride, 'You know, dear, it looks to me for all the world like a *ball* gown.' The family felt, 'Isn't this a little too *mature*?' There is a general sense that wedding gowns should be not naive but present-day-denying, as if your wedding were going to take place in a magical fairy-tale dreamland. But I thought that the husband should see her as the beautiful woman she is now. At the wedding, she *was* attractive, and it made everyone a little nervous. Because she was in control—the bride was in control. Another reason I didn't want to do the whole froufrou thing is that I didn't want the groom to be underdressed. What you find today is the bride all done up and the rest of the party rather causal. I wish people dressed up more, but I understand why they don't, because unless the whole crowd is going to play the game it's hard to get people into it." Long took the groom shopping for a navy-blue two-piece suit: "Classic, simple, you fill in the third word."

Given the options for men, a suit is probably in better taste than something more formal. In England, chances are that the groom who wears a morning coat already owns it, and that the male guests who own morning coats will turn up wearing theirs. But in America the groom who wears a morning coat has hired it for the occasion, and the guests wear suits, and this serves only to distance the stars of the show from their audience.

John Loring, the design director of Tiffany & Co., says that Americans, lacking the pageantry of court life which prevailed in Europe, have had to invent their own ceremony—something democratic, built around an event that could serve as a common denominator. And so the American imagination came to be focussed on the wedding, as a sort of Everywoman's coronation. The danger in this, of course, is that the bride and groom, and even their parents, may approach the event as if it were a state occasion.

Isaac Mizrahi, who has designed wedding gowns for friends and private customers, as well as two dresses this season for Bergdorf Goodman, says, "Tulle and seed pearls are the absolute antithesis of what a bride should be. She has to be the symbol of purity, which gets lost in all that froufrou. You achieve purity mostly by sculpting out of the most beautiful satin. When you make a wedding dress out of satin, it has to be satin that the Pope would wear."

Though Pat Kerr's dresses are generally more ornate than Mizrahi's, Kerr agrees with him in principle. "In most of my designs," she says, "the complexity comes from the lace, which lies flat. I almost never do a ruffle."

The bride who is overdressed may be unconditionally excused, because her excess is interpreted as a measure of how much she's in love. But the bride in a simple dress shifts the focus from herself to the occasion; there is something winning about a woman who turns her back on the chance to be queen for a day, and who knows the difference between her wedding's private significance, which may or may not be the fulfillment of some childhood dream, and its significance for the guests, who were never privy to the bride's childhood dream in the first place and who would probably rather be out playing golf.

ASKED TO recall the bridal gowns that are among the greatest of the genre, de la Renta cited the last dress Balenciaga designed—a white satin princess dress, austere in its lines, embroidered with ropes of pearls—for Franco's granddaughter, when she married the future Duke of Cádiz, in 1972. Herrera, too, thought of wedding gowns by Balenciaga—"for the purity of the line." More recently, the most memorable bridal gowns have been those by Yves Saint Laurent: the Shakespearean bride (fall, 1980), covered in red-and-gold damask and brocade, and the black velvet and pale-gray satin Goya bride from the Picasso collection (fall, 1980), escorted by two harlequins. The white ottoman-and-satin patchwork dress Saint Laurent designed for the Duchess of Orléans, in 1969, is staggeringly elegant and faintly homey.

Azzedine Alaïa recalls the dress Worth made in 1904 not for the bride but for her mother, the Comtesse Greffulhe: a gold brocade-and-tulle dress, jewelled and embroidered, with a train edged in sable—a dress that at that time was more resplendent than any queen's. "C'était la limite," Alaïa says. It's not the dress he admires so much as the fact that the mother's entrance at the church stole the show.

Mizrahi's favorite gown is Maria's in the movie version of *The Sound of Music*, with its enormous skirt and long train.

I asked de la Renta what relation a wedding dress should have to what is going on in fashion. "Absolutely none," he said. Alaïa disagreed. "A bridal gown must correspond to its time," he said. "What's the point in doing something old?" When Gale Elliott got married, Alaïa made her a long white stretch bustier dress; the groom wore a black suit by Comme des Garçons.

Most of the women who opt for a so-called traditional wedding dress, I suppose, are hoping—consciously or not—to steer clear of fashion, to buy a dress that won't ever look dated or ridiculous, in retrospect. The sentiments attached to a wedding are meant to be eternal, and therefore, we think, the dress should be eternal, too. The trouble is, this stepping outside time almost never works, so that twenty years down the road the dress we now consider traditional looks not like something timeless but like 1989's idea of a traditional dress.

De la Renta says that white is not reserved for virgins. Pat Kerr likes to work in off-whites, candlelight, champagne, and even a blush pink, which she overlays with écru lace—she calls this a wonderful color for "the girl who married at eighteen and divorced at eighteen and a half, and now she's thirty-two, she has a career, and she wants a train and a headpiece and a gorgeous gown, because in her mind this is the real wedding."

The choice of colors for the last wedding dress Long designed was between white and oyster: the bride wanted oyster, he says, but "I just kept holding up this white. I would go out the door and come back in again, and the gasp value was so much higher on the white that in the end that was what we used—for reasons of pure theatrics."

Mizrahi favors white; he says that he finds it "spiritual." Now that black has become so commonplace, for both day and evening, white looks somehow transcendent. The effect of white is heightened by black. "It's like in this new production of 'Swan Lake' at American Ballet Theatre," Mizrahi says. "Take away the black swan, and the white swan doesn't stand for anything. It's the contrast that gives the symbol its meaning." If black no longer signifies mourning, it still connotes absence, evil, doubt, darkness, misery, the void, and white is our way of saying no to black.

The critic and translator Wallace Fowlie, the author of *Love in Literature*, contends that in literature men are ennobled by war and conflict, and women are ennobled by love. I'm not wild about the implications of this, but I see that what he says has historically been true, and that the male counterpart of the bride—jubilant, triumphant, in her glory, at her peak—has been not the groom but the conquering hero leading his army home from some fresh campaign. For centuries, the story has been that men are fulfilled in their relationship to God and the world, and women fulfilled in their relationship to men. Both literature and life are, of course, infinitely more complicated than this. But the desire to create something absolute in a world where nothing is certain seems to me perfectly human, and if the attempt isn't always successful the symbol, still laden with hope, is no less powerful. If weddings reflected all the ambiguities of married life, the bride would wear gray.

January 1998

Shirt Wars

With a loyalty usually reserved for alma maters and hometown baseball teams, New York men are rallying around their English shirtmakers, two of which have lately set up shop here.

Turnbull & Asser's Fifty-seventh Street store faithfully reproduces the clubby atmosphere of its venerable headquarters on Jermyn Street, in London. The prestige of its off-the-rack models is undoubtedly enhanced by the firm's reputation for bespoke shirts. Founded in 1885 by Reginald Turnbull, a shirtmaker, and Thomas Asser, a salesman, Turnbull & Asser now casts itself as the keeper of a distinguished sartorial tradition, an arcane code that reduces buttons, cuffs, and collars to matters of right and wrong. Faithful customers include aristocrats, movie stars, and the Prince of Wales. Also, Ben Bradlee, former executive editor of *The Washington Post*: as a valedictory tribute on his last day of work, several hundred members of his staff turned up in the style that had become his trademark—a striped shirt with a white collar.

Turnbull & Asser's genteel decor and the somewhat aloof demeanor of its sales staff are in sharp contrast to Thomas Pink's new Madison Avenue emporium, which, like *its* Jermyn Street store, greets the average shopper with an open-armed embrace: bright lights, jazz playing in the background, a specially commissioned scent that smells like freshly pressed linen. Pink is ahistorical: to the extent that the past is evoked, it is a restructured one. Even the name has been appropriated, from an eighteenth-century London tailor best known for his scarlet hunting jackets. (His customers were said to be "in the pink.") The present company is the brainchild of James Mullen, a thirty-seven-year-old business-school graduate, in partnership with his two brothers. With more than one hundred and fifty designs available in seventeen different sizes, Thomas Pink hopes to render custom shirts unnecessary, if not obsolete. The amalgamation of Old World sophistication with aggressive marketing—a mail-order catalogue!—has earned the upstart brand a large following of clients (among them, Tom Wolfe, Viscount Linley, and John F. Kennedy Jr.) who contend that Pink is more daring and modern than the pedigreed competition. The shirts, as it turns out, are remarkably similar. Nevertheless, the rivalry continues, with one side claiming to own the past and the other, the future.

Men Will Be Men

THE NINETEEN-SIXTIES were full of hope, and in fashion the hope was men. The "peacock revolution" was at hand, led by a vanguard wearing turtleneck sweaters, fitted suits (dignified by historical adjectives—Edwardian, Napoleonic), voluminous cloaks, even jewelry and handbags. Oleg Cassini, Pierre Cardin, Bill Blass, Yves Saint Laurent—the leading designers of women's clothes rushed headlong into menswear, liberating the victims of tradition. *Vogue* decided to issue men's editions. After nearly a century of plodding along in dark, drab flannel suits, men seemed at long last ready to cast off their inhibitions and strut.

Here we are some fifteen years later, and men's clothes look as staid as ever. Has nothing changed? Well, clearly something has, if not to the extent that designers predicted. Consider men as they appear in two recent advertisements:

The current campaign for Aramis men's cologne depicts a man in a tuxedo and a woman in an evening gown; they are in the kitchen. It could be his kitchen, it could be their kitchen, but somehow you get the idea that it's hers, if only because the situation implies that she is on her own turf. She stands facing the man, who is backed up against the refrigerator, pinned between her outstretched arms. Coming upon this couple in a magazine is like opening a wrong door and surprising two strangers. What saves the picture from being just another loaded situation, what makes it so striking, is that the woman is the instigator.

Ads for Calvin Klein underwear are of a different sort. The photograph, taken from the vicinity of the model's knees, forces the viewer to look up to a man so sun-bronzed, so hard-muscled, that he appears to be hewn out of rock. Is he a lawyer, a bank teller, a real-estate agent? It doesn't matter, because this man is made for sex. Obviously strong but at the moment inert and completely vulnerable (his eyes are closed), his sex appeal is strictly man-to-man.

Consider *American Gigolo*, a movie in which Richard Gere plays a high-priced young man who services the women of Beverly Hills. He takes great pride in dressing impeccably and keeping fit; it's all in a day's work. To the accompaniment of disco music, in a scene so charged with rhythm and energy that it becomes a dance, he lays out the coming week's worth of shirts and ties. Clothes provide this man with a means of expression. His character is skin-deep. "Everything worth knowing about me you can learn by letting me make love to you," he tells one woman.

The gist of all this is that men are sex objects now—a new, though not unexpected, development. When women became self-supporting and more forthright, they could supposedly choose their men the way men have tradition-ally chosen their women; men, it stood to reason, would then dress to call atten-tion to themselves. As it turns out, most men, even those who play the siren role, still follow the advice dispensed by English tailors, which has it that a man's clothes should go unnoticed. They dress for their careers, not for romance. To look at them, you might think men had made no sartorial progress in the past ten years. But that rote style is only half of the story.

THE OTHER is that while many men have reverted to the safety of tradition, some have gone on to explore the possibilities of fashion. The promise of the peacock revolution has been fulfilled in the articulation of a style that is decid-edly homosexual. Its leading exponents include Calvin Klein, Alexander Julian, Claude Montana, and most Italian designers, notably Giorgio Armani and Gianni Versace, who design clothes fitted closer to the body than tradition allows. Jackets come with imposing shoulders, the waist suppressed; pants are cut narrow in the hips. The silhouette is Y-shaped. Armani tailors a suit to taper so drastically from shoulder to waist that the man who wears it takes on the dimensions of a member of some super-race, impervious to the cares that weigh so heavily on other men and make them stoop-shouldered. Montana pro-duces a high-priced, fast-selling, tough-looking line of leather outerwear, char-acterized by outrageously broad shoulders, tassels, prominent hardware—nail heads, buckles, steel zippers with big teeth—and other S.S. overtones.

Several designers today make clothes that correspond directly to the fan-tasies in which gay men cast themselves. As far as I can tell, these include overtly masculine, usually outdoor roles, such as lumberjacks, firemen, cowboys; the military, or any other occupation in which a uniform imparts authority and anonymity; and prep school, which may recall male bonds formed early on or suggest innocence waiting to be corrupted. Gay chic in its present form is essentially an exaggerated masculinity, an advertisement for virility and youth.

The stock in The Crow's Nest, Camouflage, High Gear, the Loft, and other New York City boutiques that cater to gay men's tastes in clothes is disproportionately casual: what the shops lack in suits, dress shirts, and ties, they make up for in a large and varied supply of shorts. Now what, one wonders, leafing through the racks in these stores, do the men who shop here wear during the day? Any man who doesn't work, or whose job is as a lifeguard, might find his entire wardrobe here, but chances are that most men would need something more formal, such as a suit, to wear to the office. What these boutiques sell is romance, or a least the clothes for it—the romance of a way of life apart from the demands made by society. The style is not functionally casual, as, for instance, L.L. Bean's is, but casual in spirit. The real aim is to make the man not comfortable but alluring.

It would be convenient to think that gay men, by rejecting a way of dress prescribed by tradition, were choosing for themselves a more individual style, but that doesn't seem to be the case. The so-called clone look—leather bomber jacket, flannel shirt, blue jeans, and hiking shoes—is every bit as ubiquitous on Christopher Street as the gray sack suit is on Wall Street. Many gay men seem to have exchanged one uniform for another.

As for the old uniform—the drab colored, utterly conformist suit—it is as commonplace today as it was before the revolution of the sixties. Granted, men now have more leeway when it comes to the color of a shirt or the stripe of a tie. They have a new wealth of advice on buying clothes and getting dressed available to them in several books (the best, *Making the Man*, is written by a designer, Alan Flusser). Yet the overall look of men's clothes has hardly changed at all. Today's tuxedo is a fairly accurate facsimile of the one Griswold Lorillard first wore to a country club in Tuxedo Park, New York, in 1886. There is not much room for personal variation.

The three-piece suit as we know it dates to the 1850s. By that time, the dandyism that had taken hold in London and Paris thirty years before, when men adopted an effeminate silhouette—bosoming chest, pinched waist, and curved hips, often achieved by corseting—was on the wane. (The colorful, snug-fitting knee breeches men wore regularly through the 1700s had become taboo, as a symbol of aristocracy, after the French Revolution.) By mid-century, the "ditto" suit had arrived—a coat, waistcoat or vest, and trousers, all matching. Color was restricted to the waistcoat and tie, often made of such sensuous fabrics as silk brocade and dotted velvet. In the nineties, creased trousers came into vogue, when Edward, Prince of Wales, tried on a pair that had been lying folded at his tailor's and liked the slenderizing line.

By the turn of the century, the new civilian uniform was more or less complete, dictated by the Industrial Revolution and the changes it had brought to men's lives and work. The fabrics were sturdy and usually dark, in order to camouflage the soot and dirt produced by locomotives and factories. The age of specialization had dawned: all life would be more efficient. Men would see to reality, women to fantasy. Men would deal in numbers and ideas, women in images. Men agreed to run the world, women to decorate it.

By the early nineteen-seventies, that arrangement seemed to have outlived its usefulness. Women would pursue their ambitions, men their vanity. For a time, both sexes dressed alike, in blue jeans, muslin shirts, and Wallabees. Pitched in some sexual no-man's-land, these "unisex" clothes could be as noncommittal as a cassock but revealing enough to convey the shape of the body underneath. Men and women had hit on an interim style, a bid for more time to consider their new roles and how to dress for them. It was never intended to last.

Now, having thought the matter over, the majority of men seem to have declined the freedom to dress more imaginatively. Apparently, they don't want fashion. But why not?

In 1938, Elizabeth Hawes, an outspoken fashion designer and writer busy waging her own campaign for livelier menswear, asked the men she knew why they dressed the way they did, which was, for the most part, pretty boring. Because, they nearly all replied, it was the way women wanted to see them. (Mind you, their wives and mothers bought them their clothes.) And why didn't they rebel, strike out and wear something a little more stylish, whimsical, flattering, colorful? Because they were afraid of being thought effeminate, they said.

When, in the course of my own highly subjective research, I asked those same two questions of a number of Brooks Brothers-looking men I know, their answers were: 1) because this was the way respectable men had always dressed, they guessed; and 2) because they were afraid of being thought effeminate. Most of these men bought their own clothes. Not one of them admitted to dressing for women, though all of them wanted women to find them attractive.

Asked how they thought women wanted men to look, they said: successful (seven out of nine men polled), prosperous, powerful, tall, strong, fatherly, boyish, and (one vote) lost. The discrepancy between what men think women want in a man and what women actually do want in a man (a list that may include some of the same adjectives but would more likely start with wise, intelligent, kind, remarkable but unspectacular) is hardly new. But the signals, however crossed, get through nonetheless. A straight man may not dress expressly to attract women, but he declares by the way he's dressed that it's women he wants to attract.

After a few long looks around, you can't help but come to the conclusion that men's attire is primarily an expression of solidarity. Styles are polarized according to sexual preferences. Sometimes these are stated in terms that leave nothing open to question, as in the case of Montana on the one hand and Brooks Brothers on the other. Sometimes the statements are qualified: Calvin Klein and Jeffrey Banks cut clothes that look traditional but really aren't, because their fit is so close. Paul Stuart takes the Brooks Brothers mold and jazzes it up—only slightly—with more distinctive fabrics and a cleaner fit, for men who are interested in clothes but pretend not to be. Perry Ellis's suits are almost a caricature of the Brooks look—oversized jacket and baggy pants that pay tongue-in-cheek tribute to the sack style.

But no matter how modified the stereotype, it is rare that men's clothes manage to sidestep the issue of sexual preference. That this should be such an important factor in the way men dress day in and day out strikes a woman as peculiar. To the extent that lesbians dress in a style of their own, it resides mainly in the way they wear their clothes, not in the clothes themselves. Whereas most straight men shy away from band-collared shirts or skinny bow ties, for example, because of what they might imply, no woman decides against a particular kind of skirt or color in a blouse for fear of coming across gay.

Obviously, women get away with a lot more, and always have: "A woman impudent and mannish grown," says Patroclus in *Troilus and Cressida*, "is not more loath'd than an effeminate man." A woman can wear pants as a matter of course, but a man in a dress is still a transvestite. Why do men's clothes get so bogged down in double meanings? Why is it that men feel so compelled to assert their sexuality in the way they dress? "It did seem to me once that without questioning men's entire upbringing, one could question men's clothes," Hawes wrote. "But I am beginning to doubt it."

According to many psychologists, men's sexual identity is more fragile than women's. The caretakers of children of both sexes in our society are women. Both boys and girls initially identify with their mothers; for girls, that identification continues, uninterrupted, into womanhood. Boys, on the other hand, must eventually separate themselves from their mothers in order to find their masculine identity. As a result, becoming a man is at least in part a process of eradicating the feminine, of refusing to side with women any longer, of setting oneself apart. This could explain a lot of things—among them, men's collective resistance to the notion of fashion, which has been women's territory, and women's privilege to dress in men's clothes without incriminating themselves.

Even the words men and women use to talk about their clothes differ. A woman aspires to dress with style. But men speak of being "properly dressed"; one of the recently published clothes manuals for men is titled *Dressing Right*. Men, according to Carol Gilligan, the Harvard psychologist and author of *In a Different Voice*, tend to make more categorical decisions than women. Precisely because a man's experience in growing up is one of separating himself, he emerges free to think in abstract terms and inclined to live according to principles. But a woman, who has never had to sever those first bonds, sees the world as a place where everyone is connected, where no principle is without its repercussions in people's lives, and consequently, where no issue is ever as black-and-white as is looks on paper. When the invitation says "black tie," a man knows exactly what to wear—and what not to; a woman might wear a dinner suit, a cocktail dress, or an evening gown. For women, there are half-tones, more shades and degrees.

To think that this fundamental difference in the way men and women look at life should be so apparent in the clothes they wear is at first startling but, come to think of it, only fair. Men and women, wrote Randall Jarrell, "understand each other worse, and it matters less, than either of them suppose." Getting men to participate wholeheartedly in that process of rapid change we call fashion begins to look harder than ever, and the world probably wouldn't be all that much better off if they did.

Natural Settings

The jellyfish's domelike, phosphorescent surface is perfectly rendered in moonstones interspersed with tiny diamonds; its curling gold tentacles, paved with amethysts, dangle below. The thought of a wealthy woman, well dressed, sporting on her lapel a creature commonly regarded as a menace and a pest must have delighted Jean Schlumberger, the jewelry designer whose work is currently undergoing a revival of interest inspired by a magnificent exhibition, "Un Diamant Dans la Ville." ("A Diamond in the City"), at the Musée des Arts Décoratifs, in Paris. While others applied the principles of modernism to the craft of precious stones—streamlining the shapes, creating "abstract" settings—Schlumberger resolutely pursued his own course, a serendipitous parade of flora, fauna, and everyday objects. Surprisingly, it is the sleek art-deco necklace from Cartier that now looks dated and conventional and Schlumberger's brooch of a giant ruby pierced by gold arrows that has proved to be not only timeless but subversive.

He was an unlikely revolutionary. Born in 1907, in Alsace, to a well-to-do family of textile manufacturers, he defied his mother's warning that by becoming a jewelry designer, he would forfeit the right to dance with his clients. When he worked, he wore a smock made for him by Balenciaga, the great couturier and a friend. From

1956 until his retirement, in the late seventies, he was ensconced at Tiffany & Co., in New York.

He deplored the flatness of most jewelry, designing in three dimensions. He abhorred the idea that the value of a piece was the monetary worth of its stones, protesting that he "might as well pin a check to someone's lapel." Whereas most precious jewelry conjures up ballrooms and opera houses, a rarefied world whose inhabitants are acquainted with the great outdoors by reputation only, Schlumberger's work pays homage to the wonders of nature: hand-chased gold tulips, diamond bees, ruby-eyed catfish. Waging a campaign against jewelry-as-status-symbol—the family heirloom, the love trophy—he created jewelry that can afford to make fun of its own importance, suggesting that the ultimate luxury may be a sense of humor. Among the sketches on display is one for a pair of earrings: the right, a devil; the left, an angel. Each whispers his encouragement in the ear of the woman who wears them, as she hesitates, torn between virtue and sin.

✳ ✳ ✳

April 1990

Landscape with Figures

THE STREET-CLEANERS here in Paris are dressed in bright-green jumpsuits that match the long green brooms they use to sweep the gutters, and the green motorbikes on which they patrol the sidewalks, vacuuming up what the dogs have left behind. On café terraces, the cane chairs and small round tables are arranged in rows, like boxes at the opera, all turned to face the passersby. Everything, right down to the dirty ashtrays on the tables, is unmistakably French. Franco Moschino, the Italian designer, says that the dirt in Rome is real but the dirt in Paris is theatrical dirt.

Among people who work in the fashion business and travel the circuit—Milan, London, Paris, New York—the standard assumption is that these four cities now constitute one great big community: that New Yorkers wear clothes by Giorgio Armani, and Parisians shop for shoes at Manolo Blahnik, in London, and the Milanese carry Hermès bags, and Londoners wear Levi's. There is supposedly no longer any such thing as national style: there is only the international style, a kind of fashion Esperanto. And yet anyone who travels and takes along clothes that at home seem perfectly appropriate, or even fashionably elegant, knows what it's like to wear those same clothes in Paris—or for that matter, in any other city—and to seem out of place, clearly identifiable as a foreigner.

The visitor to Paris feels at times like the answer to a "What's wrong with this picture?" puzzle. There is an astounding consistency to the French style—a consensus of color and texture and shape within any given period which makes for a kind of seamlessness in the surroundings. A pants suit by Giorgio Armani, stylish and "international" as it may be, looks slouchy and even sloppy in Paris—at odds with the aesthetic that built the Palais-Royal and laid out the Avenue de l'Opéra and furnished the Grand Véfour. At a time when more and more of the world is being colonized by Hyatt hotels and McDonald's restaurants and Benetton boutiques that are all interchangeable, and in the midst of endless speculation about a united Europe in 1992, it's reassuring to find that local distinctions still exist.

The notion of the elegant Parisienne, born with style in her bones, is not, as one might suspect, an American invention, an outgrowth of our national inferiority complex: the French played a big part in creating the idea, and when it had grown into a legend they subscribed to it themselves. Colette extolled the "little working girls" in the garden. "For the most part their hair is immaculately done, with a sense of modesty and dignity that restrains them from anything over-elaborate, from outlandish ornament, even from artificial coloring," she wrote. "They have slim figures. They wear starched white collars, blouses with the cuffs turned meticulously back at the wrist. They display a wise distrust of plaids and stripes, and their plain skirts would age them a trifle if they did not wear them a little short: because they have shapely legs and impoverish themselves buying stockings." Valerie Steele, in her recent book *Paris Fashion: A Cultural History*, quotes Louis Octave Uzanne, a Frenchman and the author of *La Femme à Paris*, published in 1894. "In every class of society, a woman is *plus femme* in Paris than in any other city in the universe," he declared. These observations have with time become clichés, but a mystique of sorts still surrounds Frenchwomen, and anyone with an interest in human nature can't help wanting to take that mystique apart in order to find out what it's made of and how it works. Riding on buses, sitting in cafés, walking down the street here, I study the way people dress. Suppose you took that woman there, in the leggings and the jacket, or the one in the tweed suit, and set her down in New York City: what is it about her that would identify her as French? It is probably foolhardy to try to talk in general terms about fashion in a country that is home to designers as artistically far apart as Hubert de Givenchy and Jean Paul Gaultier. But the gulf between Givenchy and Gaultier is in many ways not nearly as great as the distance between the attitudes they share and the attitudes that back home we take for granted. It is these differences that occur to an American in Paris several times a day, and they strike me as more interesting than the similarities.

For one thing, the French respect fashion as a profession, as a diversion, as a topic for serious discussion in ways that Americans generally don't. Philosophers like Roland Barthes have delivered themselves of lengthy disquisitions on the subject; Pierre Bourdieu, one of France's leading sociologists, has undertaken an exhaustive investigation into matters of taste as they relate to social class; the semiologist Jean Baudrillard has examined the premises of seduction. One tries in vain to imagine an American market for a book like Gilles Lipovetsky's *L'Empire de L'Éphémère*, a hefty treatise on *"la logique de l'inconstance, les grandes mutations organisationnelles et esthétiques de la mode"* (no pictures), or even for a handy reference volume like *Les Mouvements de Mode: Expliqués aux Parents*.

Much of this discourse at the highest levels of thought is in fact buoyed by hot air—by an often exasperatingly pedantic elaboration of what seems as if it ought to be self-evident. At other times, the ideas and the statistics mustered to support them are a source of idle fascination. In Bourdieu's *Distinction: A Social Critique of the Judgment of Taste*, for example, we read the results of a 1976 survey in which Frenchwomen, grouped according to the occupation of the head of the household, were asked to rate their own features. The women in the "Farmworker" category rated their skin and their noses the highest; women under the "Clerical, Junior Exec" heading liked their hands best; and women in the "Executive, Industrialist, Professions" division were the most satisfied with their hair, faces, eyes, teeth, and bodies. Even when the theory or the information is useless to someone trying to make some larger sense of the French tradition in fashion, the mere fact of this discourse is telling.

David McFadden, who was the curator of "L'Art de Vivre," last year's exhibition of the French decorative arts at the Cooper-Hewitt Museum, in New York, says of France, "The surface is understood better than in other countries, because it's meaningful information—what people see in your house, in your dress, is who you are. The philosophy is that you are what you create around you." The information encoded in the surface of things here goes beyond the usual socioeconomic particulars that help people to know something about one another before they've exchanged a word; French objects and furniture and clothes also contain instructions for their use. In an essay in the book published in conjunction with the "Art de Vivre" exhibition, the art historian Suzanne Tise quotes from a 1925 luxury-goods catalogue describing French curios: "They contain our souls, they assume the most exquisite form of our thoughts. It is the virtue of the curio that it secretly influences our ways of feeling, and perhaps acting." An object's function is for us its reason for being, and its design is something extra; for the French, good design, even at its most decorative, is not a luxury. Even their everyday objects encapsulate a lesson in civilization.

A Louis XIV *bergère* reminds us to sit up straight; a narrow suit by Yves Saint Laurent teaches us to make our movements small and close to the body.

In New York, people are often described, if not defined, according to the designers they ally themselves with, and even to the untrained eye the labels are fairly easy to identify: "She's tall, blond—a real Ralph Lauren type," or "Who was that woman across the table, the one in Lacroix?" Here in Paris, the labels are more often illegible. Women tend not to dress right down to their shoes in clothes by a single designer. Yet snobbery is alive and well, McFadden says. "In France, if something is mass-produced—truly mass-produced—it loses its popularity, because it doesn't have that cachet of being special. The French want pieces made by hand of fine materials, with beautiful workmanship. But the French artists working in small studios, the craftspeople, have a difficult time of it, because the average buyer wants an *objet de luxe* by a firm that has a name. You don't go to some unknown artist's studio to buy handmade glass, you don't go to Saint Gobain and buy mass-produced glass—you do go to Baccarat and buy cut glass. The objects the French want fall right in the middle, between craft and industry."

Yvonne Brunhammer, the chief curator of the Musée des Arts Décoratifs in Paris and a consultant for "L'Art de Vivre," says that France is a terribly conservative country, and that its conservatism is the climate necessary for the growth of an avant-garde. If the course of French fashion is, as Brunhammer defines the course of the French decorative arts, "a constant dialogue between tradition and innovation," then the course of American fashion seems to be a constant dialogue between fashion and non-fashion. In a nation of immigrants, eager to fit in, fashion is the local game that newcomers play to get accepted, with the result that people who follow fashion come under suspicion for being conformist, and fashion itself is seen as pernicious, coercing people to look alike. So the cult of the individual in America is, when it comes to clothes, the cult of non-fashion, and this rejection of all the things that fashion stands for gets played out, ironically, in the mainstream of American fashion, with designers devising clothes that manage to be both fashion (fancy fabrics, famous name on the label) and non-fashion (functional articles from sporting-goods and other "legitimate" realms).

The French find our love-hate relationship with fashion mystifying—it's the "hate" part that they don't understand. Their ability to recognize innovation presumes a certain familiarity with what has gone before. The French, convinced that fashion is not only something they do better than anyone else but something they invented, feel collectively obliged to follow its progress, the way an American who isn't a baseball fan might watch the World Series. Among the people here who have asked me for an eyewitness account of events on the runways were a taxi-driver and a professor at the Sorbonne. During the semi-annual rounds of fashion shows in Paris, highlights of the day's collections are shown each evening on the TV news.

An American here is struck by how strong the herd instinct is among the French when it comes to fashion. Frenchwomen of a certain age habitually dress in suits by or after Saint Laurent. Young Frenchwomen express their solidarity in trends—a sudden rash of black lace stockings or knitted shawls bordered with a ribbed ruffle—that usually last no more than a season or two and rarely make their way abroad. The latest discoveries are telegraphed on the street, and the air is charged with the exchange of fashion information.

And yet Frenchwomen, even when they're wearing the same skirt or carrying the same handbag, somehow succeed in looking one of a kind, usually by virtue of some small detail. Living in Paris, one comes to realize that there are an infinite number of ways to tie a scarf or comb one's hair. These little flourishes remind me of tales of the Paris Opéra Ballet a century ago, when every dancer in the corps went out of their way to distinguish herself from every other dancer in the corps, for the benefit of the members of the Jockey Club in the audience, who often selected their mistresses from the stage. Writing half a century later, Edwin Denby imagined "a Paris fan's dismay at the sight of our clean-washed girls, looking each one as like all the others as possible, instead of (as in Paris) as *un*like," and he added, "As for the Americans, when they see a huge gifted company on the vast stage in Paris, they wonder that the Opéra public likes its dance pleasure of so small a kind, inspected as though through an opera glass, a limb or a waist at a time." As attention-getting devices go, the ones deployed by Frenchwomen are remarkably subtle, drawing the viewer in, requiring closer study. This is an art not of first impressions but of lasting ones.

THE INSTITUTION of the demimonde is, of course, defunct, but the attitudes that gave rise to it live on. The *grandes horizontales* had an enormous influence on fashion in their day, and that tradition survives, unreconstructed, in clothes designed by Emanuel Ungaro. To our minds, sex is, on the one hand, something furtive and naughty (there has always been a place in American culture for designated "bad girls"—sex symbols like Marilyn Monroe and Madonna), and, on the other hand, something organic and good for your health. To the French, sex is something exquisite, to be led up to and orchestrated—an aesthetic experience that takes place amid ruffles in a tufted-satin setting, like the inside of a candy box. This idea is, in its way, curiously sentimental, leaving no room for heavy breathing, no room for sweat—and it seems a far cry from America, where the sexiest genre in fashion these days is exercise clothing.

If the way a society keeps sexual behavior under control is one of its organizing principles, then fashion, being the language in which sexuality (among other things) is expressed, is a key to something basic. The clothes Frenchwomen wear are nearly always fitted, if not tight and sometimes downright constricting. (A suit by Saint Laurent indicates the body underneath it more precisely than, say, a suit by Bill Blass.) Perhaps because they seem to be "held" by their clothes, Frenchwomen walk and sit and carry themselves as if they thought they were sexy. (My friend Lucie, an Englishwoman living in Paris and a thoughtful observer of the local landscape, has a related theory: that Frenchwomen feel sexy because they still wear such elaborate underwear—an idea corroborated by the fact that there are nearly as many lingerie boutiques in Paris as there are bakeries.) When Frenchwomen dress in something big and loose, it is more often than not a man's sweater or sports coat borrowed from a boyfriend's closet and worn as a trophy. An American in Paris eventually arrives at the conclusion that the differences in the way the French and the Americans dress—or, more accurately, between the way Parisians and New Yorkers dress—come down to differences in relations between men and women in Paris and in New York.

Surely the most glaring of these is that American women still feel conflicted about being regarded as sex objects, whereas if Frenchwomen aren't regarded as sex objects they're insulted. American men rarely compliment a woman on her looks, for fear of activating her suspicions about their motives; Frenchmen compliment women routinely. (Lucie says that in twenty years in England the highest compliment she ever received from a man was "You're looking well this evening"—a remark ambiguous enough to be interpreted as a comment on the state of her health.) We American women want to be loved for ourselves, for who we are, and if it so happens that we're pretty, that's a bonus. This attitude may have its origins in our Puritan heritage, but the feminist movement has recently given it a big boost by reinforcing our conviction that it's wrong for a woman to trade on her appearance. Also, the worship of beauty doesn't sit well with the tenet that good looks constitute an unfair advantage in a society in which all women are supposed to be created equal.

The French are astonishingly free of such qualms. Soon after the film festival last year in Cannes, the magazine *Télé 7 Jours* devoted its cover to Josiane Balasko, one of the stars of Bertrand Blier's *Trop Belle pour Toi*, in which Gérard Depardieu, though he is married to the beautiful, young, refined Carole Bouquet, falls in love with Balasko, his dumpy middle-aged secretary. Alongside a closeup portrait of the pudding-faced actress, the cover line proclaimed that Balasko seduces Depardieu despite her *"physique banal."*

If Frenchwomen, by the clothes they wear, seem to endear themselves to men in ways that would make an American woman uncomfortable, their style of dress is often contradicted by their extraordinary self-possession and by their manner, which can seem remote by our standards. Depending on the circumstances, a Frenchwoman may pout or sulk or stalk out, but she does it in clothes that declare her willingness to please a man on his own terms. Frenchwomen would seem to be more aware of what Valerie Steele in her book calls their "erotic responsibilities."

THERE IS an everyday formality, a routine decorum, to life in Paris which permeates the clothes people wear. It is, as Aldous Huxley once wrote, simply another form of democracy: "In America the cowhand addresses his millionaire boss as Joe or Charlie. In France the fourteenth Duke addresses his concierge as *Madame*." In America, one dresses down; in Paris, one dresses up, and that is not the same as overdressing.

The vanity threshold is higher here, for men and women alike. No woman would think of going to the grocery store on Saturday morning without first putting on her makeup and maybe high heels. Almost consistently, Frenchwomen present themselves as if they found themselves attractive, regardless of their attributes, and almost consistently the presentation is convincing. Maybe the French criteria for beauty are more elastic than ours, capable of encompassing what in America would be a nose too big or lips too thin. At any rate, Frenchwomen seem to regard beauty both as something they were born with and as something to be achieved. "As for the women of the dominant class they derive a double assurance from their bodies," Bourdieu writes. "Believing, like petit-bourgeois women, in the value of beauty and the value of the effort to be beautiful, and so associating aesthetic value and moral value, they feel superior both in the intrinsic, natural beauty of their bodies and in the art of self-embellishment and everything they call *tenue*, a moral and aesthetic virtue which defines 'nature' negatively as sloppiness. Beauty can thus be simultaneously a gift of nature and a conquest of merit."

Honesty is not nearly so highly prized here as it is at home, but that is not to say that the French are dishonest; it's just that for them artifice is a means of expression. I would be willing to bet that honesty is not very high on the list of what French men and women are looking for in each other: reality, to their way of thinking, is not an aphrodisiac. Nor is "natural" beauty considered a virtue, even when it comes to nature—the French plant the trees in their gardens in a matrix and coax their shrubs into poodle-like topiary. It is not uncommon in Paris for a Frenchman to compliment a woman on her makeup—the kind of comment that horrifies most women who have just arrived from the States, where makeup, if it's well applied, is supposed to be imperceptible, and where most men instinctively know to pretend that it is. There is something fully realized about the way Frenchwomen look, as if they had envisioned a certain image of themselves and had taken the necessary steps to arrive at it. By comparison, American women look like works in progress, if only because we can't admit to having done anything to improve on our appearance. The glamour we see in a self-righteously drab actress like Jessica Lange is beyond the French, who prefer a woman to look more "finished," as Catherine Deneuve and Isabelle Adjani do. Most American women figure sooner or later a man is going to have to see their face naked anyway, and that when that day comes the makeup will be recognized for what it is—a mask. (The irony of this, of course, is that American women wear as much makeup as Frenchwomen, if not more.) The appeal of the straightforward, clean-scrubbed look, unfalsified by "paint," is essentially moral: we admire a woman for the courage to show herself to the world as she is, and in the end it's the courage we find attractive.

For their part, the French are comfortable when they know that what they're wearing is appropriate. The notion of comfort, the cornerstone of American style, is not alien to the French (despite their frequently ridiculous attempts to look casual), but theirs is essentially a cerebral comfort, not a physical one. Women in New York walk to work in their suits and running shoes, for the sake of their feet, and change into their "real" shoes when they get to the office. In New York, one has the sense that on the street one is not only anonymous but invisible.

Stephen de Pietri, who died in February, and who had been the director of exhibitions for Yves Saint Laurent and a resident of Paris for five years, used to lament the effects of this notion that comfort comes first—a notion that has taken hold in the decades since America freed itself from the supposed tyranny of Paris designers. He said once, "In many ways, you could say it's hostile, or, anyway, antisocial, this independence from fashion—that it becomes an aggression, to say that you don't care about clothing, because, really, dressing well is a social grace, and something you do for someone else."

SOME OF the most important designers in the history of French fashion have, of course, been foreigners who settled in Paris: Charles Frederick Worth, an Englishman; Cristobal Balenciaga, a Spaniard; Elsa Schiaparelli, an Italian. In the end, their styles were all seen as French, and so was their success. In recent seasons, some of the liveliest ideas advanced on the runways here have been proposed by designers who aren't French: Martin Margiela, a Belgian; Katherine Hamnett and John Galliano, from London; Romeo Gigli, from Milan; Issey Miyake, Rei Kawakubo, and Yohji Yamamoto, who with a dozen or so other Japanese designers now account for the first two days of the fashion-week schedule.

The current debate here is about the state of French fashion and its fate in a world dominated by business conglomerates, with giant corporations having bought up a number of the most famous haute-couture houses in the hope of following Chanel's example and building a successful empire on the name of a dead founder. When the word got out last year that the new management at Dior was looking for a designer to replace Marc Bohan, who had directed the house since Yves Saint Laurent's departure, in 1960, rumor had it that the short list included two Italians—one of whom, Angelo Tarlazzi, was living and working in Paris—and only one French designer, Claude Montana. In the end, Tarlazzi—whom the French now claim as their own—went to design the haute couture for Guy Laroche, Montana went to do the same for Lanvin, and the job of the Dior ready-to-wear and haute couture was given to the other Italian, Gianfranco Ferre, who is based in Milan. If at first some French fashion enthusiasts found it galling that the house of Dior, the cradle of the New Look, had passed into the hands of an Italian, their misgivings were allayed by Ferre's first couture collection—a resounding success, for which the French press awarded him the Golden Thimble. The reed-thin tailleurs, the frothy blouses, and even the evening gowns looked like the Ferre we know from his collections under his own name, but the focus was somehow sharper: the shapes were less exuberant; the materials were more restrained; the sexiness was not quite so forthright. The overall effect was more disciplined than what we had come to expect from Ferre, and that in itself seemed to indicate that he had arrived at some deep and sympathetic understanding of a creative tradition that is indigenously French.

Whether or not you accept the theory that the French, having grown up surrounded by beautiful objects, are incapable of bad taste (a theory that any recent Thierry Mugler collection would go a long way to refute), it is at least safe to say that the French are probably more sensitive than anyone else to the panorama in which they're seen. In Paris, where the city itself jealously commands so much attention, where conversations and trains of thought are continually interrupted by the sight of some rooftop or passageway or window, a human being is a mere figure in the landscape. From time to time, at dinner parties and on the street, one sees American expatriates who persist in dressing exactly as they did back home, completely oblivious of the fashion going on around them. This is the sartorial equivalent of never learning the language.

Five years ago, a man I know, an American who was living out West at the time, made a trip to Paris. Walking one afternoon along the Esplanade des Invalides, with the Grand Palais at his back, he saw coming toward him an impeccably dressed Frenchman, who looked as if he'd stepped right out of Charvet's windows; on his arm was a sleek and impeccable woman. The American, who had never given much thought to his or anyone else's clothes, was turned out in a ragged lumberjack-plaid flannel shirt, grease-stained khaki pants (the ones he always wore when he worked on his car), and scuffed-up hiking boots. He felt the Frenchman's gaze steadily on him, taking in every fraying edge, every splotch of oil, and as the distance between them narrowed it seemed to him that he was entering a force field of disapproval. Finally, from a few feet away, the Frenchman looked him in the eye, shook his head, and, without breaking his stride, said, simply but firmly, *"Non."*

Fanfare in a Minor Key

YVES SAINT LAURENT celebrated the thirtieth anniversary of the opening of his couture house with a party here in Paris at the Opéra Bastille the other night. A program of arias, sung by the soprano Katia Ricciarelli and Dmitri Hvorostovsky, a baritone, culminated in a *grand défilé*—a retrospective of one hundred and four outfits, beginning with a suite of Saint Laurent's famous variations on the tuxedo and progressing to a group of sumptuous evening gowns, worn by a fleet of models advancing on the audience as the opera orchestra played Berlioz' "Marche Troyenne." The best retrospective, however, was mounted by the guests—loyal clients, friends, members of the press, and twenty-seven hundred present and former employees—who had delved into their closets and dressed in their most beloved clothes from Saint Laurent's collections over the years.

The evening began with film clips from interviews and with black-and-white footage of the house's second collection, including scenes in the *cabine* ("*Vite, vite, vite!*" an assistant urged as a mannequin was helped into the bridal gown for the finale) and out front, in the salons, where fashion editors seated on either side of the runway craned their necks to follow each new outfit as it passed ("*Merveilleux, hein?*"). Then backstage congratulations: Zizi Jeanmaire, Eugenia Sheppard, Lee Radziwill kissing the twenty-six-year-old Yves. A few veteran journalists in the audience at the Opéra spotted themselves in the audience in 1962.

In an excerpt from a 1968 interview, Saint Laurent was asked how he felt about Chanel's remark that he was right to copy her, and that he was the heir designate to her tradition. He replied that he was very flattered that she saw a resemblance between her work and his, but then he went on to make a few distinctions: for one thing, he was completely enamored of what was going on at the moment, he said—"*Moi, j'adore mon époque*"—whereas a Chanel suit was like a costume from the era of Louis XVI, a "*document.*"

In the same interview, Saint Laurent said that there are three kinds of couturiers: *les grands*, who know how to produce a *coup de coeur*; those who work honestly at their métier (these, he said, he found very boring); and, finally, those who present their dresses with Mickey Mouse ears and various other whimsical gimmicks (the Opéra audience laughed at this, no doubt recalling the black felt Mickey Mouse ears that Karl Lagerfeld had sent down the runway at Chanel only last year). The meaning of such shenanigans, Saint Laurent confessed, escaped him totally. In his opinion, there were then only two living examples of the first type of couturier: Balenciaga and Chanel. In the second and third categories, he named no names. Clearly, he himself aspired to the rank of *les grands*, and there can be no doubt in anyone's mind that he attained it.

His favorite color? Black, he replied. He deplored *les bourgeoises*—their esprit, their taste, their carefully coiffed hair. Would "elegant" be an apt word to describe the woman he designs for? Saint Laurent told the interviewer that he preferred to think of her as "*séduisante*"—seductive, a woman who dresses to please men. He defined a dress as "a scenario, a story." He called the future "full of hope." Asked to name the worst misery, he responded, "Loneliness." He said he'd like to go away for a long time, with nothing to do.

As time went by, Saint Laurent became a recluse, retreating from the society he dressed. For several years now, the more skeptical members of the fashion press have come away from his collections with the feeling that there was nobody home. There were rumors that Saint Laurent himself was no longer designing the ready-to-wear, and then that he was no longer designing the haute couture. If these suspicions had been based on nothing more than hearsay, they might have been easier to dismiss. But there were the clothes: a pastiche of bits and pieces from Saint Laurent's greatest hits, a rehash of his former inspirations. Long after other designers had moved away from the swaggering, broad-shouldered silhouette that prevailed during the late seventies and early eighties, Saint Laurent continued to insist on it, and the house named for the designer who had once professed to adore his own era began to appear hopelessly stuck in a rut. The clothes seemed to bear out the notion that Saint Laurent had abdicated and that, for the sake of the business, which went public on the Paris stock exchange two and a half years ago, no one was letting on. His appearances four times a year, at the end of his collections, did nothing to reassure us; looking bloated and heavily medicated, he made his way unsteadily down the runway with the dazed air of an animal let out of its cage.

In interviews in the French press within the past year, Saint Laurent has openly acknowledged his alcoholism and his addiction to cocaine; he has discussed the emotional trauma of growing up homosexual in Oran, Algeria, and of his two bouts of clinical depression, one right after the other, for which he was hospitalized. The gist of these articles, and of statements by Pierre Bergé, Saint Laurent's business partner from the beginning, is that the crisis is over—that he has put his problems behind him. But although Saint Laurent appears to be in better shape now than he has been for years, these bulletins have the vaguely hollow sound of a publicity campaign to prop up the colossus.

Christian Dior and Jacques Fath had the good fortune to die before they ran out of ideas. Madeleine Vionnet, having closed her house at the age of sixty-three, lived long enough to become a cult figure. Chanel in her old age augmented her reputation as a designer by setting herself up as an oracle, issuing Dorothy Parker-style pronouncements on matters of life and taste. Successful designers, as they grow older, have three options: to change with the times, to retire, or to continue quietly to dress their faithful clients. At the height of his glory, Saint Laurent articulated a vision that many women of all ages aspired to. But now that his collections have failed to move forward, his house attracts mostly middle-aged women whose prime coincided with his own, who continue to adhere to the style they dressed in during the years when they felt at their most attractive. Saint Laurent is not the first designer to outlive his moment—Paul Poiret died penniless as well as forgotten. But few have outlived it in so tragic a manner. Much of the fanfare on the occasion of this anniversary had the final-sounding ring of an obituary—as if Saint Laurent were already dead.

He was in the audience, seated halfway back in the parterre, beside Catherine Deneuve, his longtime friend and the recently appointed model for Yves Saint Laurent skin-care products. (She was wearing an emerald-green-and-turquoise sequined dress and jacket from his spring haute-couture collection, shown the week before.) Welcoming the guests and announcing the order of the evening's program, Pierre Bergé seemed to address Saint Laurent directly. The people there that evening, he told him, had come not only to take part in the festivities but also to demonstrate their admiration and their affection. Later, when Bergé, whose political ambitions have been the subject of much speculation here (and who last year published a book of essays entitled, after a poem by Paul Éluard, *Liberté, J'écris Ton Nom*), talked about "this house that became an empire," it called to mind his emergence from behind Saint Laurent's throne. It was said that Bergé had wanted the Ministry of Culture under Mitterrand; he was given the directorship of the Opéra instead. This was his own stage that he was standing on.

The throng of dresses as they came toward us revived images of others, stored away in memory's attic. This was by no means the most comprehensive retrospective of Saint Laurent's designs we'd ever seen, nor was it the most impressive. Exhibitions like the one mounted at the Metropolitan Museum of Art, in New York, in 1983, made a more persuasive case for the breadth of his work and included more outright showstoppers. But for those of us who lived through the years when Saint Laurent was supreme, this *grand défilé* served to recall the basis of his greatness.

Saint Laurent has found raw material for his imagination in the work of Picasso, Braque, Bonnard, Matisse, and van Gogh; in Bakst's designs for Diaghilev's Ballets Russes; in the folkloric traditions of Russia, Spain, Africa, India, and China. His sense of color—his gift for bizarre but felicitous combinations, which have been widely imitated, with less success, by other designers—seems to derive from painting rather than from fashion. In the press, he has been portrayed as a cultivated man, with a mind that ranged far afield of fashion. He often cited the authors he loved most, particularly Marcel Proust—another neurasthenic too sensitive for this world, with whom he identified. When travelling, he sometimes assumed the name of Swann.

That Saint Laurent, a mere designer of what the English contemptuously call frocks, took himself so seriously struck some people as presumptuous, but those who were susceptible to the clothes he turned out were willing to forgive him his pretensions. In an essay in the anniversary souvenir program Bernard-Henri Lévy, France's most conspicuous celebrity intellectual, argues the case for conferring on Saint Laurent the status of artist. Other fashion designers—Mario Fortuny, Charles James, Romeo Gigli—have been called artists, too, usually in terms insinuating that their work is too esoteric for the masses. But in Saint Laurent's case it is simply that for the better part of his career he has been virtually the only couturier who could qualify as one of *les grands*. If his achievement didn't fit our definition of fashion, the problem was not so much that the clothes he designed were so exalted but that our notion of fashion had become so debased.

I have friends who would be surprised to hear that a thinking person could be moved by the sight of a dress, but I have been, and it has happened to me most often at Yves Saint Laurent. When I try to analyze what it is that gives his clothes this power, I always arrive at the same conclusion: something to do with the cut. In his collections we have watched a brilliant mind tackling the perennial problems of dressmaking. (His Mondrian dresses, in 1965, cut in rectangular panels and pieced together with horizontal and vertical seams, were an exercise in eliminating the darts that had been the traditional means of conforming the fabric to the breasts.) The interest inherent in the cut of Saint Laurent's clothes is, however, not only technical but sexual. The tenderness with which the fabric is made to drape around the body is so painstaking and attentive that the dress is, finally, like an act of lovemaking.

"If he has a religion," Anthony Burgess is quoted as saying in the souvenir program, "its divinity is surely woman." Some people see in Saint Laurent and his work one of fashion's most confounding ironies—that of the homosexual designer who loves women's bodies with an intensity bordering on lust, who celebrates women and renders them more beautiful and, in the end, more attractive to the men around them. There is something idolatrous in Saint Laurent's attitude toward women, as if they were the keepers of life's sacred flame.

Loyalists declared his spring haute-couture collection a success—a return to feminine loveliness, an assortment of clothes that were eminently wearable, if not groundbreaking. But my skepticism was revived, rather than put to rest, as the parade wore on. The daywear, at the beginning, looked all too familiar; the ideas were so sparse and so random, with no development and no continuity, that at the finish it seemed as if the ninety-one numbers had been conceived by almost as many different people. The hardest thing about designing a collection, Saint Laurent told *Le Monde* in an interview that appeared the day of his show, is to find what he called "the line"—to keep from losing one's way. In his best collections over the years, he has presented a theme or a set of ideas which he then went on to develop with the curiosity of a research scientist and the rapture of a poet. That sense of investigation was missing, and, apart from a handful of numbers—among them a strapless evening gown sculpted in black gazar—the majority of the clothes looked perfunctory. If in fact Saint Laurent had a hand in this collection, as the recent articles imply, I could perhaps be convinced that he had sketched his ideas, which were then passed on to his atelier to interpret, but nothing could persuade me that he had resumed the method he often used in the past, conceiving a dress directly on a model's body. Whether he can eventually find his way back to his original fascination and the satisfaction he once derived from his work remains to be seen. This season, I couldn't decide which was sadder: to think that Saint Laurent himself had had nothing to do with this collection or to think that he had actually designed it.

At the end of the *grand défilé*, Saint Laurent walked from all the way upstage down to the footlights, and for an instant he looked utterly lost. Then Bergé and Deneuve emerged from the wings and flanked him. Saint Laurent took the microphone in one hand, seeming choked up or confused, or both, and tried to say a few words of gratitude. Deneuve clasped his other hand, behind his back; Bergé steadied him with a hand on his shoulder. In the end, he managed a statement—that his had been a life of love (*"une vie d'amour"*) in a house that had been founded on love, and that he believed that in his collections he had expressed what was for him the most precious thing in life: the love of a woman. Then Bergé seized the mike and thanked everybody from the bottom of his heart. The audience breathed a collective sigh of relief: Saint Laurent had got through the program without any mishaps.

What we have witnessed in his collections over the past several years is a man's ongoing struggle with himself—a struggle that he was evidently losing as he tried by diverse means to satisfy his longing for oblivion. Like so many other members of the audience that night at the Opéra, I went to pay my respects to a designer who had shown me and others of my generation, whose experience of fashion was shaped by ready-to-wear, the haute couture's reason for being— a precision and a subtlety that can only be custom-made. But my mind kept straying from the vigorous young man in the film to the broken-down man in our midst, and the notion of promise and its fulfillment, which other people seemed to find so exhilarating, only served to deepen my sense of loss at the prospect of such an enormous talent eclipsed by some private pain that in the long run has proved to be even larger.

Survivors

THIS YEAR marks the one hundredth anniversary of the birth of Charles de Gaulle, a milestone that the French chose to commemorate one night in June by booming the "Appel du 18 Juin"—his famous rallying cry broadcast over the BBC in 1940—from a giant model of a radio console erected in the Place de la Concorde. Also, as it happens, it was fifty years ago this June that the Nazis occupied Paris—an anniversary that passed unmarked. At the Louvre's Musée des Arts de la Mode, however, the liberation of Paris and the end of the war are being celebrated, in an exhibition dating from that era and titled "Le Théâtre de la Mode."

In the spring of 1946, some two hundred dolls, dressed by fifty-three French couture houses in outfits from their spring/summer collections (the first available for export since the war) and displayed in sets created by twelve painters and designers, including Christian Bérard and Jean Cocteau, set sail for America to prove that Paris fashion was alive and well. They were not without precedent: French dressmakers had been outfitting dolls in the latest styles and sending them off to private clients all over the world as long ago as the seventeenth century. The "Théâtre de la Mode" was conceived in the fall of 1944, after Paris was liberated but before the war ended—when the street lamps in the City of Light had been turned back on but were dimmed. In 1945, after an opening stint at the Louvre's Pavillon de Marsan, the dolls made a goodwill tour of the capitals of Europe; the following year, wearing a new updated wardrobe, they travelled to New York (where the exhibition was housed in the Whitelaw Reid mansion, at Fiftieth Street and Madison) and San Francisco (to the de Young Museum). The proceeds went to Entraide Française, a war-relief organization.

Once their mission was accomplished, the dolls were retired, but they were not forgotten. In 1951, when a young woman named Susan Train arrived in Paris to work for American *Vogue*, people were still talking about them. No one seemed quite sure what had become of them, however, and as time went on, it was assumed that they had been destroyed. Train's inquiries were met with characteristically French shrugs, and replies to the effect that *"la mode est si éphémère"*—fashion is so ephemeral. Five years ago, Train (by then Condé Nast's Paris bureau chief) was visited in her office by Stanley Garfinkel, a professor at Kent State University, who told her that he had discovered the dolls in Goldendale, Washington; they had been rusticating at the Maryhill Museum of Art, a formidable-looking poured-concrete mansion built in 1914 on a bluff overlooking the Columbia River by a wealthy American eccentric named Sam Hill, who moved in international circles and numbered among his friends Queen Marie of Romania and the dancer Loie Fuller. Garfinkel was determined to remount the "Théâtre de la Mode." Train went to investigate, and found the dolls in decent condition. Resolved that they should be shown at the Musée des Arts de la Mode, which had recently opened, she returned to Paris, where she enlisted the help of Pierre Bergé, the president of Yves Saint Laurent, and began to make arrangements for their passage home. It is through Train's persistence that the "Théâtre de la Mode" has come into being for a second time. After hearing about it for all these years, she says, she simply wanted to *see* it.

The "dolls"—which are not the kind of dolls that little girls play with, or the kind that certain grownup women proudly display in lighted curio cabinets, but, rather, twenty-seven-inch-tall wire figurines that look like the ones in Giorgio de Chirico's paintings—arrived back in Paris in a jumble. Their heads and some of their limbs had been detached, and it was often impossible to tell which shoes, which gloves, which hat had gone with which clothes. Train compiled photographs from the original exhibition in order to document every outfit and match it with its proper accessories, and Nadine Gasc, the head of the Musée des Arts de la Mode's department of textiles and fashion, consulted the fashion magazines of the time. Like Train, Gasc had been hearing about the "Théâtre de la Mode" for ages. At a *bouquiniste* in Angers a few years ago, she bought a copy of the original program—a souvenir of an event she would like to have attended. The late Stephen de Pietri, who was the artistic director of the current exhibition, and to whom it is dedicated, began the task of recreating the sets.

Eliane Bonabel, who in her early twenties designed the dolls and chaperoned them on their original tour, was called in this time around to perform what Gasc calls "a little plastic surgery." By late 1944, Bonabel was already embarked on a successful career as an illustrator; she had also worked with marionettes. Her assignment, she recalls, was to devise a mannequin that would not be a cutout. She decided against solid figures, and using the measurement charts found in fashion magazines as the basis for the proportions, devised a body contoured in wire—one that would look as if it had been, as she puts it, "drawn in the air." The wire had the added advantage of permitting some flexibility: the arms and legs could be manipulated to make each doll look a little different from the rest and to introduce the idea of movement. Joan Rebull, a Catalan sculptor living in Paris, molded the heads, and replicas were cast in plaster, with the features left unpainted. (At some point over the years, lipstick was added, but the conservators removed it.) Bonabel says that the idea was to make dolls that would be "a little too thin and a little too pale," like the fashion models of the time. The hair varied: it was real or it was string or silk thread or wool, sometimes glazed with glue. (Alexandre de Paris, the coiffeur, was called in to refurbish the hairdos, most of which looked as if they'd been slept on for forty-five years; he reset the limp tresses on tiny rollers and rewound the curls with tiny hairpins.)

Each of the fifty-three couturiers was asked, in 1944, to dress one doll at the least, five at the most, for different scenes, to be set in the morning, at the cocktail hour, and in the evening. In some cases, the process of miniaturization was particularly complicated. The stripes in the fabric for one dress by Carven were too wide for the scale of the dolls, so the fabric was cut and resewn to make the stripes narrower. At Patou, a special weave was recreated in miniature. There were miniature hand-stitched buttonholes for miniature hand-covered buttons, which could actually be unbuttoned; there were tiny zippers, which opened and closed; and there were real pockets and exquisite linings. According to Bonabel, the instructions to the houses were to provide only the clothes, which, they were told, would be augmented by hats, but some of the houses got into the spirit and furnished matching shoes and gloves and umbrellas, and in no time a competition developed, with one or two ateliers in the end going so far as to produce lingerie.

Two years ago, when all the crates were unpacked at the Musée des Arts de la Mode, some accessories were missing. "We had twenty ladies in *tenue de ville* who had no shoes," Train says. She called on Massaro, the custom shoemaker on the Rue de la Paix, in the rather faint hope of persuading him to recreate what was missing. Then she spotted some miniature shoes in a showcase there, and took heart. One of his best clients, Massaro told her, had been Mrs. Gilbert Miller, a famously elegant American who collected dolls, and in filling her orders for shoes he had been obliged to make shoes for her dolls as well. He agreed to Train's request. Two missing plastrons by Cartier (one of a jewelled bird in a cage, designed as the symbol of the Occupation) were recreated by Yves Saint Laurent's costume jewellers; François Lesage reproduced Van Cleef & Arpels' jeweled epaulets in embroidery for Schiaparelli's evening gown; Chaumet remade a matching necklace, hair ornament, and bracelet.

As it turned out, the dolls had stayed on in San Francisco after their tour, in the basement of a department store called the City of Paris. Other cities had wanted the exhibition but had been unable to come up with the financing. No one, even in France, was willing to pay to have the dolls shipped back to Paris. "Thank God," Train says. Chances are that they would have been dispersed and sold, for lack of storage space. In the archives of the Chambre Syndicale de la Couture Parisienne, the trade association that still organizes the shows every season, she found the minutes of a meeting of the executive committee in September, 1951, recording that the president of the City of Paris, insisting that the dolls must not be destroyed, proposed to send them at his own expense to the Maryhill Museum; the committee agreed. But even more remarkable than the fact that the "Théâtre de la Mode" survived, perhaps, is that it came about in the first place. Fashion designers have never been known for their solidarity; that so many of them agreed to participate in a project like this probably says less about the designers themselves than it does about the circumstances that united them.

IN MOST fashion histories, the years from 1940 to 1944, so painstakingly examined by historians of every other field, are summarized briefly, and only, one feels, as a setup for the voluptuous dawn of Dior's New Look, in 1947. There has been a sense that the less said about the behavior of many fashion designers during these years the better. In Paris, Chanel, who closed the doors of her couture house in 1940, is alleged to have had an affair with a Nazi officer, and among the designers who stayed in business were several who apparently behaved no better; it's said that Marcel Rochas would cross the street rather greet his former Jewish clients. As for the clothes, it is taken for granted that the war years weren't fashion's finest hour, given the restrictions under which the couturiers were forced to work, to say nothing of the daily matters of life and death which must have eclipsed questions of style. We assume that under the circumstances practicality won out over fantasy—that the immediacy of an occupying army and ration coupons must have prevented the imagination from wandering very far. If anything, the Occupation of Paris is routinely regarded by Americans as the event that launched American fashion on its own course, with New York cut off from the French inspiration on which its designers had previously relied. It's only now, with the publication, in Paris, of Dominique Veillon's *La Mode Sous l'Occupation*, that we learn how valiantly Frenchwomen's impulse to express themselves in the clothes they wear adapted itself to their straitened lives, and how narrowly the French fashion industry escaped extinction.

Veillon, a historian and the author of two other books on the Occupation, describes a city that woke up with a champagne hangover one morning in September, 1939, and found itself at war. The *caves* of the Ritz were transformed into air-raid shelters, complete with fur coverlets and Hermès sleeping bags. A new fashion was born, and, with it, a new adjective, *utilitaire*, to describe innovations like Schiaparelli's enormous pockets, designed to take the place of a handbag. The conscientiously stylish woman would request a *vélo-taxi*—a go-cart of sorts, pulled by a man on a bicycle—that matched her outfit.

According to an essay by Nadine Gasc in the "Théâtre de la Mode" catalogue, the system for rationing clothes which went into effect in the summer of 1941 was a complicated one. In some cases, two old garments could be bartered for one new one. Since men's clothes could be exchanged for women's, newspapers published patterns for turning a man's three-piece suit into a woman's. Gasc quotes Colette: "I feel I ought to save this diary, so that I can open it again at a later date to attest to the fact that in February, 1941, even as we stood in line for our milk, our rutabagas, and our mayonnaise made without oil or eggs, and even though we had no crêpes to celebrate Candlemas and wore leatherless shoes, Paris went on accomplishing its most characteristic feats, producing a figured velvet dress . . . a very dressy pink lamé blouse."

Colette was perhaps the most impassioned witness to the ways in which Frenchwomen of the time made do, psychologically as well as materially; she memorialized an era when "three wisps of straw, a furled handkerchief, a scrap of waxed cloth, a domino tile, and a dog's leash" could add up to a hat. Veillon documents hats made from blotting paper and from newspapers—the latter executed in a range of different dailies, and worn as a means of advertising the wearer's political views. A fashion for plaid sprang up, as a declaration that the wearer sided with the British. From time to time, women working for the Resistance, receiving shipments of arms from London, gave in to the temptation to make a blouse out of silk from a parachute, even though it might signal their ties to the English or the Gaullists. On exhibit at the Mémorial de la Paix, an excellent new museum of the war, in Caen, is a bridal gown made from a parachute.

That life went on we knew, but that it went on with such goodnatured vigor—that couturiers produced outfits called Coal or Black Coffee, or an entire collection with each number named after a stop on the Métro; that they turned their hands to disguising culottes as a skirt; that a *"journée de l'élégance à bicyclette"* was organized as an open-air fashion show of stylish clothes for getting around town on a bicycle—comes as something of a surprise. To the American mind, particularly after the sartorial free-for-all of the seventies and eighties, the effort required to sustain an elegant appearance seems like a luxury in peacetime, let alone in time of war. How staggering, how amusing it is now to come upon photographs (in the exhibition catalogue) of Parisian women in a beauty salon where the hair dryers, for lack of electricity, were powered by two men on a bicycle in the basement, pedalling the equivalent of three hundred and twenty kilometers a day to dry the hair of one hundred and fifty clients. The instinct for fashion, put to the test during the war by relentless indignities and deprivation, proved to be fundamental to the French character. Veillon recognizes that for most women the act of making a dress out of an old tablecloth or going to the hairdresser as usual constituted not only a refusal to give in to adversity but a means of safeguarding the identities they had built for themselves in a world that, morally and physically, was being reduced to rubble. She calls the hats they wore a provocation, a *"manifestation d'insolence,"* that did not go unnoticed by the occupying soldiers in the streets; in 1944, the Germans tried to close down the milliners altogether.

Meanwhile, Veillon reports, the leaders of the Third Reich had a plan for the fashion industry: the French couture houses would be integrated into the German enterprise, based in Vienna and in Berlin, which was to take the place of Paris as the cultural capital of Europe; the French ateliers would provide the specialized handwork; the French couturiers would be transferred to these new centers of fashion, where they would find reserved for them *"de brillantes situations."* Lucien Lelong, the designer who was then the president of the Chambre

Syndicale de la Couture Parisienne, replied that the Germans could, of course, impose anything on the French by force, but that the haute couture could not be transferred, either as a whole or in part—that its creativity was "not only a spontaneous outburst but also the consequence of a long tradition cultivated by specialized workers" in diverse *métiers*. In November, 1940, Lelong went to Berlin to argue that since the Germans considered fashion a cultural activity, every country should have the right to create its own. Eventually, the Germans relented and allowed the French couture to continue but under constant surveillance, on the premise that, deprived of its foreign outlets and of choice materials, it would find its creativity weakened and would finally, in Lelong's words, "die of asphyxia." The houses now worked under a system of *"dérogation"*—a special dispensation that, according to Lelong, was called into question fourteen times during the four years of the Occupation. The Germans imposed a series of restrictions, limiting the number of couture houses in operation and eventually forbidding photographs of the clothes (in order to curb sales). Lelong stalled for time, and fought to have the number of couture houses increased. In March, 1942, he organized a group fashion show in Lyons, in the Unoccupied Zone. In 1944, the Germans closed the houses of Mme. Grès and Balenciaga, on the pretext that they had exceeded the quotas set for fabric.

Evidently, Lelong had the foresight to recognize that France's economic future lay in a continuation of its long-standing role as the provider of luxury goods to the rest of the world—that the luxury-goods industries, of which fashion was the most highly visible, would be France's bread and butter. Veillon relies on Lelong's own account of his dealings with the Germans, from the archives of the Chambre Syndicale. Susan Train, who came across it in her research for the "Théâtre de la Mode," was moved to translate it, and it is her translation I quote. In his report, made in 1944, Lelong writes, "The maintenance of this industry in activity and the survival of its skilled workers represents for France the immediate possibility of earning a great deal of foreign currency in exchange for very little raw material, very little transport, a great deal of invention and hard work. Before the war, it was calculated that one exported haute-couture model enabled us to purchase ten tons of coal; the export of one litre of perfume, two tons of oil; one bottle of champagne, three kilos of copper."

As for the clients of the haute couture during the Occupation, Veillon reports that, contrary to popular assumption, they were not predominantly the wives of German officers. In 1941, the Chambre Syndicale registered around twenty thousand couture cards (required for access to the shows), of which two hundred were reserved for the "authorities of the Majestic" (the hotel that served as Nazi headquarters in Paris). In the spring of 1944, the number of cards in circulation had fallen to about fourteen thousand; still, there were only two hundred set aside for the Germans. The majority of the customers, by Veillon's description, were French, wealthy Parisians and residents of Neuilly, Versailles, and other surrounding towns, or rich foreigners—South Americans, Spaniards—who moved in what she calls "a protected universe." It was not unheard of for two friends who wore the same size to go in together on a suit and take turns wearing it. As the war went on, a new contingent began to appear, opportunists the French called "*les BOF*," for "*beurre-oeufs-fromages*," the scarce products that these entrepreneurs sold at scandalous prices, amassing fortunes. Veillon passes along the story, recounted by a journalist of the time, of the woman who arrived in the salons of one couture house with her daughter, for whom she bought four dresses at eight thousand francs apiece; these new clients were the wife and daughter of a man who had come by the service stairway and offered to sell the designer butter at three hundred francs a kilo.

Under the leadership of the octogenarian Marshal Pétain, who habitually made pronouncements to the effect that a woman's place was in the kitchen, and who had only got around to taking a bride at the age of sixty-four, the Vichy government launched its own attempts, more modest but no more successful, to manipulate fashion as a means of propaganda. In keeping with the sturdy pastoralism that Pétain, from his office in a hotel at a health resort, promoted as France's salvation, the state encouraged couturiers to work in *le style campagnard*. Among the wartime photographs that accompany the "Théâtre de la Mode" exhibition is one of an outfit with a dirndl skirt and puffed sleeves, titled "The Milkmaid." Every once in a while, a client would order one of these outfits—something to wear on vacation or while working in the garden.

A WEEK before the recent opening of the "Théâtre de la Mode," the floors of the galleries at the Louvre are strewn with wood shavings and scraps of wire; the windows looking out over the tops of the chestnut trees in the Tuileries are open to let in some air; a visitor steps out of the elevator and is greeted by the smell of paint. A steel ladder towers above Jean-Denis Malclès's scene of a Surrealist garden, still under construction, where some of the dolls will go for a moonlit promenade. Among sawhorses, toolboxes, a sewing machine, and a portable generator, Anne Surgers, a young woman in a white smock, who has recreated the sets on the basis of the original designs and photographs, shuttles between Joan Rebull's carrousel—a Dionysian merry-go-round populated by mermaids and centaurs—and André Dignimont's set, where the dolls will congregate in the arcades of the Palais-Royal. André Beaurepaire, the painter and set designer, has arrived—a vigorous man who looks to be in his sixties, wearing a plaid shirt and sporting a backpack. He is reviving his own original décor, "La Grotte Enchantée."

Meanwhile, the dolls are gathered in the conservation laboratory, where they hang, headless, by their clavicles. A doll in Jacques Heim's tropical floral-printed cotton bandeau bra, diaper, and tulip overskirt—the wire cage of her midriff exposed—is dressed for the beach at Biarritz. Balenciaga's full-skirted black wool suit with a fitted jacket and a fringed back faille sash draped at the hips looks as glamorous today as it must have in 1946. Jacques Fath's black velvet mermaid dress with a skirt of sequin-dotted black tulle over pale-pink satin is still being imitated. Mme. Grès's black silk-organdy evening gown, with a series of pleats pinched at the waist and falling open over a bright-green organdy underskirt, has lost none of its impact. (In many cases, Alexandre says, it's the hairdo that looks dated, not the clothes.)

Note cards on which are written the specifications for the various outfits dangle from satin ribbons that attach the dolls' shoes to their feet. On tables in another room, more shoes are arranged: thumb-size gold leather ankle boots in three scalloped tiers with platform soles; red-and-ivory platform saddle oxfords with tiny red leather tassels at the ends of the laces; ankle-strapped black suede sandals with black leather piping no wider than the line made by a pencil. There are miniature pocketbooks and ruffle-edged umbrellas that open; suede gloves with nearly microscopic topstitching around the fingers; belts that actually buckle, for four-inch waists. The dolls' heads—immaculately coiffed, hats already in place—are on pikes driven into boards. Seen all together, they form a disembodied crowd. One blonde with shoulder-length hair is waiting until the last minute for her black straw picture hat, which is sitting in front of her.

Everyone who has worked with the dolls, it seems, has fallen under their spell. Train claims that each doll has a distinct personality. Bonabel talks about how some of the dolls looked instantly chic and others needed some fiddling with—which, she adds with a laugh, is the way it is in life. David Seidner, whose still-life photographs of the dolls, taken for the catalogue, are featured in the exhibition, says that for him the mere idea of the dolls seemed "charged some-how—atavistic and pagan, full of fantasy and voodoo." Working in the museum at night and on weekends, Seidner would find himself spending an hour posi-tioning a sleeve or coaxing some movement into an eighteen-inch-long skirt intended, in the life-size original, to drape and fall several feet. Exasperating as all this was, however, he found the dolls "expressive" and "dear." There is, he says, "something vulnerable about their being so small." In his portraits they are shown against a backdrop of wooden doors that were found in the basement of the Louvre—chosen, he explains, because he finds old textures "narrative"— or against pieces of zinc and lead that remind him of the rooftops of Paris, or against shards of plate glass. By the end of the project, he says, his role and the dolls' role were reversed: Seidner stiff and tense, hunched over a tripod, and the dolls set free, running through a carpet of dried leaves.

Once the exhibition opens, the dolls seem back in their element. Animated and graceful, their heads held high, they revisit the Pont des Arts in Georges Douking's view of the Île de la Cité, veiled in mist. The skyline of Montmartre— the windmill of the Moulin Rouge and the dome of Sacré-Coeur outlined in black wire beneath small wire cumulus clouds—looms in the distance in Jean Saint-Martin's set, "Croquis de Paris." In Louis Touchagues's scene of the Rue de la Paix and the Place Vendôme, seen in one-point perspective, the square is in motion, full of chic Parisiennes window-shopping at the jeweller's, hurrying to meet a friend at the Ritz, en route to the box office at the Opéra.

In Cocteau's "Ma Femme Est une Sorcière (based on René Clair's movie *I Married a Witch*), dolls in evening gowns occupy a burned-out maid's room under the eaves. A basin and a mirror are still left standing in one corner. Marcel Rochas's bride, in white satin, is stretched across the iron bed. Pierre Balmain's witch, in a gown of gray tulle embroidered at the bodice with gray pearls, is poised in midair on a broomstick. Through holes in the roof are visi-ble glimpses of Notre-Dame and the ink-blue night sky.

From the balcony of the eighth-floor galleries, visitors look down on Bérard's opera house as if from the theater's top tier, closer to the scaled-down crystal chandelier than to the stage. Downstairs, other visitors, like late arrivals finding their seats in the parterre, walk inside the set, where the stage is filled with dolls in evening gowns, and more dolls in full formal dress watch from the boxes. They have worn their jewels, their turbans, their evening gloves, their furs—including an ermine stole fringed in very small tails, and a full-length ermine cape, scalloped at the hem and lined in pale-pink satin. One doll, in Balmain's pink satin strapless gown encrusted with rhinestones and silver sequins, wears long gray tulle evening mitts embroidered to match.

Gasc calls discovering so many dolls all from the same season the find of a lifetime. Train agrees. "This is something that no museum in the world has," she says. Gasc remarks on the "cohesiveness" of the clothes: it was a time when designers worked—and women dressed—in harmony, if not in outright unison. Bonabel recalls that people then had a different notion of fashion: it was, she says, "like a set of regulations, and we dreamed of submitting to them." The smaller couture houses, Train says, had their eyes on what the big ones were doing. The level of quality not only of the workmanship but of the designs, even by those couturiers whose names are long forgotten—Annek, O'Rossen, Blanche Issartel, Georgette Renal, Calixte, Véra Borera, Ana de Pombo—is astonishingly high. The clothes of the "Théâtre de la Mode" fill a gap in our understanding of fashion, providing a transition from the mannish silhouette of the war years to the literary grandeur of the New Look. In Lucien Lelong's turquoise-and-white polka-dot day dress with a draped bodice and a full skirt, and in his ivory tulle strapless evening gown embroidered with slate-gray leaves and flowers over a white satin underskirt—both designed by Christian Dior before he left Lelong and formed his own house—there are unmistakable intimations of the revolution that Dior would soon launch, and they prove once again, Train says, that "fashion is an evolution." The New Look didn't materialize out of thin air; it was on its way. Dior simply accelerated its arrival.

Paris had survived intact, its bridges and landmarks still standing. The fashion industry had held its ground. As it happens, the "Théâtre de la Mode" depicts a world without men. There is something touching about these dolls, so painstakingly turned out in sumptuous clothes made possible by peace, as if the wool suits and fur coats and festive ballgowns were Frenchwomen's just reward for the dignity with which they went about their lives, for their makeshift chic. While the men who had fired guns and flown warplanes were driving their tanks down the Champs-Élysées in V-Day parades and getting medals pinned to their chests, these dolls were being created—a passing monument to a more domestic heroism.

✳ ✳ ✳

Wrap Star

*In the fall of 1997, Diane Von Furstenberg revived her famous wrap-dress,
a best-seller in the seventies.*

Once upon a time, there was a princess with an idea. The idea was a dress. Not a taffeta ball gown like the ones fairy-tale heroines usually wear—this was a drip-dry, cotton jersey dress that wrapped in front and tied at the waist. The princess devised cunning prints in vivid colors and arranged for the dress to be manufactured and sold. In no time, women all across the land were buying the dresses—five million of them—and wearing them. And even though the princess was a member of the jet set, famous far and wide as a glamorous party girl, her dress was seen as evidence of an uncanny knack for identifying with her customers: they felt that she must have understood them to have invented something so comfortable and practical, so suitable to their own everyday adventures and to their newfound sense of independence.

For the women of the land had gone to work. Hi-ho! It was the seventies, and en masse they left their sculleries and their hearths for careers in finance, law, and other fields that had been the province of men. Wearing a wrap-dress by the princess—an entrepreneur herself—the women went on job interviews; they went straight from the office out to dinner; they went around the world, washing the dress at night in the sink in their hotel rooms. Requiring no help with a zipper in back or with hard-to-reach hooks and eyes, the wrap-dress epitomized not only the spirit of women's liberation but of sexual liberation, too: in two minutes flat, a woman could be dressed and out the door; she could be undressed in even less time.

Years passed, and the princess moved on—to books on decorating, a deal with Avon, a clothing line sold on QVC and the Home Shopping Network. The women of the land had come to regard her as one of them. (And indeed, after her divorce from the prince, she was demoted from royalty to mere celebrity.) Until one day her son took for his bride a damsel who cherished the dress that had long been forgotten. She and her friends searched thrift shops for vintage versions; the populace was under the spell of the seventies. And so it came to pass that the wrap-dress, after a long sleep, was reawakened. The (former) princess put it back into production—this time in silk jersey and in a new range of colors and prints. The calendars had been turned to the fall of 1997. And all the signs and portents said that the now-classic dress would live, happily, ever after.

Camelot

THE CONTROVERSY (did he or didn't he have AIDS?) that surrounded Perry Ellis's death, two years ago, and drowned out the eulogies has lately been stirred up all over again by Jonathan Moor's biography, *Perry Ellis*, which belabors the issue. There is no doubt that Ellis's career was cut short or that his death was awful and demeaning, but today the question of how he died seems nowhere near as important as the sad fact that he is gone, and that much of what he stood for in fashion seems to have died along with him.

Ellis's life was not the stuff of which epic biographies are made. He grew up in Virginia—in Portsmouth, and later, in suburban Churchland—and his childhood was, by his own account, contented and uneventful. Success came to him relatively late, when he was nearly forty, and the life he led from then on, though extravagant in some respects, was hardly grandiose or fancy; his close friends weren't movie stars or intellectuals or millionaires or artists. There was no mystery about him, according to Patricia Pastor, his longtime assistant who succeeded him as designer for the line that bears his name. He had, she says, "a plain old life," and he was happy in it.

His route to success on Seventh Avenue was a roundabout one. His background was in marketing: he earned a bachelor's degree in business from the College of William and Mary and, after a brief stint in the Coast Guard, a master's in retailing from NYU. He had no formal design training. In 1963, he went to work at Miller & Rhoads, a department store in Richmond, and eventually built its junior sportswear department, one of the smallest in the store, into the biggest money-maker—"bigger than the furniture department," he proudly told an interviewer—on the strength of the Shetland sweaters and matching knee socks, the plaid skirts, and the Peter Pan-collared shirts that were the staples of such manufacturers as John Meyer of Norwich and The Villager. Representing a large constituency, Ellis wielded considerable influence with these manufacturers. Often, they asked his opinion on colors and design changes, and he advised them so well that in time he was hired away by John Meyer. In 1974, Ellis joined Manhattan Industries as vice-president and merchandise manager of its Vera Sportswear division, and was assigned the task of turning Vera Neumann's bright-colored silkscreen paintings into sportswear. Two years later, he was given his own line, called Portfolio, and, two years after that, his own division, with his name on the label.

Several of Ellis's collections achieved instant landmark status: the swirling wool challis dresses and skirts printed with ducks, geese, and pheasants; the twenties-style linen and eyelet chemises that coincided with the movie *Chariots of Fire*; the kaleidoscopic mixture of tartan plaids; the geometric patterns inspired by Sonia Delaunay. In every collection, there were buttonless blazers, worn open or anchored by a belt; trompe-l'oeil one-liners (a sweater with a "belt" knit into the waist or a "pendant" at the neckline); woolly tights and patterned socks; flat shoes. Single-handedly, Ellis revived hand-knits, bringing to sweaters peplums, ruffles, and other details usually reserved for fabrics, and purveying such oddities as a two-piece knit bathing suit with Argyles down the sides. He waged a campaign to bring back culottes, as a more flattering alternative to pants and a more comfortable alternative to skirts, and he turned them out in all varieties; cossack pants, knickers, and bloomers; box-pleated, streamlined, or full; ankle-length, mid-calf, or mini (a combination of shorts and skirt, formerly called a "skort"). He created width at the shoulders by means of a pleat at the top of the sleeve or a ruffle around the armhole. Though the antecedents of his clothes often came from menswear, the silhouette was unfailingly feminine. However voluminous the skirt or coat or culottes, the waist was always clearly defined. His clothes moved gracefully.

Ellis believed that if you weren't having fun doing your job you were in the wrong line of work. The good times that he and his assistants—Pastor, who joined him in 1976, and Jed Krascella, who was hired two years later—had designing his collections spilled over into the clothes and onto the runway. Early on, the three of them settled into their special roles: Ellis supplying the ideas, Krascella getting them down on paper, and Pastor calculating how to make the designs work in fabrics and on a body. The themes, Pastor says, were never preconceived; they simply emerged from the clothes as the collection evolved. Planning a collection dominated by flared boleros and highwaisted matador trousers, the three of them talked in Spanish accents all day long.

For the fall show of 1978, they engaged the Princeton football captain and cheerleaders to appear, and this prompted a string of free associations—an oversized raccoon coat, saddle oxfords, snug little sweaters, and chrysanthemum corsages—that all together celebrated life on campus.

Ellis emerged in the late seventies, at a time when the names on designer labels had suddenly become household words and the designers themselves had been elevated to the rank of celebrities, signing their names on the rear pockets of blue jeans. Their living rooms, their dinner menus, their dogs were routinely featured in "lifestyle" stories; their opinions on matters of taste were duly recorded; they were photographed at parties in the company of glamorous clients wearing their designs. And the public was reassured to know that at the center of those images lived a real person: Ralph Lauren, the silver-haired, smiling urban cowboy; Calvin Klein, the boyishly handsome entrepreneur; Bill Blass, the wry, debonair man-about-town. But the Perry Ellis image was uninhabited. Ellis believed that the designer's name belonged inside the clothes. He preferred to go about his life in private, in the company of a few close friends, and refused to allow a personality cult to be built around him. When, from time to time, the press tried to bestow on him a blue-blooded past, making him out to be a preppy Southerner from an Old Dominion family, who lived in a West Side town house furnished with heirlooms, he didn't bother to set the record straight.

He was an obstinate perfectionist, who paid excruciating attention to detail. One season, when all the post offices in New York were sold out of a new issue of flower stamps he wanted for his invitations, he sent someone on his staff to New Jersey to buy them—to buy twice as as many as he needed, because he liked only two of the four designs. Rea Lubar, who handled Ellis's publicity for the first few years, claimed that though he drove her staff crazy they loved—and respected—him for being such a stickler. Trying to find extra seating for one of his shows, she consulted the Yellow Pages and came up with a Staten Island company that rented bleachers. She was prepared to make the arrangements over the phone, she says, but Ellis insisted on seeing the bleachers. So off they went, in his big white Pontiac. The bleachers were fine, he said when he saw them, but a little rusty—could they be painted orange? There are stories of flowers being too short for a vase, of a custom-designed dining-room table for his apartment being a quarter of an inch too wide. Yet somehow he managed to escape being tyrannized by his own good taste—a common fate in the fashion business. Robert McDonald, who shared a brownstone with Ellis for fifteen years, recalls that their house was the kind of place where there are dog hairs on the sofa and you can put your feet up on the coffee table.

In his book, Jonathan Moor, with nothing more than scraps of information, constructs a picture of an average, unassuming guy who loved Frank Sinatra's singing and Frank O'Hara's poetry, who was a good cook and a good dancer, who never learned to drink Scotch. According to other sources—people who knew him well—he was a homebody, an intensely loyal friend, and something of a snob, impressed by other people's celebrity, though not by his own. He appreciated humor but couldn't tell a joke well. He played squash regularly (always doubles), more for the company than for the exercise. McDonald characterizes his taste in music as "lite classical." His taste in books ran to biographies, mostly of historical or literary figures; after reading Beryl Markham's *West with the Night*, he sent copies of it to some twenty people he knew.

His friends contend that Ellis was an introvert. In an interview in 1980, he said that his favorite childhood pastime had been reading, "because you do it by yourself." An only child, he remained on close terms with his parents. His mother wrote him a letter once a week, enclosing five dollars. Sometimes she sent clippings, usually inspirational, with the important parts underlined. Pastor has one of these taped up on the bookshelf behind her desk: "What a man is and does depends entirely on the use he makes of his indwelling power. Right thinking plays the most important part in our lives."

Ellis himself was an inveterate, assiduously thoughtful note-writer—most comfortable expressing his feelings in writing, one friend believes, than in person or over the phone. Another friend remembers a note Ellis sent to thank him for a gift he had sent to thank Ellis for a weekend at his house. An acquaintance of Ellis's who worked as a lowly copywriter at *Vogue* once got a note from him saying that while he was riding his bike to work he'd spotted a woman walking down Columbus Avenue looking wonderful in his clothes, and then realized that it was she.

FOR ALL Ellis's refusal to advertise himself, his clothes were an open book, and in them one could read aspects of his personality. Looking at videotapes of his collections recently, I was struck again by how prolific he was, and how unstinting. Often, he would spend several ideas on a single outfit when most designers would spread them out and call attention to each of them. He preferred the durable to the luxurious, the casual to the formal, the understated to the showy. When, in 1979, he began designing furs, he chose to work in sheared beaver, not "glamour" skins like fisher and sable. Ellis's furs were dyed moss green or slate blue or eggplant, to match the color range of his clothes, and they were treated as fabric, cut along the same lines as his jackets and coats—with capelet collars or dimple sleeves. In the collection inspired by Sonia Delaunay, he showed sheared-beaver coats in vivid geometric patterns. These were furs that aspired to the status of mere cloth—furs with a grandeur so self-effacing that it didn't register at first glance.

Ellis brought to everyday, casual clothes a level of invention in the cut, a richness in the colors, and a complexity in the mixing of prints and textures which are usually reserved for more sumptuous fabrics and for statelier clothes—for haute couture. He never outgrew his affection for the collegiate style—the matching-sweater-and-knee-socks sets and the pleated plaid skirts— that had served him so well in his first job. Like most designers, Ellis had his weaknesses, and, as is often true, they were the converse of his strengths. His men's suits looked downright jokey, as if he couldn't quite bring himself to do something so conventional with a straight face. His evening clothes for women were lacking in conviction; the best of them were generally softer, more luxurious versions of the sweaters and skirts he did so well. The theatricality, the role-playing, the fantasy inherent in the most dramatic evening dressing went against his nature. He was a pragmatist, at home in the here and now, and the woman his clothes projected was an ingénue, not a femme fatale.

When Laughlin Barker, Ellis's lover and the president of Perry Ellis International, died of AIDS, in January, 1986, Ellis asked Robert McDonald, who was then working in the film industry, to come into the office a few days a week, "just to keep the paper flowing." In March, Ellis asked him to step in as president, a job for which, McDonald says, "I couldn't have been less qualified." But Ellis's own health was failing, despite public statements to the contrary, and he clearly wanted to leave his business in the hands of a friend. McDonald complied, assuming that he and Ellis would have a year or so together, during which he could learn the ropes. Ellis died that May—not, however, before dictating a stack of thank-you notes to friends for the flowers they had sent him during his illness.

Patricia Pastor says that the transition was smooth, because Ellis had always included her and Jed Krascella in decisions. "We were so much a part of the business that there was no waking up one morning and wondering, 'What would Perry have done?'" Her collection for this fall is exuberant and quirky, with wool check suits whose jackets are fringed like a cowgirl's, scallop-edged blouses and ballerina skirts, cable-knit cashmere scarf-necked sweaters, blanket skirts, and a trenchcoat lined in Russian squirrel. The clothes are not, perhaps, as whimsical as Ellis's, but some of the signature themes—the mixture of patterns, the culottes—are still there, and the style is in keeping with the one he devised. Pastor says that there is bound to be a resemblance between her designs and his, because in the course of working with him she came to believe most of what he believed about clothes.

For years, Ellis dressed in the same uniform daily: khaki pants (no belt), a blue oxford shirt, and Top-Siders (sometimes no socks). If clothes could be said to have a purpose, it was, to his mind, to give people a sense of well-being—to put them at their ease, so that they could go about the business of their lives. He had no interest in turning out sartorial objects of art. He wanted to bridge the gap between fashion, which seemed aloof, meticulous, and forbidding, and the discombobulation of everyday life—between the frozen image and the body in motion. What mattered finally wasn't the clothes themselves, or even the way they looked, but the way they could make people feel. Anyone who doubted the validity of this theory had only to watch his models and the way they moved in his clothes. They strode—sometimes skipped—down the runway, breezy and sure, arms swinging at their sides.

In his collections, Ellis showed a bias toward the natural—little or no make-up, hair that fell into place, an image that hadn't been fussed over. He made clear the distinction between self-respect and self-adoration, between self-awareness and self-involvement; even at its most elaborate, his style was remarkably free of the vanity implicit in so much of high fashion. In the late seventies (which to all intents and purposes lasted until 1983 or 1984), the height of the Beige Decade, Ellis leaned toward a palette of rich colors: teal and periwinkle blue, eggplant, forest green, garnet. While the rest of fashion was awash in silk crêpe de chine, he chose to work instead in wool, linen, and cotton—rough-textured, unpretentious fibers that didn't require people to be on their best behavior. At a time when clothes were getting more and more explicit, when many designers subscribed to the notion that the best wrapping is the one that divulges the contents of the package, Ellis proceeded on the assumption that a woman's sex appeal resides in her sense of herself—in her wit and energy and confidence and humor—and that in the end the sexiest clothes are the ones that put her at her ease.

When Perry Ellis and Ralph Lauren were mentioned in the same breath, as they often were, it was usually to make a point about American fashion—about its being such a mass-market industry, bereft of artistry, that a designer who couldn't even sketch (as Ellis couldn't, and as Lauren can't) could nevertheless become a staggering success. What Ellis and Lauren had in common was a knack for merchandising, an instinct for what a certain customer wanted, and in both of them this understanding was subjective, an outgrowth of their own tastes and yearnings. The clothes Lauren designs are, to all appearances, an attempt to invent for himself the life to which he aspires; Ellis, in the clothes he designed, recreated for himself an idealized version of the life he remembered. For those of us who grew up in circumstances like the ones he invoked, his clothes became the means by which we could revisit our past, glossing over the lousy time we had at the prom, or the tedious summer we spent working at the five-and-ten. And for people who knew no more of this world of small towns and tidy suburbs than what they'd seen in the movies, Ellis's fantasyland proved to be no less compelling. While Lauren caters to our popular fascination with the aristocracy, Ellis reaffirmed our faith in the middle class. He celebrated Middle America at its most ordinary: homecoming parades, covered-dish suppers, summer camps, Scout troops, and paper routes.

Our memory when it comes to fashion is short and selective. The clothes we wore twenty or thirty years ago seem comprehensible and appealing, however quaint. But the clothes we wore ten years ago strike us now as impossibly remote, and the years when Ellis flourished have been consigned to oblivion for the time being. His name has quietly slipped into history, until that day in the distant future when some museum mounts a retrospective exhibition and revives his reputation. In the meantime, for those of us who witnessed his career there is something poignant and a little painful about recollecting the clothes he designed. In them we see how much the world has changed in these past few years, and how we have changed along with it. Ellis's clothes are full of optimism, of laughter, of innocence. He presented us with a vision of what politicians and editorial writers call the youth of America—student-council presidents, cheerleaders, varsity athletes, yearbook editors, valedictorians—and of the future stretching out before them, unfolding at their feet like the clean white paper down the middle of the runway.

Ralph Lauren's Achievement

IN THE little more than a year since Ralph Lauren's flagship Polo store opened in the old Rhinelander mansion, at Seventy-second Street and Madison Avenue, in New York, it has become a cultural landmark, an "instant classic," to borrow a term Lauren's publicists once used to describe the success of his women's perfume. Tourists overheard planning their rounds of the Upper East Side museums now include the store on their agendas: "Today we're doing the Whitney, Ralph Lauren, and the Frick...." On any given afternoon its many rooms are filled with people milling distractedly about, their steps slow, their eyes anxious for fear that they might miss something. They are, to all intents and purposes, on a house tour. They call each other's attention to the antique steamer trunks stored high on shelves above the display cases, to the violin resting alongside a scroll of sheet music, to the antique Waterford crystal chandelier; they admire the art deco green glass panels etched with polo players (relics of the Westbury Hotel's Polo Lounge, before its recent renovation) and the gilt-and-mirror vitrine (from Cartier in Paris); they smile when they come to the boys' department, where antique model racing cars are strewn on the bottom of an armoire, like toys on the floor of a closet; they climb the magnificent hand-carved mahogany staircase, its walls lined with gilt-framed hunting scenes and portraits of somebody's ancestors; they sign the guest book, lying open beneath an enormous arrangement of fresh flowers on a table in the entrance hall. Every last detail is perfect, right down to the books left scattered about as if someone had just been reading them: the leather-bound *Nicholas Nickleby*, resting on a table next to the elevator; the three-volume *Birds of the British Islands*, stacked on an ottoman in the boudoir; the collectors' edition of the works of Eugène Sue, standing on the mantel. Throughout the store young, pink-cheeked men and women greet the crowds, seeming less like salespeople than members of the family, quietly steering visitors away from the private quarters. "How are you today?" they say, or "Good morning," but never "Can I help you?" With tidy fires burning in every grate, the beds (on the top floor, the home-furnishings department) turned down for the night, the teacups on the end table, the house looks lived in, like a home. One begins to wonder what it must be like after closing, when the soigné inhabitants surely retire to their rooms and dress for dinner, reconnoitering for drinks among the men's shoes in the library before going upstairs to dine among the suits.

This house is the grand seat of Lauren's far-reaching empire, a monument to his phenomenal success, which has been praised by some people and decried by others, often for precisely the same reasons. He is either an impassioned connoisseur or a shameless plagiarist, appropriating objects, eras, and styles and signing his name to them. (Last December, *The New York Times* ran a story about "the Laurenization of New York," documenting his influence on other merchants' displays, as if the notion of Victorian Christmas had never existed until Lauren discovered it.) Either he has brought the classic virtues of men's tailoring to bear on women's clothes or he has consigned women to wearing modified versions of the clothes that men wear. He epitomizes American fashion either at its best, easygoing and glamorous, derived in equal parts from the great outdoors and Hollywood movies, or at its worst, contrived, based on received notions and images, with no affinity for the body and no flair for design. Either he is the Great American Success Story (a biography is under way), a self-made man, now personally worth more than $300 million, living in a world he has envisioned, outfitted, and furnished, or he is a playactor, a Jew pretending to the life of the landed gentry.

Lauren was born Ralph Lifshitz, in the Bronx, in 1939, and raised in a four-room apartment overlooking Mosholu Parkway. His surname was changed when he was seventeen—by his father, according to some versions of the story, by Ralph and his brother Jerry, according to others. He studied business at the City College of New York, worked as a salesman at Bloomingdale's and Brooks Brothers, and peddled ties. In 1967 he persuaded Beau Brummel, a men's clothing manufacturer, to let him design a line of neckties, which were four inches wide at a time when the standard width was two and a half, and made from patterned silks that looked like upholstery fabrics. Building on the ties' success, Lauren branched out into a line of men's wear; then women's wear; and eventually fragrances, linens, leather goods and luggage, shoes, and—last year—

furniture. Apart from a financial crisis in 1978, which prompted him to restructure the business, Lauren's expansion has been brisk and uninterrupted. And as his business has expanded he has consolidated his image.

Lauren's men's wear was admired early on for its quality (he insisted on all natural fibers at a time when other designers routinely used synthetic blends) and its cut, which seemed to be for an opinionated Brooks Brothers customer who had traveled the world and brought home a few improvements. For the movie of *The Great Gatsby* he outfitted Robert Redford as Jay Gatsby, the man with shirts by the dozen. Lauren established himself as an authority in men's tailoring just as the notion of androgyny was beginning to seem sexy and appealing. Women dressed in men's tuxedo shirts and pants, ties, and hats, as Diane Keaton did in *Annie Hall*, wearing clothes designed by Lauren. He offered women scaled-down models of fine men's shirts, fitted tweed hacking jackets, skirts pleated at the waist like men's trousers.

In the early seventies Lauren also laid claim to the western style, with chambray shirts, corduroy prairie skirts, separates in denim, chamois, and suede—a rugged, casual look that celebrated the frontier spirit and nicely dovetailed with a then widespread longing on the part of thousands of city-dwellers for a pair of cowboy boots. Soon Lauren appeared in his own advertisements, silver-haired, suntanned, smiling, wearing a work shirt and faded dungarees, at home on the range. The folk-artsy, loving-hands-at-home side of his work— sweaters depicting a schoolhouse, lace-collared blouses—has gradually merged with this western look in a category that might best be labeled Americana, perpetuated now in a separate collection, called Roughwear.

Lauren is still turning out high-class haberdashery for men and women, but lately its style has come to be indistinguishable from his Anglophilia. Lauren's English phase got off the ground around the time of *Brideshead Revisited* and has run right up to the present, seemingly encompassing such cultural milestones as *Chariots of Fire, Out of Africa*, and the "Great Treasure Houses of Britain" exhibition at the National Gallery of Art, in Washington.

Lauren occasionally works in other veins, among them a bright-colored, splashy printed style of resort clothing that at its most casual suggests the beach in the Hamptons and at its most formal calls to mind Rick's Bar in *Casablanca*. In some years, some seasons, his references are pointed. In others they are as generic as the monogram embroidered last spring on his women's blouses, a tangle of lines that look as if they ought to form letters but don't. Still, time and again Lauren returns to the tunes he knows best—one an American anthem, the other a stately hymn to the upper class—and it is in these that his voice is heard most distinctly.

LAUREN HAS persistently denied that his clothes are fashion, and while it's true that he doesn't engage in the seasonal variations on hemlines and silhouettes that occupy most couturiers, there is something disingenuous about this claim. More, perhaps, than any other designer of our era, he has anticipated our collective longings with such split-second timing that he has managed to produce what we wanted next, just before we realized that *that* was what we wanted. In this sense his work has consistently been at fashion's very height. Lately our appetite has been for tradition, as we've struggled to make the past somehow continuous, to keep it alive in the moment at hand. This effort manifests itself in any number of ways, from campaigns to preserve our architectural heritage to a newfound enthusiasm for debutante balls to the rediscovery of silent films. For his part, Lauren makes clothes distinguished by a certain dapper stodginess, reprising a style long associated with old families and old money, and designing furnishings that appear to be antique but nonspecific, so that they manage never to look like exact reproductions.

But neither do they have any life of their own. Wandering through his store, one can't help but be struck by how incidental the clothes, which are totally lacking in "hanger appeal," seem to the overall picture. Even his home furnishings are best seen in context. It is the setting that makes sense of them for us. In fact, the full complement of Lauren's achievement can best be seen not in his products but in his advertisements and his stores, in which he fully articulates the vision he is marketing.

Lauren's ads, ingeniously photographed by Bruce Weber, depict fair-skinned, fine-boned people of all ages—or rather little girls, young women, and men of all ages—but none of the Third World types chosen to be the Benetton stores' ambassadors to the public, or the frowsy white trash that inhabits the ads of Georges Marciano. The scenarios, which generally run to ten or twelve pages, have in the past included a visit to a family swathed in pinstripes, herringbones, Harris tweeds, silk paisleys, and fur-collared cashmeres, as they lounge about what looks to be one of the stately homes of England, complete with chintz-slipcovered chairs, back issues of *Country Life*, a canister of walking sticks in the hall, and two resident yellow labs; and an African safari, the slightly sunburned participants resplendent in straw hats and khaki, white linen, and suede, the tea table set with a silver service, a Land Rover in the background, a cuddly lion cub draped over one man's shoulders. The most recent was a field trip to an artist's weathered studio somewhere in the tropics (in the grand tradition of Gauguin's sojourn in Tahiti, perhaps), a room strewn with old rattan furniture and picture frames, a half-finished canvas on the easel, the painter himself wearing a shirt and tie, Prince of Wales plaid trousers, and navy-blue Keds-style sneakers, the woman at his side (his model, his muse?) in a strapless flower-sprigged sundress and thongs. In stark contrast to the freneticism that prevails in most fashion photography, Lauren's people exude dignity, tranquility, and preoccupation—their minds are elsewhere, far from the clothes they're modeling. They look as if they've simply been observed during the quiet course of an average day—at home, at the club, on vacation. They are, clearly, private people, not in the least flamboyant, and yet when faced with the camera's gaze, they meet it steadily; at other times they stare off into the middle distance, deep in thought.

In advertisements for Lauren's Home Collection there are no people. Still, the rooms look less like decorators' showrooms than like living quarters conveniently glimpsed when the occupants were out. Among last winter's designs was one for a slate-blue room dominated by a huge Victorian carved mahogany bed, dressed in paisley, pinstripe, and windowpane-plaid sheets and topped with a claret velvet comforter, on which a fur coat is nonchalantly draped; in the background stands a zebra-patterned wing chair, a pedestal displaying a marble sculpture of a man's head, and a grand piano topped with pictures in silver frames and a vase filled with white peonies. One half expects to see Noel Coward seated at the keyboard. But whether the rooms are empty or occupied, the approach is the same—always photojournalistic, persuading us that this world we see before us actually exists, that events are taking place in it even as we peruse a magazine. These pictures are the visual equivalent of eavesdropping and, better than anything else he has produced, they illustrate Lauren's conscientious efforts to create what he has called "the whole atmosphere of the good life."

The message telegraphed by these ads is that Lauren's clothes are for people whose lives are privileged, satisfying, comfortable, tasteful, leisurely, even luxurious—in short, better than the average person's life may be at the moment, but not beyond imagining. Here is a paradise, but one that is possible on earth, inhabited by people who qualify as aristocrats—if not by their blue bloodlines, then by their refined and sensitive natures. They are also WASPs. Not since

Mainbocher dressed the young society matrons of the forties and fifties has a designer explicitly invoked such snob appeal in his clothes. Some critics have roundly condemned Lauren for marketing a fantasy package of the WASP life, as if it were his to sell; some have looked the other way. But deep down there seems to run a current of resentment, grounded in the bitter notion that a Jew from the lower middle class isn't entitled to the style of the Connecticut gentry. One executive of a tweedy New York men's store told me not long ago, "We *are* what Ralph Lauren is trying to be." Remarks like this have a dismayingly anti-Semitic sound, but they also beg a question: Is it objectionable for someone to affect a style he admires, if he wasn't born to it? It is, after all, a free country.

When Lauren recreates the look of an English country house, or of the Adirondack "camps" that were wealthy New Yorkers' wilderness retreats in the early part of the century, or of the manor houses on the north shore of Long Island, the result is always recognizably Lauren's, not to be mistaken for the real thing. His renditions are more emphatic and spiffier than the originals, his colors bright instead of faded, his effects a little too studiously achieved. Like a lot of Americans, he probably formed his first impressions of the world beyond his immediate neighborhood at the movies. One imagines that his Paris is the Paris of *Gigi*, his Wild West that of *High Noon*, his Main Line Philadelphia the house where Katharine Hepburn lived in *The Philadelphia Story*. His career may indeed be the Great American Success Story, not so much because he rose from hand-me-downs to vast riches as because he has recreated the world according to his imagination and then recreated himself as the sort of person who would live in it.

"I was a New York kid playing basketball, playing baseball," he told one interviewer. "The clothes were a dream . . . a setting, part of a world." He told another of his job as a glove salesman, driving around Long Island with his box of samples strapped into the passenger seat of a used Morgan: "I was twenty-two, and I was wearing custom-made suits. I thought I was Douglas Fairbanks." At one point he considered becoming a history teacher, because he liked the idea of dressing in tweed jackets with suede patches at the elbows and smoking a pipe.

"My clothes sell," he contends, "because I'm the consumer, and I haven't lost touch with that." What makes his images so resonant is not only that they embody our fantasies of what it must be like to lead a certain kind of life but that they seem to embody his fantasies too. His inspirations are intensely personal. His Home Collections have closely paralleled his own houses: a tropical retreat in Jamaica, a six-thousand-acre working ranch in Colorado, a beach house in Montauk, an apartment in Manhattan. Those who know him report that he has never lost his childlike delight in a new toy. On the desk in his office are miniature models of the racing cars he owns.

Lauren is in a sense the quintessential designer for the newly rich, proving by his own example that enough money can buy anything, including the semblance of tradition, a facsimile past—not a pedigree, perhaps, but the things pedigreed people own. And that is what counts, according to Lauren's view of the world. The crux of a person's identity, the experience of being that person, the aura of urbanity or erudition or sportsmanship that surrounds him, resides in the trappings, not in the person himself. There are shortcuts. One needn't ride to the hounds, for example, to wear jodhpurs. (Lauren wore them to cut the ribbon at the opening of his New York store last year.) One needn't be well read, so long as one surrounds oneself with books. One needn't play the piano, so long as one has a piano. In short, one can be whoever one wants to be. Or—more accurately—one can seem to be whoever one wants to be. There is in all of this something touchingly naive.

In the window of his store on Madison Avenue, on a royal-blue flag edged in gold silk fringe and draped over a table, Lauren displays his Achievement. According to W.A. Copinger, in *Heraldry Simplified*, a man's Achievement is defined as his "coat of arms with all the exterior ornaments of the shield, together with the quarterings duly marshalled in order," and it signals his identity and ancestry to any passing armorist. According to a friend in London, an amateur expert, the motif—or, frankly, heraldic pastiche—Lauren has chosen for himself would be entered in the registers of Garter King of Arms, kept at the College of Arms, on Queen Victoria Street, in London, in these terms:

Crown. A circle of gold, issuing therefrom four crosses patée and four fleur-de-lis, arranged alternately: from the crosses patée arise two golden arches ornamented with pearls, crossing at the top under a mound, surmounted by a cross patée, also gold, the whole enriched with precious stones. The cap is of crimson velvet.

Arms. Quarterly: first, Azure, two lions passant in pale, or; second, Gules, a gridiron, or; third, Or, a bend sinister, azure; fourth, Azure, three fleurs-de-lis in chevron, or; the whole encircled with a garter, azure, ensigned "EST MCMLXVII," or.

Compartment. A triumphal wreath of laurel, argent.

Motto. POLO.

Lauren's Achievement was probably pieced together by one of his art directors, whose concerns, we may imagine, were purely graphic. Nevertheless, it is laden with meanings, among them the implication that Lauren's ancestry on his father's side can be traced to two lions (a variation on the Romulus and Remus story, perhaps); the improbable claim that his mother is somehow descended from Saint Lawrence, a martyr grilled over red-hot coals (the gridiron) and a monk; the assertions that Lauren is also descended from a bastard (the bend sinister) and, lastly, from a roly-poly Capetian king of France. In heraldry, groups of three are almost always laid out in a triangle, reflecting the coat of arms' origin as a medieval T-shirt—two symbols at the top, indicating the width of the shoulders, the point of the triangle at the waist. Lauren's arrangement in the fourth quarter—one fleur-de-lis at the top, two at the bottom—is upside-down, thereby conjuring an image of Humpty-Dumpty.

Lauren apparently takes it for granted that by divorcing symbols from their contexts, he can unburden them of their specific meanings and yet somehow leave their general sense intact. If his coat of arms isn't meant to be taken literally, its suggestion of aristocratic glamour surely is. Likewise, he strips objects and clothes of their function and expects them to retain their integrity. But a ranch hand wears dungarees because they're practical for roping cattle, not because he likes the way they look; an English country gentleman wears flannels and tweeds because they're suited to his climate and his leisure; an artist wears what's comfortable; a fisherman, a golfer, or a huntsman wears the gear appropriate to his sport. At first glance Lauren's approach to these many genres strikes us as purely superficial, but on second thought it seems to spring from some deep restlessness and discontent. Like a lot of people who make their living in the fashion business, Lauren is ironically enamored of people for whom clothes are not a self-conscious means of expression but a function of the lives they lead. Oh, to be all caught up in something other than fashion and still have style! The instinct behind this notion is, I think, a sound one, an attempt to affirm that there's something more to life than clothes. But, sadly, Lauren's only notion of how to go about getting beyond clothes to whatever else life might have to offer seems to be to dress the part of someone who never gives clothes a second thought. This, of course, changes nothing.

Lauren is not so much a designer as a connoisseur, calling our attention to the things he appreciates. Other designers, masters of fashion, like Yves Saint

Laurent, Emanuel Ungaro, Valentino, Galanos, Geoffrey Beene, trade on images that are specifically upper-class but work in terms that are inventive and abstract. Lauren deals in the familiar, and his terms are loaded. One looks at an outfit by Saint Laurent and is informed by the sophistication of its cut and sumptuousness of its fabric that the woman wearing it must be wealthy. One looks at an outfit by Lauren and concludes that the woman wearing it is wealthy because that is the way wealthy women supposedly look.

In books like Sinclair Lewis's *Dodsworth* and almost anything by Charles Dickens, in movies like *Alice Adams*, *The Promoter*, and *Stella Dallas*, in *Pygmalion* and, more recently, in *Me and My Girl*, people imitate their betters, only to be punished for their ambition (sometimes) and to learn that their betters aren't really better off after all in any of the ways that matter. In Lauren's version of the story, however, upward striving not only goes unpunished, it is applauded as the apotheosis of a self-made man. He ascends to the realm of the rich and discovers it to be a far nicer world than the one the middle class inhabits; he savors its every detail. This is the romance, an American parable in the manner of popular fiction like *Ellis Island* and confirming that America is still the land of opportunity, that the path to the top may be narrow but it's open. We look at Lauren in his various poses and think, Oh, come off it, but all the while some sentimental voice in our head is saying, Well, good for you. And the moral to be drawn from his story is reassuring: if he has acquired all this for himself, then it's accessible to us, too.

Lauren plays on our ambivalence about the upper class. We grant him the license to pretend to a grandeur that isn't his by birth because we are disillusioned with the rich. The trials of Claus von Bulow, the contest over Seward Johnson's will, the indictment of Ivan Boesky, and *The Two Mrs. Grenvilles* have taught us that the upper class is corrupt. The rich, who occupy that place on high that the rest of us have been striving to get to, are steadily slipping in our esteem, disinheriting themselves from the appurtenances of their class. These people, we think, don't deserve what they've got. Their houses, their clothes, their antiques, their cars, should be in the hands of people who can appreciate them. If the rich won't play their part as stewards of the finer things in life, then those things should be awarded to people who will. This is, appropriately enough, the age of "the democratization of polo," with members of "a new breed of wealthy people" taking lessons at the Greenwich Polo Club, according to a recent article in *The New York Times*. Lauren picks up our fantasy of the rich where the rich themselves have left it off. Look, he says, good news! The things you've always coveted, things that in the past belonged exclusively to a privileged few, are now in the public domain. Help yourself. It is up to you to carry on this exquisite tradition.

And yet there is something faintly absurd about the people who heed this call, and about Lauren himself. Their presumption may go unpunished by us mortals, but built into the unwritten laws that govern this life is the gods' revenge: that a working ranch and dungarees do not make a cowboy or an estate and a walking stick a country gentleman; that the trappings of another person's life cannot impart the dignity of his experience; that an identity is not acquired but earned. In the end there is something oppressively sad about the flotsam of the upper class that has washed up on the deck of Lauren's flagship: the photographs of prep-school crew teams, rows of staunch-looking boys whose names nobody knows; the now meaningless trophies that must once have loomed terribly important; the lovingly chosen presents to commemorate some special event, the people and the day long forgotten. In a showcase on the first floor, in the men's department, is a horn tobacco canister, silver-trimmed, on the front of which is engraved, "To father on the occasion of his silver wedding, 15th October 1910." It is for sale.

❋ ❋ ❋

Shoe Crazy

NEW SHOES can't cure a broken heart, a tension headache, or iron-poor blood, but they can temporarily relieve the symptoms. That shoes can serve as a home remedy—and a highly effective one—is something that women know in their bones and men never seem to learn.

Why shoes? Why not gloves or handbags or hats? In *Shoes Never Lie*, the most comprehensive treatise on shoe fanaticism to date, the cartoonist Mimi Pond theorizes that, given the choice, disconsolate women will buy shoes before anything else, because when you buy shoes, A) you have someone waiting on you at your feet and B) you don't have to look at your pasty-white skin in the dressing-room mirror. Also, c) shoes always fit, no matter what you weigh.

Many men, witnessing the rapport women have with their shoes, sense that they are missing out on something, though they would be hard-pressed to say exactly what. *Women and Shoes*, a one-act play by Nina Shengold, presented in 1984 in New York by Manhattan Punch Line, opens with two men, Willis and Seb, sitting in a bar. Willis says,

> I got a question. You ready for this? It's a question. I wanna know how come it is—and I want you should think about this—there's not one single female woman on earth that can walk past a shoe store without looking in. Never happen. I ask myself. You're out there walking, this woman and you, you're out taking the air in a strolling along kind of walking kind of way, or not even. You could be *going* somewhere. You could be walking along with a purpose, some kind of intentional purpose, she's *still* gonna look at that shoe store. Now you could be talking about anything, right, with this woman you're with here, like *sex* you could be talking about and she's still gonna check out those shoes. The day that a woman walks right past a shoe store I tell you, Seb, hell will grow ice pops. Now what I'm intending to ask

myself here is just how come this is. Who looks at their feet? *You* look at their feet? I never look at their feet. You ask what my wife stuck her feet in the last five days running, I have not a clue what my wife stuck her feet in. . . . My wife she got shoes like if there was legs coming out of each pair and a girl coming out of each legs I'd be set up for life. And yet and in spite of all of this and in spite of the fact that I don't give a rat butt what shoes she got stuck on her feet that I don't even notice, we walk by a shoe store, that's death. I mean we could be talking about *sports*. Go and figure it. *Shoes.*

Seb concurs:

My wife likes em too.

THE PATHOLOGY OF SHOES

Because psychologists and men have tended to view shoe craving as a crippling addiction, most shoe-dependent women are furtive. Pond documents their techniques for making their closets appear normal, by stashing their shoes in unlikely places—in the freezer, under the cushions on the sofa, in the oven.

Many men would jump at once to the conclusion that such women are in obvious need of help. But those men are wrong—in part because they have yet to recognize the intricate and varied roles that shoes play in the matrix of our civilization.

SHOES IN LITERATURE

Marcel Proust wrote in *À la Recherche du temps perdu* of the Duke and Duchess de Guermantes, leaving their house on their way to a costume ball. The Duchess, wearing a red dress, is about to get into the carriage when the Duke sees that she is wearing black shoes. He sends her back upstairs to change into red shoes, to match her dress. "Well," he announces to his guests, "we poor, downtrodden husbands, people laugh at us, but we are of some use all the same. But for me, Oriane would have been going out to dinner in black shoes."

SHOES ON THE STAGE

Dona Prouhèze, a beautiful religious young woman and the heroine of Paul Claudel's *Le Soulier de satin*, is drawn into a liaison with Don Rodrigue, though she is already married—to an impassive, elderly man. For the better part of the play she resists temptation, but by Scene V her resolve is flagging. Knowing full well the disastrous ramifications in both this life and the next, she leaves the house of her husband to consummate her love for Rodrigue, but not before praying to a statue of the Virgin Mary. She takes off one of her shoes. "While there is still time," she says, "holding my heart in one hand and my shoe in the other, I put myself into your hands! Virgin Mother, I give you my shoe!" And she places the shoe in the statue's hand, in order that her progress will be halting and undignified as she runs toward evil. Prouhèze will limp into adultery.

SHOES IN THE MOVIES

In Preston Sturges's classic comedy *The Lady Eve*, Barbara Stanwyck connives to attract the attention of Henry Fonda, an oblivious bachelor millionaire and fellow passenger on an ocean cruise. After watching other female contenders demurely drop their handkerchiefs in front of his table at dinner or try sweetly to engage him in conversation, neither to any avail, the resourceful Stanwyck sticks out her foot and trips him. He breaks the heel of her shoe. She seizes on his apologetic eagerness to make up for the damage and invites him to her stateroom. "The shoes are in there," she says, gesturing toward a trunk containing fifty pairs. "Because you were so polite, you can pick them out and then put them on, if you like." Fonda selects a pair of high-heeled slingbacks. "Doesn't seem possible for anybody to wear anything . . . that size," he says sheepishly. He slips them on her feet, and then one thing leads to another.

Each of these instances in its own way attests to the power vested in shoes—power to put a wife in her place, to redeem a wayward soul, or to seduce a stranger.

THE SHOE-SEX CONNECTION

Freud and his followers advanced a variety of theories, cited by Valerie Steele in her book *Fashion and Eroticism: Ideals of Feminine Beauty From the Victorian Era Through the Jazz Age*, to explain foot fetishism, the sex appeal inherent in the foot, and the sexual significance of shoes. Most of them revolve around the heel or the toe, or the entire shoe, as a phallic symbol, except for those times when the shoe could symbolize "the vagina into which the phallic foot is slipped." William A. Rossi, the author of *The Sex Life of the Foot and Shoe*, hypothesizes that "foot and shoe eroticism derive in part from the intrinsic sensitivity of the foot, especially the soles and toes, to tactile stimulation," to quote Steele's paraphrase. Presumably, these theories account for the thrill some men get out of the shoes women wear, but none of them, it seems to me, satisfactorily explains the thrill *women* get out of the shoes they wear. No woman with a normal, healthy shoe drive would content herself with a closetful of phallic symbols. The fact, known to all shoe-crazed women, is that the appeal shoes hold encompasses sex but is not limited to it. When new shoes speak to a woman, the message they whisper in her ear is not a proposition but a promise.

THE PSYCHOLOGY OF SHOES

From earliest childhood, girls are told stories of other girls who grew up to have shoes change their lives. Cinderella's marriage to a handsome prince turned on a glass slipper that would fit no one's foot but her own. Judy Garland in *The Wizard of Oz* was given a pair of ruby slippers that could help her get to the Emerald City and, when the time came, transport her instantly back home to Kansas. So it is not surprising that grown women, when they are hoping that their lives will change dramatically, look to shoes.

Not all shoes are empowered to bring about sweeping change, however. Of those that are, some have been designed by Manolo Blahnik, some by Susan Bennis and Warren Edwards, others by Salvatore Ferragamo, Vittorio Ricci, and Yves Saint Laurent. But the shoes that consistently look as if their range extended to the miraculous are the work of a man who is justifiably famous within fashion circles and virtually unknown outside them: Roger Vivier.

THE FABERGÉ OF SHOES

What Fabergé is to the eggs in the dairy case of your supermarket, Roger Vivier is to the shoes in the window of your local department store. Vivier studied sculpture at the École des Beaux Arts, in Paris. In 1937 he created the shoes for Elsa Schiaparelli's collection; among them was the first platform shoe. In 1947, after several years in New York under the auspices of Delman, a chain of shoe salons licensed to department stores, Vivier returned to Paris and entered into a collaboration with Christian Dior, designing made-to-order shoes to complement Dior's haute couture. Over the course of his career Vivier has also designed shoes for Balenciaga, Jean Patou, Mme. Grès, André Courrèges, Hermès, Yves Saint Laurent, Emanuel Ungaro, and private clients including Josephine Baker, Maria Callas, Elizabeth Taylor, Rudolf Nureyev, and the Rolling Stones. In 1953 he designed a golden kidskin shoe studded with rubies for the Queen of England on the occasion of her coronation.

It has been sixteen years since Roger Vivier had his own boutique in Paris. But last summer, encouraged by the response to a retrospective exhibition of his shoes mounted by the Facade Gallery, in New York, he opened a boutique on Madison Avenue, where his entire current collection is sold, along with an occasional remake of one of his designs from the past. Come fall, Vivier shoes will be available through some department stores, as well. This is good news for shoe mavens.

SHOES YOU CAN BELIEVE IN: DISTINGUISHING FEATURES

Vivier's shoes exhibit a sculptor's preoccupation with texture and three-dimensional form. He executes paper maquettes as models for certain of his designs. There is nothing mundane about these shoes. They are characterized by seamless vamps and elongated, often flattened toes; a voracious use of materials not ordinarily found in shoes, including unusual leathers like antelope, turtle, and pony skin, and delicate fabrics like silk mousseline, organdy, and panne velvet; and novel heel styles, many of them picturesquely named—the "comma" heel (whose profile is shaped like a comma, curving inward toward the arch), the "spool" heel (with the pyramid inverted), the "escargot" heel (in the shape of a snail). For Marlene Dietrich, Vivier designed the "globe" heel, a narrow high heel with a rhinestone-paved ball at the base.

To any woman of a suggestible turn of mind, Vivier's shoes conjure up a Disney-like image of tiny fairy hands embroidering satin with threads of gold, of squirrels scurrying through the forest bearing a cargo of faceted glass beads, of bluebirds with satin ribbons in their beaks, swooping and circling around a fairy-tale heroine's ankles, tying the final bow.

SHOES YOU CAN BELIEVE IN: SOME EXAMPLES

From the dozens of Vivier shoes in the permanent collection of the Costume Institute at the Metropolitan Museum of Art, in New York, and others on display at the Facade Gallery, these few examples may serve to give an idea of the sort of shoes that justify a woman's placing her hopes in them:

From the nineteen-fifties, tartan-plaid wool-twill slingbacks with an ankle strap, a stiletto heel, and a tasseled brass bow on the vamp; and sky-blue ankle boots covered with blue Chantilly lace and embroidered with blue and white sequins, clear, yellow, and light- and dark-blue beads, with a narrow high heel and a blue satin bow at the front.

From the nineteen-sixties, evening shoes of black satin completely covered with hummingbird feathers, with a high convex needle heel; and peach satin pumps inspired by Goya, covered with peach tulle, through which copper threads are woven in a loopy, latticework pattern, with teal blue and gray beading, rhinestones, a narrow pointed toe, and a beaded Louis XV heel.

From the nineteen-seventies, red satin shoes inspired by the Duchess de Guermantes, embroidered with red crystal beads, ruby rhinestones, and red crystal paillettes, with a sole in the shape of a mandolin, the square toe as the base; and high boots with a clear plastic vamp, the shaft and heel covered in red satin and embroidered with red metallic thread and ruby paillettes, and ruby headlamp rhinestones at the ankle.

And, from the nineteen-eighties, black satin spike-heeled evening shoes with an open toe, a band across the instep, four rhinestone "bracelets" for ankle straps, and a zipper up the back of the heel; and white low-heeled sandals with straps that cross at the instep and wings, like Mercury's, appliquéd at the heel.

HOW SHOES WORK

That there exists a direct connection between new shoes and an abrupt improvement in a woman's state of mind has long been established, but exactly how that turn for the better comes about is a matter of some speculation. Roger Vivier believes that shoes set off a chain reaction. It is "something very mysterious," he says. "Shoes are in one way very earthy. They are the part of us that touches the ground. And yet by changing a woman's balance, the way she stands, they can change her frame of mind, her spirit, her soul."

An alternative—admittedly far-flung—hypothesis, which a friend and I cooked up as we set out on a recent shoe reconnaissance mission, takes as its basis the "science" of reflexology, which contends that various areas on the sole of the foot correspond to various parts of the body—a spot on the bottom of the big toe to the pituitary gland, the area at the base of the ball of the foot to the stomach, the crest of the metatarsal to the eyes and ears, the rim of the arch to the spinal column. Reflexology seeks, by stimulating these areas on the foot, to restore the body's metabolic balance when it has been upset by injury, illness, or stress.

If reflexology's premise is true, and I am content to think that it is, then it stands neatly to reason that a new pair of shoes would make a woman feel better all over.

But however shoes bring their change about, the women who love them recognize in each other a sameness of approach, a common faith.

OUR CREED

We believe in shoes as a force for change in the world, as a talismanic means of putting the past immediately behind us, of buying into the future and hastening its arrival.

We believe that the world is a disconcerting place to live; that, despite considerable evidence to the contrary, everything may yet turn out all right; and that there is no telling what tomorrow might bring.

In buying new shoes we signal to the gods that though we are down, we are not yet out.

Designer Genes

In the fall of 1995, medical researchers announced the first successful gene transplant as therapy for a congenital disease.

WASHINGTON, Dec. 2—Doctors announced here today the momentous results of an experimental procedure performed on three patients with defective "style genes." The treatment has proved "successful beyond our wildest dreams," said Dr. Ernest Arbiter, who headed the team of physicians and scientists at the National Institute for Corrective Elegance (NICE).

Two men and a woman were chosen to participate in the study on the basis of what was diagnosed as a congenital inability to put together an outfit. Researchers removed some of the subjects' red blood cells, inserted a healthy style gene, then injected the altered cells back into their veins; the procedure was repeated twelve times over twenty months.

One of the men, whom the study identifies as a laughingstock since childhood, has overhauled his wardrobe and shows no signs of remission. The other, notorious for wearing "the worst ties on the planet," is now a wardrobe consultant to rock stars. The woman, whom scientists classified as "mousy" at the study's inception, has since manifested proficiency in tying a scarf twelve ways.

The findings were the talk of the International Congress of Geneticists, an annual conference being held here this week, and seemed sure to alter the course of treatment for the severely style-impaired—an estimated twenty-three percent of the adult population, for whom until now there has been little, if any, hope.

Only a decade ago, a lack of style seemed an intractable affliction, one that doomed its victims to a life of drabness and contempt. Traditional therapies, which focused on improving the patient's taste by means of supervised shopping, nearly always failed. In 1988, however, researchers looking for the gene for slim thighs stumbled on the style gene, sparking a series of developments that culminated in the news today.

On Seventh Avenue, the mood was one of guarded optimism. Oscar de la Renta pronounced the breakthrough "a potential victory over tackiness." Bill Blass said that "it is still too soon to tell" whether the results would be lasting, but he praised the efforts of scientists "doing battle to eradicate the tragic bad taste that strikes so many families."

* * *

Fat Pride

No horizontal stripes. No knits. No drop waists. No bright colors. No large prints. No pastels. No shiny fabrics.

These are the rules by which fat women have traditionally been advised to dress, handed down like folk wisdom, in confidential tones, in fitting rooms and in the pages of women's magazines. The clothes available have usually been inexpensive and poorly made, of cheap materials, on the grounds that fat women wouldn't spend as much as other women on their clothes, because they don't take the same pride in their appearance and because they don't intend to stay fat for long. To the extent that the clothes have been at all remarkable, it's been for their reticence, an absence of style, which was thought to be for fat women's own good and, perhaps, for everyone else's as well. By following the rules, a fat woman might camouflage her size and come off looking somewhat smaller. In which case one might flatter her by remarking that her outfit was "slenderizing."

"Slenderizing" is no longer the supreme—albeit backhanded—compliment it used to be, now that fat women are being exhorted to stop trying to look like what they're not and to celebrate themselves as they are. In *Breaking All the Rules*, Nancy Roberts sounds the call, brightly insisting that it isn't a woman's size or shape but the pride she takes in herself that makes her attractive, urging fat women to forget the old rules, to invent a style all their own, "to create positive images of big women." Dressing well is "just the beginning," she contends. "It's the beginning of saying to ourselves and to the world. 'We're OK. . . . We're going to go out there and grab what the world has to offer. We're entitled to the same choices that smaller women have, not only in respect of our clothes, but ultimately in respect of our lives as well." This rhetoric has a vaguely familiar ring, a dim echo of the "Black is beautiful" movement, which freed black women from aspiring to Caucasian standards of beauty. Now, as then, the issues are more political than aesthetic, but the front line of the battle is being fought in matters of fashion.

Roberts would have fat women believe that fashion in all its variety is available to them for the taking. As if to prove her point, a whole new crop of specialty stores has sprung up in recent years. Surveys differ, but the estimates are that as many as one third to one half of the women in this country wear a size 14 or larger. As the baby-boom generation ages, the large-size share of the market is, surprisingly, growing, dispelling any hopes that the fitness craze is winning out over our national tendency toward obesity. The majority of women (and men, for that matter) still put on weight as they age. One manufacturer of large-size clothing told me recently, "We figure that time and gravity are on our side."

Of the new large-size boutiques, the best known is probably The Forgotten Woman, founded in New York ten years ago, at Sixty-sixth Street and Lexington Avenue, by Nancye Radmin, a Riverdale housewife who had failed to lose the "substantial amount of weight" she had gained during her pregnancy and went into business because she couldn't find anything to wear. By the end of the first week she had sold half her inventory, confirming her suspicion that "something was happening out there." Since then Forgotten Woman boutiques have opened in eighteen other cities, to lines around the block.

Radmin's was by no means the first large-size specialty store, but it was the first to cause such a sensation. Its success was based on a formula whose time had come: clothes by famous designers in large sizes. Persuading the designers to oblige has, Radmin admits, been "a slow road," but it is growing wider and better travelled all the time. Her store now stocks an impressive, if potluck, array of designer labels, including, on one recent visit, Givenchy, Laura Biagiotti, and Albert Nipon. The Forgotten Woman also sells the kinds of clothing often hard to find in large sizes, such as active wear (golf and tennis clothes), bathing suits, lingerie, and blue jeans, and an extensive selection of evening wear, in which the store does a vigorous business. A beaded gown by Bob Mackie, who made his reputation designing the slithery, glittery dresses Cher used to wear on television, is available in size 22, for $12,000. "Now that," Radmin says proudly, "is truly a first."

Half a block away from The Forgotten Woman on Lexington Avenue is Ashanti, another large-size boutique, run by Bill Michael and his wife, Sandra.

The Michaels launched their store in 1968, at 132nd Street and Seventh Avenue, in Harlem, selling clothes that ranged in size from 4 to 24, but after several years they dropped the small end of the spectrum in order to dedicate themselves to their most faithful customers. "A size eight or ten has a lot of places she can go to find clothes," Bill Michael says. "The woman who wears a size twenty can't shop around so much." Ashanti's strength—and the better part of its inventory—lies in its own label, designed by Barbara McCaine and distributed wholesale to a number of department stores and specialty shops.

What The Forgotten Woman and Ashanti share is a conviction that fat women want to express themselves through clothes, as other women do; that if they can't set trends, they can at least participate in the trends as they happen; and that they want quality in their clothes and are willing to pay for it. This new attitude, ratified by the commercial success of these and other specialty stores, has emboldened many manufacturers of misses clothing to enter the large-size market.

Gloria Vanderbilt, for one, has shrewdly capitalized on the credibility she acquired by being a stickler for fit in misses blue jeans and has launched a large-size line, for which seventy-five percent of all her misses designs for a given season are simultaneously translated into large sizes. Bernard Holtzman submits the four hundred or so pieces he designs each season for the Harvé Benard line to Baron Abramson, a licensee that manufactures some sixty percent of them in large sizes. Even Fred the Furrier has branched out into large-size furs.

Most of these clothes, like Vanderbilt's group of casual pieces in black acid-washed denim, look surprisingly up-to-the-minute, not at all like those that fat women have traditionally had to choose from—caught in some stylistic limbo, outside fashion, outside time. Dark-colored shapeless tents made from synthetic fabrics are gradually giving way to large-scale versions of the clothes of the moment.

Even Lane Bryant, for years the bastion of noncommittal budget-priced clothing in large sizes, has refurbished its image since being bought, five years ago, by The Limited, a national chain selling youthful, spirited sportswear. Like many other retailers, Lane Bryant has now stopped using large-size resources and has turned instead to misses and junior manufacturers, commissioning them to produce their current designs in large sizes. According to a spokeswoman for the company, "We always keep our eye on The Limited, to see what's selling well."

Ironically, one of the hallmarks of this new era in large-size fashion is that most of the designers no longer work specifically with fat women in mind. Of those I talked to, only Barbara McCaine, at Ashanti, conceptualizes her clothes for fat women, catering to four figure types: the balloon, who's widest in the middle; the barrel, large all over; the pear, bottom-heavy; and the figure eight, with a pronounced waist. While other designers are busy transposing misses styles into large sizes, and boast that they make few, if any, concessions to fat women, as if to design clothes explicitly with fat women in mind would be somehow patronizing, McCaine calls attention away from the torso by focusing on the neckline or the sleeve, or uses a horizontal seam in a shift to suggest a waistline. Though the results may not always look like the zenith of fashion, they serve as an interesting reminder that the old rules had a purpose beyond keeping a fat woman in her place: they were founded on the premises of optical illusion, which, given the chance, still works to any women's advantage.

FOR ALL the recent sweeping changes within the large-size industry, the world beyond has been slow to respond. More department stores have taken to carrying more large-size clothes—notably Macy's, which now devotes an entire floor to large sizes. But others serve their large-size customers with apparent reluctance, for fear, probably, that a prominently placed large-size department will compromise their prestige. Bloomingdale's large-size boutique is on the basement "Metro" level, near the entrance to the Lexington Avenue subway. In what seems like a cruel joke, the only route to the large-size department at I. Magnin in San Francisco is through the petites.

Many optimists, enumerating all the ways in which the large-size world is changing, cite the fact that *Vogue* now runs a large-size advertising supplement, called Fashion Plus, twice a year, and that a handful of large-size modeling agencies, with names like Big Beauties and Plus Models, are thriving. But the *Vogue* supplement, which is paid advertising, signifies no change in editorial policy. And, according to T. Zazzera, the director of the Today's Woman department at Ford Models, of which the large-size division is a part, most of the bookings for large-size models are for catalogues or advertisements featuring large-size clothes. Both L'eggs and Hanes have waged vigorous ad campaigns in print and on television on behalf of their large-size pantyhose, but the day when a fat woman will be swathed in black velvet to sell a classic whiskey or draped across the hood of a car is yet to come.

There's been a lot of talk lately about the new fuller-bodied ideal. *Vogue* and *Elle* have heralded breasts, now back in style; *Vanity Fair* paid tribute to the actress Valérie Kaprisky's derrière, pictured in a molded sequined sheath. But do these developments constitute a more enlightened attitude toward the diverse sizes and shapes that women's bodies take? Leafing through magazines, looking at the images that express our current fantasies about women, one realizes that what all this comes down to is not that we now recognize fat as beautiful but that anorexia is no longer the ideal—that it's okay to be normal.

I asked a friend, a size 20, whether fashion seemed to her off limits to fat women. "Well, of course," she replied. "Nobody wants to look like us, and nobody wants to look *at* us." Though fashion has gotten more democratic over the past fifteen years, some people still choose to see it as a club and designers as its membership committee, cruelly insisting that the women who would join first conform to an image.

But to the extent that coercion is at work in fashion today, it is generally subtle and even, it seems to me, well meant, based on a superstitious conviction that if it weren't for the constant vigilance that fashion requires, most women would simply let themselves go to seed. This may be true for the woman whose weight fluctuates by five or ten pounds, but it seems clear that few women are obese for lack of incentive. We know better than to think that anorexia nervosa, bulimia, and other eating disorders can be solved by a little self-improvement. Still, it's hard to kill off the impulse to prod. One plump woman I interviewed reported finding a dress she liked at a fancy New York store and, not seeing it in her size, asking the saleswoman, "Can you get this for me in a fourteen?" "Yes," the clerk answered, "but if you were really good, you could wear the twelve."

It is only within the past few years that large sizes have been standardized from 18w to 24w, as a continuation of misses sizes, which stop at 14 or 16. (Previously, large sizes were based on waist and bust measurements, with one size range for tops and another for bottoms, and neither bearing any relation to the misses numbers.) But sizing is still highly subjective—even in the misses range. Most European sizes run a good deal narrower than their supposed American counterparts, and all vary from one manufacturer to the next. When the sizes run small, it's as if to insist that the customer meet the designer on his or her own exacting terms; when the sizes run large, the clothes seem to flatter the customer by suggesting that she's thinner than she is. Generally speaking, the higher the fashion, the less ingratiating the sizes.

THERE ARE very few women—and none I know—who are strangers to the despair and self-loathing that come of failing to measure up to the ideal they've set for themselves. Most of us have scrutinized ourselves and rated our body parts in a way that most men, however vain, would never think to do; we then proceed to dress so as to camouflage what women's magazines used to call our "figure flaws." The language magazines used to talk to women has changed, but the aim—the notion of helping a woman attain her best—hasn't. With careers of our own and less of an obligation to conform, we may no longer try to be all things to all people, or to all men, or even to one man in particular, but on the whole we still strive to please. Self-improvement is a longstanding feminine pastime, and it is one that draws women together and gives them a sense of community. Fat women share in this but in varying degrees, and they often localize their energies, concentrating on elaborate makeup, exotic perfume, or a perfect manicure.

Of the tonics the rest of us rely on, at least one—one of the most effective—doesn't seem to work for fat women at all, and that is shopping. Those of us who wear standard sizes may, if we're feeling downhearted, go browsing or buy something new, but the fat women I talked to described shopping as a demoralizing ordeal, a desperate search they dread and postpone as long as possible. Most shop alone, not wanting anyone else to witness their difficulty in finding something that fits, to say nothing of their shame at having to face their own bodies in a three-way mirror. Bill Michael told me that on those rare occasions when a fat woman walks in the door of his boutique with a size-6 companion, who's come along to give advice, he and his sales staff know that trouble isn't far behind, especially if the thin woman is the fat woman's mother. The women I interviewed told poignant stories about their experiences shopping. Most said that sales people in department stores often condescend to them, and that in designer boutiques, such as those that line Madison Avenue, fat women are ignored as a matter of course. Most steer clear of fashion magazines; those who read them report exercising their alter egos by looking at photographs of the latest styles and saying to themselves, If I were thin, I would wear *that*. For fat women the rewards of shopping are scant, even now that the selection of large-size clothing is better, even when something fits. One woman, whose weight has yo-yoed all her adult life, told me, "When I was a ten, I would see something and think, That'll look great on me. As an eighteen, I see something and think, Oh, well, maybe."

Stores like The Forgotten Woman provide a safe haven for these women and a decent array of clothes in their sizes. And yet, the design of these clothes is still a far cry from high fashion. For one thing, there is far too much glitz, as if, now that the old taboos have been lifted, the time has come for fat women to embark on a binge of self-decoration. Before I began my research for this piece, a linen suit with a rhinestone-studded bodice would have been unthinkable, but now I know where to go to find one.

If the current changes in the large-size clothing industry constitute a revolution, it is, it seems to me, one that is bound to be limited, because fat activists underestimate fashion. If our shifting preferences in styles of dress or in body types were capricious and purely visual, they might be easier to dismiss and, finally, to overcome. But there's more to it than that.

We interpret physical features to be manifestations of the character traits we particularly admire. Not so long ago we favored women who were rail-thin and flat-chested not simply because we like their looks but because their looks connoted someone streamlined, who lived a fast and active life, making her way in what has been a man's world, unencumbered by the old conventions of femininity. This idea is being supplanted by that of a woman whose body is more emphatically female, shapely but solid and lean, well exercised, as our notions of womanhood and women's place in the world are changing. If we haven't yet come around to finding fleshy, heavyset women, like those in eighteenth-century paintings, attractive, it may be in part because they signify for us docility and lethargy, and these are traits we just can't bring ourselves to sanction.

We discuss the tides of fashion—what's in or out—in terms that imply that they are subject to forces outside us, beyond our knowing. One hears women talk, for instance, about the new preoccupation with breasts as if breasts were making a comeback of their own accord. But fashion is one of the means by which we dream collectively, and whether or not the shape those dreams take suits us personally, it has a tacit logic that makes sense deep down to us all.

Musclebound

Brian Moss, the brains behind Better Bodies, in Chelsea, conceived of his gym as a club—not a health club, like the New York Health & Racquet Club, with a pool and tennis courts, but a nightclub, like, say, the Limelight or Nell's, with low lighting and funky décor. At thirty-five, Moss looks pretty much the way he did when he appeared five years ago on the cover of *Playgirl*—tall, with long dark hair in a ponytail, four silver rings in his right ear and one in his nose, and a few days' stubble; on an average winter weekday at his office, he is wearing a black sweatshirt cut out at the neck, several silver charms on leather thongs around his neck, torn jeans, and motorcycle boots. The entrance to the gym is through a café, with marble-top tables and wrought-iron chairs, an Ionic column, and empty gilt picture frames on the walls. There are vitamin supplements for sale at the counter, including one called Fat Burning Complex; also, water bottles, carrot juice, bagels, T-shirts, and magazines with names like *Ironmen* and *Flex*. The stairwell leading to the gym, in the basement, is strewn with graffiti, "like the subway," Moss explains.

Downstairs, the walls, ceiling, and floor are black, and the equipment, all raw metal with a clear finish, is arranged according to body parts: arms, legs, back. The swirl-patterned rug in the cardiovascular-training area, cordoned off by velvet ropes, was acquired from the Tropicana Casino, in Atlantic City. At the center of the room, under a crystal chandelier, are a yellow tufted sofa and chairs, slipcovered in plastic to deflect sweat. A man in gym shorts and a tank top is sitting on the sofa, taking a snooze, his head lolling on his shoulder. As for the murkiness, interrupted at intervals by overhead spotlights that cast dramatic shadows and make muscles stand out in stark relief, Moss thinks of it as an essential part of the atmosphere. "I'm sure there are some people who love 7-Eleven lighting in a gym, but I'm not one of them," he says.

The men are wearing a variety of getups. A plaid flannel shirt with the sleeves ripped off at the armholes, loose-fitting jeans, a Walkman, and construction boots. A sleeveless cut-off T-shirt, a wide leather weight belt, black tights, black-and-fluorescent-green half-gloves, and construction boots. A red "Gold's Gym" tank top, biker shorts, a Walkman, a clunky stainless-steel watch, a weight belt, and construction boots. One guy with his key ring threaded on his bootlace walks by, jingling with every other step. "I've always worn boots in the gym," Moss says, not only for support in heavy squats but also because he likes the "punkiness" of the way boots look. "Within the last year or so, they've been adopted by the gay community," he says. "These guys all come in here with heavy footwear. Sneakers are totally out."

Most of the people who work out at Moss's gym look as if they've been busy with their scissors—lopping the legs off their sweatpants and cutting short their tank tops, sawing off the sleeves of their shirts, hacking their necklines wider and deeper. There is, he says, a progression that people who come to get into shape inevitably go through: "When they first start, they're not willing to expose anything. And then, as they begin to change, they want validation, to show you they're changing—guys will go sleeveless, girls will start to wear little skimpy things. Some people might stay at that point. But if they really go to the extreme and build a lot of muscle, they cover up. They just become secure with it. They know they have a great body, and they don't have to show it. I think how people dress is a function of where they are in the quest for their bodies." In Moss's opinion, the baggy look that prevails at his gym these days is "a backlash" against spandex and cotton Lycra.

Moss opened Better Bodies in 1982, and two years later he founded the first modelling agency for bodybuilders. Since then, the fitness business has changed considerably, and, Moss believes, so have the bodies of the people who work out. If bodybuilding has failed to find the broad audience that he and others envisioned, it has perhaps nudged the mainstream in the direction of a bit more muscle. As for the guys who start working out and announce that they don't want to get too big, Moss thinks that that's an inferiority complex talking—that they're rationalizing their bodies' limitations. "If tomorrow they could have twenty-inch arms," he says, "they'd buy a new wardrobe."

These days, Moss surveys his clients—men and women alike—with a satisfied air. "In the beginning, I don't remember ever walking into my gym and thinking how great everybody looked," he says. "But now everybody has a little muscle happening somewhere." He thinks that it has now become not only acceptable but even sexy for women to have muscles. Look at Madonna, whose videos have documented the conversion of her baby fat into sinew, or at the Coors Light beer commercial that shows a girl flexing her biceps on the beach. Linda Hamilton, Arnold Schwarzenegger's co-star in *Terminator 2*, was the best advertisement Moss could ever have hoped for, he says. These are bodies that have come about by means of a combination of aerobic activity (for reducing fat) and weight training (for shaping the muscle), an approach that the sneaker manufacturers have seized upon and promoted as "cross-training."

Moss says that he wanted to create a place where men and women could train side by side and inspire one another, but on this winter day the women are definitely outnumbered. There is a blond model in black toreador tights and a midriff top. A redhead who, according to Moss, has posed for *Playboy* and appeared in lingerie ads walks by carrying a pair of free weights; she is wearing black tights that accentuate her minuscule waist, and a red-and-white-striped T-shirt, cut away at the shoulders to expose her deltoids. "And I don't think those muscular arms make her large breasts any less attractive," Moss says appreciatively.

AT JEAN PAUL GAULTIER's men's show for the current winter season, presented in Paris last year, the models strode the runway in clothes that showed off their carefully cultivated physiques. There were vests worn open over bare chests, leggings that clung to the calves and thighs. There was also a jersey photo-printed on the front with a picture of a muscular male torso—for the scrawny-chested who wish they were otherwise or maybe for the man who resents having to hide his Herculean assets underneath a shirt. Gaultier expresses a certain homoeroticism with such wit and humor, and such candid enthusiasm, that you can't help being fascinated and amused by it, even if you don't share his predilection for Tom of Finland fantasies. Toward the end of the show, a model came out wearing a leather bustier cut just below his pectorals, bulging like breasts, with the nipples exposed, and the audience—a conglomeration of journalists, buyers, and Gaultier groupies—burst into a chorus of whistles and catcalls.

"It is tempting to believe that people always feel physically the same and that they look different only because the cut of their garments changes—to subscribe to the notion of a universal, unadorned mankind that is universally naturally behaved when naked," Anne Hollander writes in *Seeing Through Clothes*. "But art proves that nakedness is not universally experienced and perceived any more than clothes are." Surveying paintings made over the past seven centuries, she concludes that "all nudes in art since modern fashion began are wearing the ghosts of absent clothes—sometimes highly visible ghosts." What's harder to discern is whether naked bodies are seen through the lens of the clothes they have shed, or whether the clothes came about in response to the need to see the naked body in a certain way, to depict it in a manner that is particularly timely— calling attention to some features, minimizing others.

For centuries now, the way we choose to style the naked body and the way we move have been inextricably tied to the clothes we wear, but it is only relatively recently, with the advent of exercise as a cosmetic science, that people have had the option of actually becoming the body as they choose to see it, transforming themselves into some facsimile of their own ideal. The prototypical body, male or female, toward which people have strived in art and in life turns out to be not fixed and classical but, like the clothes we wear, subject to the whims of the moment. Kenneth Clark, in *The Nude: A Study in Ideal Form*, has documented some of these vicissitudes: the "flat, rectangular chest" of the antique male nude; the late-Gothic swell of the woman's belly; the quattrocento's fascination with the planes of the man's shoulders; the slender mannerist elongation of both the man's and woman's arms and legs. Those of us who spend a disproportionate amount of time looking at models, in pictures and on runways, have witnessed the most recent shift firsthand: for women, toward a shapelier figure, with fuller breasts and a little more meat on the bones; for men, toward a more pumped-up physique, with an often exaggerated emphasis on the shoulders and arms and chest. In both cases, the general trend has been toward more muscle. As it happens, the vernacular of movement has changed, too—you see it in people's body language, in the way they dance, which is now more calisthenic and aggressive.

Marc Cavigioli, a swashbuckling, squarely built twenty-seven-year-old power lifter who works as a personal trainer in Worcester, Massachusetts, says that "there's a real masculine pride in being strong, and now some women are taking a lot of pride in it, too, which I think is great." He talks about the "elemental, barbaric pleasure in dominating people physically," and says, "The nice thing about weight training is that you can get that feeling without ever touching anybody else. And, to be honest, you can consider yourself part of the warrior class without ever putting yourself in danger."

Cavigioli met his wife, Rebecca, a power lifter and a bodybuilder, at their local branch of the Bay State Gym, where, by his account, a lot of guys were intimidated by her because she could outlift them. He finds muscles on women sexy—particularly, muscular legs and a muscular midsection. But mostly, he says, he's attracted to the image of a woman who doesn't look helpless.

A random survey of a handful of men, none of whom exercise with weights, and who rated their own physical conditions as ranging from fit to decrepit, turned up slightly different reactions to the notion of women's new muscle. One, an executive in his mid-forties, confessed that "hard body tissue of any kind" left him sexually indifferent, and that being with a woman with fabulous deltoids would only make him feel more self-conscious about the disintegration of his own. Another man, who has lived abroad, called this new development "a sign of further confusion as to what the feminine state is," and said that he found it part of a larger issue, about the loss of femininity in America—in other societies, where women are treasured for being women, this sort of obsession doesn't exist, he says, and in those societies women are much happier. A third man, an avid tennis player, hypothesized that muscular men's preference for women with muscles is predicated on narcissism, and he grappled with the apparent contradiction between his own misgivings about muscle on women and his feminist conviction that it's good for women to be capable and strong. Female athletes, he concluded, are attractive because they've developed their muscle in the service of some activity, rather than as an end in itself. All the respondents said that they wouldn't want to be with a woman who had more muscle than they do.

For all his love of women's muscles, Cavigioli says that there's not much danger of his being physically outclassed by a woman—that it's highly improbable he'd find a woman stronger than he is. "By the same token," he adds, "I think many women wouldn't want to be with a guy who's smaller and weaker than they are. I guess it's a deeply rooted cultural thing."

AT EIGHT-THIRTY on a Saturday morning on the Upper West Side, you see them—women dressed in tights and running shoes and maybe an insulated parka over their Jogbras and T-shirts, their hair pulled back in ponytails, with bright-colored stretch-terry sweatbands around their foreheads. They carry no handbags; they walk at a brisk pace, intent on a goal, never deviating from their beeline path for a glance at the shopwindows they pass, never pausing to read the morning's headlines displayed on the newsstands along the way. They are going to the Advanced Step class at Jeff Martin Fitness Studios, at Seventy-sixth and Broadway.

Morning, noon, and night, the music throbs, spilling out of the third-floor windows and into the street when the weather is warm. Pedestrians on their way home from buying groceries at Fairway look up and see rows of bouncing figures. During the multi-impact aerobics classes, the sidewalk seems to vibrate, the way it does when a subway train passes underfoot.

Jeff Martin's clients—the overwhelming majority of them diehard and female—know the rules: they call to reserve a place (each place designated by a number painted on the floor), so that there's no last-minute scramble, no unsportsmanlike scuffles over the chance to stand front and center, next to the teacher. They know the routines so well that they could do them in their sleep. They know the teachers and follow their favorites around town, to the other aerobics studios where they teach.

Martin is a former actor, who says that the decisive moment in his career came when, at age twenty, he landed a part in an Andy Warhol play called *Sky High*, and abruptly lost it because he was too embarrassed about his body to take off his shirt. That experience prompted him to get in shape: he joined the YMCA on Twenty-third Street and embarked on a program of swimming and running on the track. Downstairs, there were aerobics classes in progress. Martin watched them and thought, I could make this so much more fun. There were no aerobics studios in New York at the time, he recalls. In 1982, he opened his own studio in the loft where he was living and put an ad in the paper, announcing a class in "dance exercise." The first day, four women came; the second day, he had five. They dressed for the occasion like the heroine of *Flashdance*, which had just come out. It was five years before he had a full class of forty.

When, four years later, the hair salon upstairs closed down, he took over the space and expanded. Although Martin seems to have a devoted clientele, he regards his position in the Manhattan fitness market as embattled, now that many aerobics studios are losing their constituents to gyms with cross-training facilities. To keep up with the competition, he has added a circuit-training room upstairs, outfitted with a stationary bike, a stair machine, a rowing machine, and other equipment. But it is primarily the introduction of step aerobics that has given his business the boost it needed to stay alive. The plastic platforms are stacked at the back of the studio. "At first, you just step up and step down," Martin says. "Then we add combinations—fun little patterns that keep people happy."

Now thirty-four, balding, compact, and not particularly lean, he cuts an affable, if not especially inspirational, figure. One Saturday afternoon, an hour before the Power Jam class he teaches, he is wearing sweatpants, a brown polo shirt over a white T-shirt, and sneakers. Along a wall in the waiting area, the instructors are represented by black-and-white eight-by-ten head shots. The studio is lit with red fluorescent lights—an idea he came up with ten years ago for a Halloween party and kept, because, he says, it makes the classes "more like a performance." The cast for the class in progress—advanced multi-impact aerobics, led by a guest instructor—is costumed at the start in white socks and sneakers, biker shorts, and zippered warmup jackets and sweatshirts that say "Vanderbilt University" or "Fordham Law." The routine begins with calisthenics and some stretches. As the pace quickens and hair gets damp with sweat, the women peel off their top layers to reveal Lycra spandex racer-back leotards cut high in the rear like thong bikinis, or Jogbras and thong briefs over biker shorts, with a belt at the waist. The teacher, all in white, is rock solid, with big quads; she shouts to make herself heard over Dionne Warwick singing "Do You Know the Way to San José?" The overweight women wear black tights and big T-shirts long enough to cover their thighs. Two lone men wearing biker shorts and Ts go through the moves without a hitch. Twenty minutes into the hour, the energy in the room is surging. A Japanese woman, whose pink sweatshirt and matching sweatpants are in flagrant violation of the unspoken dress code here, gets lost early on; she stands, panicked, flapping her arms helplessly, her eyes on the instructor for some clue to what comes next. Hands on the floor, butts in the air: stretches for the hamstring and the Achilles tendon, alternating legs. When the routine ends, the students file out slowly, stoned on endorphins, savoring the sense that every cell in their bodies is awake. An emaciated woman in the back corner stays behind for the next class, her third in a row.

BILL PEARL, a former bodybuilder whose garage, in Phoenix, Oregon, houses a collection of exercise equipment that dates as far back as the 1893 World Exhibition, in Chicago, says, "The fitness industry is constantly going through cycles." Someone who thirty years ago might have spent three days a week on the ski slopes now puts in three sessions a week training anaerobically at the gym, and skis only once or twice. "Cross-training is a cycle that people will go through," Pearl says, "just like they went through jogging and running, and now they're back into walking again." Among Pearl's most prized acquisitions is a motorized contraption, manufactured by a company called Battle Creek, that took the country by storm in 1936 and 1937, with a vibrating belt that would shake different parts of the body—the idea being that fat could be jiggled away.

Of all the equipment we use to work out, weights have probably changed the most, Pearl says. At the turn of the century, there were Global barbells and dumbbells, first produced by a professor picturesquely named Louis Attila, who opened the first health club in the United States, in 1894. On either end of a bar was a globe with a plug in it; to change the weight, the plug was unscrewed and the globe was filled with sand or shot or water. It was in the mid-thirties that the barbells and dumbbells we know today came into use, and in the seventies that adjustable weights, stacked on a cam, were conceived.

In the early seventies, an inventor by the name of Arthur Jones broke up the old Universal multi-station—a standard fixture in high-school gymnasiums—into separate units, with a different apparatus for each, and called his system Nautilus. This was an improvement, Pearl contends, primarily because it made for better traffic flow at the gym. The newfangled, collapsible rowing machines that fit under the bed are no better than the bulky 1924 cast-iron-and-hardwood model that Pearl has—if anything, he says, he prefers the old one, because it's sturdier. Recumbent bicycles, the latest fad in many health clubs, existed as early as 1902, according to Pearl.

"Wellness" is going to be the next buzzword, he predicts. The high-tech chrome equipment that dominated health clubs ten years ago is now passé; Pearl calls it the Danish-modern furniture of the fitness business. The new trend, he says, is white enamel, which looks more "medical." The latest installment in this gradual transformation of the health club into the fitness clinic is a line of equipment called Lifecircuit, presided over by a computer that acts as a robotic one-on-one trainer: prescribing the amount of resistance and the number of repetitions for each exercise, setting the range of motion, correcting your pace if you're working too fast or too slow, grading your performance, telling you what you did wrong if you scored, say, eighty-five out of one hundred, and, finally, congratulating you if you've done everything right. "If you were to compare one of these machines to an old arm-curl machine from the nineteen-twenties, the basic concept hasn't changed a great deal, but the sophistication has," Pearl says. "I attribute that to the fact that there's not a lot more that you can come up with to do—that the human body hasn't changed all that much over the last thirty-five thousand years."

IN THEIR remarkably tuneless hit song, "I'm Too Sexy," Right Said Fred—guitarist Rob Manzoli and Fred and Richard Fairbrass, two brothers who own a gym in London—list some of the problems a person with a body perfected by exercise might come up against: *I'm too sexy for my car, too sexy for my car, too sexy by far.* In the song's homemade-looking video, footage of fashion shows is interspersed with scenes of the Fairbrass brothers—both completely bald and so well built that their chests look as if they were encased in armor—performing on a runway lined with groupies. *I'm too sexy for Milan, too sexy for Milan, New York, and Japan.* As the two of them walk down the street, a passerby rips off Fred's tank top. (*I'm too sexy for my shirt.*) The moral: if you want a body that drives perfect strangers wild with desire, you'd better be prepared to trade in your car, your wardrobe, your cat (your cat?), your boyfriend or girlfriend—*I'm too sexy for my love, too sexy for my love, love's going to leave me.* Wait a minute. You mean that somebody who's such a flawless physical specimen could actually get left?

DOWNTOWN, AT the Plus One Fitness Clinic, in the World Financial Center, the rush starts around seven-thirty in the morning, when corporate-looking men and women stop in before office hours. In changing rooms that are private bathrooms, each equipped with a shower and a phone, the clients shed their suits and put on gray sweat shorts and T-shirts provided by the management, or sweat shorts and T-shirts of their own. The uniformity gives Plus One the vague air of a Phys. Ed. class. There is no spandex here; the clothes people wear to exercise are almost without exception cotton, neutral-colored, and slightly baggy. The atmosphere is amiable but businesslike, with no bodies on display. Conversation takes place only among people who are evidently already acquainted—colleagues who greet each other in passing and inquire about plans for the weekend or make some remark about how yesterday's meeting went.

In the gym, decorated like a postmodern, Memphis-style ocean liner, in shades of pale yellow, apple green, and battleship gray, the tall windows and twenty-foot ceiling make for lots of light and air. The floor is covered in that rubbery, disk-patterned vinyl that now paves so many airport terminals. The equipment is arranged in long rows—free weights and benches, Cybex machines (with slabs of weights hoisted up and down by pulleys), stationary bikes,

Lifesteps, Upper Body Ergometers (like bikes you pedal with your arms), tread-mills, and a NordicTrack cross-country ski machine—interspersed with long up-holstered tables, a blood-pressure monitor, and mysterious apparatuses that look like cockpit seats, with knobs and gauges, Velcro straps, and computer screens that every so often emit a low-pitched beep. Plus One is a full-service operation, featuring not only trainers but doctors, massage therapists, and physical thera-pists for rehabilitation. A few clients come on crutches, a few others in wheel-chairs. Mike Motta, the founder of the Plus One empire (with branches on Crosby Street, in SoHo, and in the Waldorf-Astoria), brings to the fitness busi-ness advanced degrees in exercise science and applied physiology, and experience coaching college football and lacrosse, and his gym combines the latest research in sports medicine with the rigors of athletic conditioning. Most of the men look like part-time jocks, who maybe played a sport in high school or in college. The women seem out to offset a desk job's long-term effects on their hips.

Motta says that one of the biggest changes he's seen in the ten years since he opened Plus One is in people's attitudes. "They're realizing that exercise doesn't have to be an intense period of torture to be effective," he says. That, he continues, was the eventual downfall of the Nautilus system, which sold not only machines but an entire philosophy of training. "You bounced in and you crawled out" is how he summarizes it: no pain, no gain. Now that studies have proved that burning out the muscle doesn't necessarily serve everybody's pur-poses, the emphasis has shifted, to day-to-day consistency rather than high intensity. Every year, there's a new crop of aerobic gizmos introduced: underwa-ter treadmills, tub-sized swimming pools (for laps in place), downhill ski machines with a map of the slope on a video monitor, and other toys designed to keep people from getting bored. "Training is becoming a whole way of life," Motta says. "People smoke so much less, they drink so much less, they party so much less—they've got to do something with their time."

ON A Saturday afternoon in the dead of winter, at the Vertical Club, just a few blocks north of Bloomingdale's, everybody looks tanned in the light of the red neon lining the running track, which is suspended, like a balcony, overhead. A phalanx of stationary bikers—two rows, a dozen each—is pedalling furiously, going nowhere. All the stair machines are occupied, too. Some people read the *Times* or *New York* or *USA Today* as they climb; others stare at video monitors tuned to MTV or gaze at the mirrors opposite, checking out their fellow-strangers without being too obvious. There is no one on the treadwall, a revolving cliff face that works like a garage door with boulders on it—this is one fitness fad that has so far failed to happen. Upstairs, on the track, a runner is jogging backward.

Several of the men wear frayed cut-offs over biker shorts—a look that one connoisseur of the Manhattan gym scene calls "very hetero." A trainer named Kyle contends that "true jocks only wear cotton." Asked how many true jocks there are in attendance that day, he replies, "About five." Mostly, the women wear bright-colored spandex thong leotards over biker shorts, and jewelry; the men wear designer sweatsuits or Nike tank tops and gym shorts, and jewelry. A longtime regular claims that there is a direct correlation between the shape the women are in and the size of the rocks on their fingers: the prettier the face, the better the body, the bigger the diamond. In the serried lines of stair climbers, there is a thirtyish blonde with uniform features, in a hot-pink spandex midriff top and black biker shorts, who is sporting diamond ear studs, a big gold Rolex, and a diamond ring that looks to be somewhere in the neighborhood of eight carats. Her neighbor to the right, a slightly frumpy brunette in a navy Lycra leotard with bright-green racing stripes and matching tights, is wearing a stainless-steel-and-gold Rolex and, on her left hand, a Cartier rolling ring. There is more makeup and perfume and hairspray here than at most gyms. The women's hair is not so much pulled back as piled up. Even the men look coiffed. What ever happened to sweatbands? "No more sweatbands," the longtime regular says. "Sweatbands are over."

A few of the women wear belts with fancy buckles to dress up their leotards. There are off-the-shoulder leotards, leotards sprinkled with rhinestones, leotards inset with panels of stretch lace. "I've seen stuff here that looks like it came from Victoria's Secret," Kyle says.

The muscles on view are fewer and smaller than the ones at Better Bodies. There is more conversation. Two women sit side by side on recumbent bicycles and discuss the tuition at Dalton. In the aerobic area, mauve carpet gives way to a hardwood floor. A t'ai chi class, led by an instructor with a low, soothing voice, is in progress. The students look like refugees from the glitter all around them—the women in plain, full-cut leotards and the men in fleece sweatpants. A guy in good shape, wearing tricolor spandex tights sewn in diagonal panels, pauses, and sizes up the goings on. "Exercise for ex-hippies," he snorts, and proceeds to the rowing machines.

In the ladies' locker room, a young woman peels off her halter-neck span-dex unitard and changes into a white shirt, jeans, and crocodile cowboy boots. This is a good place to work out if you're single and looking for a man, she claims; she met her last boyfriend, a real-estate agent, on the treadmill. She likes meeting men at the gym, she says, because, to be perfectly honest, you can see what it is you're getting, without the benevolent camouflage of street clothes. Another woman, overhearing this, speaks up. "If you ask me, that's a problem," she says, and explains that when you meet a man at a gym, you can disqualify him at a glance on the basis of his body, whereas under other circumstances you might take an interest in his mind first, or fall under the spell of his humor, and then, she concludes, his flabby arms and the roll of fat around his middle, when you got around to discovering them, wouldn't strike you as so noteworthy and off-putting.

It seems odd now that as recently as fifteen years ago regular exercise was something most women did in private, at home alone, in front of their televi-sions, or in a group, led by a dancer who needed a steady job to pay the rent. Going to an exercise class was like going to the hairdresser—not a secret, exactly, but part of the discreet maintenance that being a woman entailed. You went off to an exercise studio and whittled away at your waist or firmed up your inner thighs, just as you went to the beauty salon and had your hair colored or your nails done. Gyms were nuts-and-bolts, sweaty, fetid places for men who played sports and lifted weights. Exercise studios were more aesthetic, with blond wood and mirrors and spider plants hanging from the ceiling. The exercises that men did were strenuous, meant to build muscle and make them strong. The paces women were put through mostly consisted of stretching, toning, and spot reducing, to make them more supple and give them better figures.

What women wore for these occasions—leotards, usually, and footless tights—made them look more like dancers than athletes. The standard models were by Danskin, in a thick nylon knit with a spongy texture; in a limited range of styles (scoop neck, turtleneck, V neck); and in basic colors like black, navy, red, pastel pink and blue. The alternative to Danskin was Capezio, which offered more necklines to choose from and, eventually, a high-cut leg, as well as lighter-weight materials and a broader range of colors. Regardless, the only options were solids—no stripes or prints—and the knits, all matte, were one hundred-percent synthetic, without a trace of cotton.

Since then, the field has been revolutionized by advances in fabric technology, particularly in stretch fibers—most recently, a fabric called Supplex, which feels like cotton and dries like a synthetic. The branch of the fashion business that these days goes by names like "bodywear" or "activewear" now encompasses not only second-skin knits but also all manner of athletic clothing. Among the trends that industry reports forecast for the near future are: Biokryl, a nylon-and-cotton blend treated with a fungicide to prevent bacteria growth; HoloTex, a holographic fabric for higher visibility; Mitrolite, a fabric that changes color as the person wearing it moves; unitards, leggings, and "bikeatards" (unitards that end at mid-thigh), with tone-on-tone embroidery or patent-leather accents; denim-look sports bras. Unfortunately, a lot of the clothes that come under this category, particularly the ones designed expressly for aerobics, are awful-looking, in gaudy, unbecoming colors, and in prints that qualify as a blight on the landscape. These recent outbursts of reckless bad taste, as if inside an aerobics studio all the rules were temporarily suspended, bring to mind the corollary question—a mystery of long standing—about why people dress the way they do on the golf course, in clothes they wouldn't be caught dead in on the street.

Sports clothes have evidently become synonymous with sportswear in a lot of people's minds. Elderly men and women who never go running dress in jogging suits to travel on a plane. Kids wear sneakers, no matter what the occasion. Suburban mothers shopping at the supermarket are turned out in leggings and T-shirts. In fact, it seems that Americans, who first put casual clothes on the fashion map, have lately gotten even more casual, wearing some form of exercise clothing whenever they're not required to be "dressed up," which by all appearances is more and more often. Probably this has to do with the fact that relaxation equals comfort, and nothing is more comfortable and unrestricting than exercise clothing. Still, there's something preposterous about the idea of an entire nation outfitted in track suits and running shoes for sitting on the couch, watching movies on video, and eating chips. Maybe by wearing exercise clothes we're assuaging our guilt about being lazy and out of shape, the way somebody who's overweight might drink a diet soda with an ice-cream sundae.

AT THE David Barton Gym, at six o'clock on a weeknight, the StairMasters, lined up four to a row, three rows deep, in front of the large-screen video monitor playing *Pee-Wee's Big Adventure*, are all occupied by men, their legs pumping like pistons. They are wearing tank tops belted over biker shorts, or cut-off chinos and sweatshirts cropped to show off their six-packs, with athletic socks and sneakers. There is a high incidence of tattoos, and baseball caps worn backward. The individualists sport do-rags, Keds high-tops, thermal leggings. An occasional woman wanders, invisible, through their midst. A mirror that runs the length of the left wall reflects a frieze of beefy men keeping a careful eye on themselves as they lift and lower, lift and lower heavy weights, their muscles rippling slowly. Conversation is infrequent and brief. The crowd, according to the receptionist, consists mostly of actors, models, fashion-magazine editors, famous hair stylists—Oribe is a regular.

The walls are white; the floor is paved with industrial-gray carpet laid in rectangles. There is no décor to speak of, only the jungle of matte-steel machines, upholstered black. There are no amenities or frills. Variety is not what David Barton has to offer. A trainer himself, he has stocked his gym with the equipment he has deemed the best, and nothing more. There is only one type of stationary bike (recumbent); there are StairMasters but no Lifestep machines. "I'm a purist about gyms," Mark Cattano, one of Barton's freelance trainers, says. "I come to the gym to lift weights. You don't need all the bells and whistles."

In the six months since it opened, David Barton's has established itself as one of the city's more "serious" bodybuilding gyms. Rich Barretta, Mr. America of 1987, now a trainer who works out of Barton's gym exclusively, puts his clients on a low-fat regimen, with protein three times a day, to build new muscle mass and to reduce the body fat that blankets it, for that lean, carefully delineated, "cut" look. He concentrates on a specific group of muscles for each hour-long session. Barretta claims that he prefers training women—that they have better hand-eye coordination, that they work more intensely, and that they aren't so stuck on the numbers. "You never hear one woman ask another, 'So how much can you bench-press?'" he explains. One of his clients, a newspaper columnist whose job it is to be out to dinner every night, on the town, admits that the diet is often inconvenient, because so many foods are off-limits; he trains with Barretta six mornings a week. A first-time observer, amazed at these Spartan ways, asked him how long he intends to live like that. "Until I get a date," he replied.

A quick glance around David Barton's gym is enough to convince even the most casual observer that bodybuilding, like fashion, is a subculture unto itself, with an aesthetic that seems incontrovertible to insiders and utterly mysterious, not to say grotesque, to the uninitiated—an aesthetic that, if the scene here is any indication, seems to have played right into a certain gay male obsession with virility and all its trappings. Among the guys working out with weights are plenty with muscles so distended that they might have been inflated with a bicycle pump—guys who would look to the layman like Popeye, although in their own and in each other's eyes they appear godly, just as fashion enthusiasts decked out in outlandish clothes might find one another attractive and witty but strike the average person as ridiculous. Fashion enthusiasts, however, put on and take off the costumes they wear, while bodybuilders become their costumes.

The use of supplements, and worse, is reportedly widespread. Cattano, who proudly volunteers that his eighteen-inch arms are all natural, deplores steroids and says that he has never competed as a bodybuilder because he's put off by the fact that they're so commonplace in the sport. "That's cheating," he insists. He started lifting weights when he was thirteen, he says, "for fear of getting beat up," and even now, fifteen years later, he claims that building muscles isn't for him an end in itself. "I don't lift weights to get onstage in a pair of bikini briefs and flex." He says he likes Barton's gym because it's down-to-business. When he first came to Manhattan, he worked out at Better Bodies, and while he says he has lots of respect for Brian Moss as an entrepreneur he claims that he prefers to work out at Barton's, if only because the atmosphere there isn't so "cruise-y": at Better Bodies, he says, he used to get interrupted on a regular basis by guys who would come up and ask him what time it was.

AT MIDNIGHT on a Thursday at the sprawling World Gym, at Sixty-fourth and Broadway, which is owned by Arnold Schwarzenegger and open twenty-four hours, the atmosphere is mellow, despite the loud, up-tempo music. The ceiling fans are still. The traffic outside has thinned. On the treadmills and the free weights and the StairMasters and the Cybex machines, upholstered in teal-blue vinyl, half a dozen clients go about their workouts quietly, with an air of preoccupation. The dress is low-key verging on sloppy—the kind of clothes people who live alone wear at home. In front of the windows overlooking Lincoln Center, a woman makes her way down the row of Lifecircuit machines. She's a picture editor at the *Times*, and says she comes here when she leaves her office, at eleven; she is wearing royal-blue spandex tights and a big T-shirt that says "I'll see you in CUBA." Her colleague, a *Times* photographer in a big T-shirt and baggy purple shorts, says he spent the evening covering a murder in Brooklyn, went home and had something to eat, then came to the gym.

Over the course of the next hour, a few more people drift in: a concierge from a building on Central Park South, who works the night shift; a production assistant at ABC News, who gets off at eleven; a financial researcher who works nine to five but often ends up exercising late at night, he says, "because I can't get my shit together." What had he done before coming to the gym on this particular night? "Took a nap, ate, talked on the phone too long."

In the ladies' locker room, an art dealer wearing red nail polish and half-gloves from Gold's Gym is popping vitamins. She says she works out late because it's when she has the most peace of mind, and she doesn't have to keep calling her office. Tonight she came directly from a black-tie benefit, a dance performance followed by a dinner; she keeps special hangers for her evening gowns in one of her three lockers.

A lawyer wearing navy gym shorts and a white T-shirt says he usually comes around two in the morning—this evening he's early. Does he work such long hours? "No," he says as he steps onto the Versa-Climber, a ladder machine. "I'm just a late-night person. I've never slept all that much. This place is tailor-made for people like me."

DURING A recent trip to New York, Franco Moschino, the Italian designer, was struck by how body-conscious and compulsive people had gotten, with their lives arranged around their exercise regimens. No cigarettes, no alcohol, no meat, no fat. No fun. When he got back to Milan, Moschino phoned his trainer. "Don't call me," he told him. "I'll call you."

The Spirit is Willing

*In June 1996, the fact that Hillary Rodham Clinton had met with Dr. Jean Houston—
a leading exponent of the human-potential movement, the author of fifteen books, and a consultant
to several major corporations—came to light. Having engaged in an intellectual role-playing
exercise, in which they "conversed" with Eleanor Roosevelt, Dr. Houston and Mrs. Clinton were
accused by some journalists of holding "séances."*

It is true that Dr. Jean Houston, the human-potential researcher and the occasional guest of Hillary Rodham Clinton, recently came to spend a weekend with me at my country retreat. I was having difficulty writing this column, and she suggested a "brainstorming" session using some of the creative thinking techniques she has developed over years of lecturing at distinguished universities and consulting with executives from major corporations. It is also true that we conducted an imaginary dialogue with Halston in order to help us grapple with some of the more difficult issues facing fashion today. But allegations that we were "channeling" Halston are completely unfounded, and any reference to our sessions as "séances" is a gross distortion of what actually took place. I have never been to a séance.

I was struggling to understand certain uncanny similarities between the present and the seventies. Caftans are back, and polyester. Dr. Houston advised me to choose a fashion expert, living or dead, who might be able to shed some light on the current revival. It was entirely my idea to go straight to the style guru whose cashmere sweater sets and Ultrasuede shirtdresses are being invoked on runways everywhere these days.

Dr. Houston and I then proceeded to conjure an image of Halston in the room with us. "Hello," we said.

"You look fabulous," he told me. "You have a big head in proportion to your body. I love big heads."

"Uh, thanks," I replied. It was impossible to tell whether he was being facetious. I asked him what he thought of Tom Ford's collection for Gucci.

"What I invented is universal and timeless," he declared. All right, fine, we continued, but the world is a different place now than it was when Studio 54 was in its heyday and America was poised on the threshold of all that liberation—women's, gay, sexual. "It's true that times have changed," he said, "but less is still more." Except, we replied, on those occasions when less is less. There is, we told him, some concern within the industry about the fact that the designer's role has changed, that designers no longer "make fashion" the way they did back in the days when his name was a household word. "Designers never made fashion," he argued. "It's fashionable people who make fashion." Yes, we agreed, but where are the fashionable people now? "That's a problem," he admitted. "Most of them have lost their glamour, and the rest are here with me."

* * *

Sackcloth
and Ashes

IN CHARLES LUDLAM's *Caprice*—a play about a highly evolved hermit who, in return for an act of altruism, is reincarnated as Claude Caprice, the leading fashion designer of his day—a character by the name of Zuni, identified as "a slave of fashion," undergoes a change of heart and renounces all that she has so relentlessly pursued. "Good-bye to ladies who lunch and *Women's Wear Daily*," she cries. "Farewell Norell, *adiós* Balenciaga. *Adieu* Dior. Schiaparelli and Chanel, farewell farewell. Howdy! Lady Wrangler." Twyfford Adamant, another couturier and Caprice's archrival, has a brainstorm. "Sackcloth and ashes!" he exclaims. "Perfect for the repentant mood of America!" In no time, sackcloth and ashes are the rage all over the world. "I have seen, in Monte Carlo, an individual dressed in sackcloth and ashes made of heavy silk and black diamonds," announces Tata, Caprice's valet and a spy for the House of Adamant.

Caprice was presented by the Ridiculous Theatrical Company, with Ludlam in the title role, in the mid-seventies—a period that in its anti-fashion sentiments bore a good deal of resemblance to our own. At the end of the play, it is neither Caprice nor Adamant but Tata—in drag, as Nicole Newfangle—who wins the "coveted" Lavender Gloves of Fashion award, presented to "the designer who best exemplifies his time," for his Je Suis Fatigué collection.

The word now is that people are tired of fashion, and that fashion is weary of its own excess. In moving to distance ourselves from the free-spending eighties, we have succeeded in putting them so far behind us that it seems inconceivable that the world could have been such a different place so recently. The shopping frenzy has come to a halt, we're told in front-page stories documenting the demise of department-store chains and President Bush's state visit to J. C. Penney, where he bought four pairs of socks. Meanwhile, members of the baby-boom generation, who were thirtysomething and single when the orgy of materialism got under way, ten years ago, now find themselves on the far side of forty, with children and a mortgage and a full set of adult-size responsibilities.

When the experts are asked to account for the abrupt shift in America's mood, they point to economics and demographics. But other factors have also conspired to bring about the change. Every day, there are matters of life and death—the environment, AIDS, the homeless—impinging on our thinking. In this context, conspicuous consumption, which during the Reagan years was regarded as a badge of personal achievement, comes off as callous and politically incorrect. The heroes of the eighties, who built junk-bond empires and casinos and shopping malls as monuments to themselves, outfitted their wives in dresses by Christian Lacroix, decorated their dining rooms with Napoleonic furniture, and in the process reaffirmed our faith in America as the land of opportunity, lately turn up in the news teetering on the brink of bankruptcy or awaiting trial or awaiting sentencing, and those of us who watched their rise with incredulous fascination can't help feeling that justice has been done. Life no longer seems like the party it was made out to be a decade ago. The people who convened every night on the dance floor of the latest club are now off to A.A. meetings. Sobriety, it appears, is the keynote for the nineties, in our wardrobes as well as in our lives.

The Chanel suit, the uniform of the eighties, with its combined message of career, money, and sex, is losing its totemic powers. Already its glamour has begun to seem quaint, and even Karl Lagerfeld, in his recent collections for Chanel, seems to admit as much, as he ranges farther afield, drawing on hip-hop mannerisms for reinvigorating the old formulas and turning out ever-broader parodies of the house themes until it begins to seem that he's contemptuous of the customer herself, a fashion victim who would buy anything festooned with those interlocking Cs. The Chanel suit (and copies of it) will, of course, remain in our wardrobes, and women will continue to wear it, but what has gradually emerged to take its place in our imagination is an outfit that falls under the category of Clothes, rather than Fashion, with a brand name, like J. Crew or the Gap, rather than a designer's signature on the label.

At the highest level, the New York fashion establishment is still going through the motions: designers parade their new collections on the catwalk, magazine editors continue to photograph and present the clothes as if they were momentous, stores go right on ordering them, and sometimes, though by no means as often as before, customers buy them. But within the industry everyone agrees that these are crisis times. The ideas this past season seemed fewer than ever and farther between; this is not the sort of climate that fosters experimentation. (Interestingly, Marc Jacobs, at Perry Ellis, and Ralph Lauren presented their finest collections to date, suggesting that they're designers who work best within the limitations of established genres—Western in Jacobs' case, nautical in Lauren's.) The Western motif was all over the place, in fact, bringing back memories of the last full-scale Western revival, in the mid-seventies—a time when people turned their back on fashion in favor of "real clothes": jeans and thousand-dollar cowboy boots.

The tide has turned in Europe as well. The clothes being shown there are in many cases getting simpler, stripped of the decoration that has bogged them down for the past decade or so. In Paris, Ines de la Fressange, the former model for Chanel, has opened a boutique on the Avenue Montaigne, selling "basics" like red velvet jeans, suede penny loafers, anoraks, and trenchcoats—clothes that are in the public domain and don't need a famous designer to conceive them. In Milan, Sybilla and Franco Moschino have abandoned runway presentations and invited buyers and editors to their showrooms instead, where the clothes are seen in a "more intimate" context.

But the fashion backlash in Europe is somehow lacking in the reactionary fervor that animates so much of the discourse here. "Is fashion dead?" the alarmists wonder aloud—again. What we tend to forget at moments like this is that although fashion in the *WWD*, designer-label sense of the word may be ailing, fashion in the larger sense—as a means of seduction, as a vague consensus about what's attractive at any given moment, as the expression of some collective fantasy, as a code for information about ourselves—won't be laid to rest until the day when we're all walking around stark naked (and what a dull world that will be).

Fashion-bashing isn't a new, or even a recent, development in our culture. There have been recurrent bouts of it all along, playing directly into our national suspicion of ornament and vanity. In the seventies, our grudge against fashion grew out of a newfound feminism: women were portrayed as the innocent victims of a handful of designers who arbitrarily tinkered with hemlines and silhouettes and colors for the sake of change. "Fantasy" was a dirty word; women were to be taken as they were, on their own terms.

"Reality is the best fantasy of all," ads for Liz Claiborne's fragrance, called Realities, now proclaim. One of the pictures shows a woman taking a bath (the bathroom is small and paved in white tile, straightforward and functional-looking—an average bathroom in a middle-class apartment, with none of the sunken tubs and the gold fixtures and the wide-open spaces that characterized the bathrooms-as-stage-sets of the eighties); she is attended by a guy wearing jeans and sneakers, and a naked toddler holding on to the edge of the tub. The glamour that emanates from a suit by Yves Saint Laurent or an evening gown by Oscar de la Renta—the evocations of the Orient, the intimations of chauffeur-driven cars and four-star-hotel suites and fancy-dress balls—is not what we go shopping for when we shop for clothes these days. "Fantasy" is a dirty word once again, but this time for different reasons. Today, we see fantasy as irresponsible, and reality, with all its attendant obligations, is marketed as its own reward.

If Twyfford Adamant were around to participate in this most recent round of fashion-bashing, he could turn out a line of hair shirts. Instead, there is Giorgio Armani's new A/X Armani Exchange collection. Of all the designers who are making the pilgrimage back to basic clothing, surely none has gone more basic than Armani. Ads posted in bus shelters for his new A/X store, in SoHo, read: "Armani. Store. Clothing. Basics. Period." The invitation to the store's opening was a big steel nut and bolt in a brown cardboard box. The A/X merchandise, displayed in wooden bins, like produce at a market, is mostly priced from thirty to one hundred dollars—considerably lower than the Emporio Armani line, which was launched in the early eighties as a younger, more casual, less expensive alternative to the designer's signature collection.

Emporio Armani was one of the many so-called bridge, or second, lines intended to meet the aspiring middle class halfway at a time when the jump from mass-market to luxury goods was just too big for most people to make all at once. There were skeptics at the time who warned against stooping to the customer—who counselled that part of any designer's appeal was the prestige attached to his or her name. But, whether out of some conviction that people would find it impossible to go back to lower-priced brands once they'd been introduced to higher quality or out of some faith that snobbery would win out in the end, designers insisted that the bridge-line traffic would move only one way: up. Now, with the economy in a slump, it appears that they didn't stoop low enough. In his A/X collection, Armani is underbidding his own bridge line, appealing to a customer who finds even Emporio Armani too expensive. The great success story in this regard, of course—the example that Armani, like other designers, continually looks to—is the Gap, which has been doing a land-office business in casual, inexpensive, simple clothes for the past several years, while the top of the market has levelled off. Most Gap clothes look as if they had always existed, as if no designer had ever messed with them beyond adding a band of contrasting corduroy to line the cuff or deciding to turn out a classic cotton turtleneck in burnt orange. The designer's hand rests lightly on Armani's A/X line, too: the clothes look not so much designed as thought out, and they make no mention of their ties to fashion.

The problem when clothes become as generic as these, however, is that it gets harder and harder to tell them apart: what is it that makes Armani's A/X different from the Gap or J. Crew or Calvin Klein Sport? What is it that a fashion designer is selling, if not his or her individual vision as it plays itself out in fabrics and colors and cut? With public interest in fashion at a new low ebb, it is not, evidently, the shape of a neckline or the placement of a pocket that is going to incite people to part with their money. The best reasons to buy these clothes are not apparent in the clothes themselves.

Often, in fact, it's the *idea* of the clothes that we find becoming. The manifesto for Esprit's new Ecollection promises organic cottons that have been bred to grow in different colors (eliminating the need for dyes), zippers made from recycled metal and plastic, and buttons crafted from reconstituted glass by "traditional" workers in Ghana. There is even a makeup line for women of scrupulous conscience: Origins (a division of Estée Lauder, launched eighteen months ago) offers products that are botanically based, including lipsticks in recyclable plastic tubes.

In recent ads titled "A Plea for Responsible Consumption," Esprit urged its customers to ask themselves before buying something "whether this is something you really need"—a position most manufacturers would regard as suicidal. While other companies may turn over some portion of their profits to a worthy cause, Esprit has cast itself as nothing less than a force for moral change, willing to take the economic consequences for the sake of "a healthier attitude about consumption."

The Gap's current ad campaign, now in its fourth year—a series of portraits of newspaper columnists, jazz musicians, photographers, actors, art directors—offers the prospect of celebrity to people who have been simply going about their business. Esprit and Levi Strauss have turned this idea into contests of sorts: TV commercials for Levi's 501s (filmed by Spike Lee) cast a spotlight on people who have called an 800 number to report what they do (spelunking, talking backward, flying kites) while they're wearing their button-fly jeans; Esprit selects the stars of its ads from the people who send in suggestions for ways to change the world.

More important than the clothes now is what the designers of the clothes stand for: advertising has become a platform for political opinion, attracting like-minded customers—as if a label were a club that the customer could join by buying the product, or an organization that stood for something for which the customer, by buying the product, could cast a vote. Donna Karan's new ad campaign ("In women we trust") features a woman wearing Donna Karan clothes being sworn in as President of the United States.

Benetton's long-running campaign on behalf of global brotherly love culminated last year in pictures of a nun kissing a priest and of a bloody, squalling newborn baby still attached to the umbilical cord; neither gives any indication of what Benetton clothes look like. The Guess campaign is a guessing game: what's the product being sold? Set in country-and-Western bars and the back seats of convertibles, and populated by the kind of women who used to be described as "fast," Guess ads, which may run to eight or ten pages, sometimes show the jeans that are the occasion for them, but more often don't. Ads for Donna Karan's hosiery depict a nude woman crouching on a beach—no hosiery. More and more, advertising for clothing is following the format established by fragrance ads, in which the product is so ephemeral as to be invisible and a moment's impression is everything.

Meanwhile, as fashion designers descend from their pedestals and flock to the low end of the market, manufacturers of luxury goods are scrambling to reposition themselves in the mind of the public. Bulgari, the Italian jeweller, is crusading on behalf of the World Wildlife Fund; Hermès on behalf of the Cousteau Society and other environmental causes. "Fortunoff would like to remind you," one recent radio ad announced, "that fine jewelry is not an indulgence or a display of wealth—it's an heirloom."

IN ALL fashion, there is surely no better barometer of the American public's inner life than Calvin Klein. He says that if his ad campaigns have met with success "it's only because people seem to want something that I'm feeling at the moment." While Klein's clothes, often minimalist to the point of anonymity, are hardly the stuff that history is made of, ads for his fragrances are. Sociologists of the future will find the hopes of the past ten years documented in Obsession's sculptural nudes, who exude a kind of locker-room eroticism (a man caught in mid-stride carrying a woman over his shoulder); in Eternity's beatific images of a family at the beach (a pileup of heads: mother, father, daughter, son); in Escape's adventure scenes (a couple lying on a rocky beach, locked in an embrace, with a mono ski in the foreground). Klein says he wanted to put to rest that fragrance-ad cliché of an ingénue running through a field of daisies— a sentimental image that is irrelevant to the future women imagine for themselves. So he put men and, later, children in the ads, as proof that the women the pictures portray have a full life; he situated them in scenes that are remote but not foreign to us. Klein's progress in these ad campaigns—from the fascination with extreme behavior of all kinds to the romance of marriage and a family to the adrenaline excitement of getaway sports—has been both universal and, by his own admission, autobiographical. Where other companies are now taking the high road, appealing to consumers' social conscience and better judgment, he has stuck to his original tactics. "I'm trying to get at people emotionally," he says. "I'm aiming at what they need and what they're feeling."

The circumstances in Klein's ads are often ambiguous, raising more questions than they answer. Klein says this is intentional. "It's more interesting if I can look at something and not know the whole story, so I can fantasize and use my imagination," he explains. "There's something else going on, and it relates to advertising as well. The whole AIDS problem has changed the way everyone lives. My daughter, all the kids—they're living a different kind of life than we did at their age. I think when people have to be more conservative, when they have to pull back and be careful, that's a time when fantasy maybe plays an even bigger role—through films, through entertainment, through advertising."

A dress by Valentino or a jumpsuit by Jean Paul Gaultier has implicit in its design a description of the sort of woman who would wear it and of the life she leads. Beyond a few dim echoes of James Dean and ranch hands, however, blue jeans have no such powers of suggestion; they've been a fixture of our wardrobes for such a long time now that it's hard to regard them the way we do articles of fashion. So it's left to the manufacturers to create a context for jeans, something to trigger the consumer's imagination.

In a one-hundred-and-sixteen-page advertising supplement to *Vanity Fair* last fall, photographed (like Klein's fragrance ads) by Bruce Weber, Klein staged a rock concert—a world in which jeans are the uniform. "I thought, who are the heroes of today?" he says. "Who are the sex symbols, the people out there that everyone gets excited about? Rock stars are these superstars who earn enormous amounts of money, they have wild crazy lives, and they all wear jeans. Denim and skin—that's what rock concerts are about. I was trying to tie the denim into what's really current, into something that would be provocative." The plot of the supplement, to the extent that there is one, revolves around a group of young men and women, members of a band, onstage and backstage, wearing jeans and leather jackets. A bare-chested guy in jeans manhandles a nude woman (a groupie, perhaps) against the backdrop of a chain-link fence; two pairs of legs, encased in jeans, are intertwined on the hood of a car; a naked man intently eases a woman out of her jeans. There are suggestions of homoeroticism, of autoeroticism—something for everyone. In an interview about the supplement on "CBS This Morning," Klein said, "Jeans are about sex." Jeans *are* about sex in some instances, but they're also about blue-collar jobs and white-collar pastimes. The response to Klein's rock-concert scenario has been, predictably, mixed, with many people finding its premise misguided and tired—like a middle-aged idea of what it's like to be young these days. Still, it picks up the tradition that Klein himself pioneered, in 1980, with TV commercials featuring Brooke Shields in his jeans. ("You wanna know what comes between me and my Calvins? Nothing.") It is Klein's stroke of genius to have portrayed an article of clothing that was essentially utilitarian and proletarian as a fetishistic object.

While most ads for the clothes that qualify as fashion are still standing on ceremony, like an over-the-hill femme fatale who makes eye contact across a crowded room, ads for sports clothes walk right up and start talking personal. Nike is out to reassure women that it knows what they've been through: "You didn't like the way you looked. You didn't like the way your parents looked. . . . You had your first best friend. You had your first date. You had your second best friend. You had your second first date. You spent hours on the telephone. You got kissed. You got to kiss back. You went to the prom. You didn't go to the prom. You went to the prom with the wrong person. You spent hours on the telephone. You fell in love. You fell in love. You fell in love. You lost your best friend. You lost your other best friend. You really fell in love. You became a steady girlfriend. You became a significant other. You became significant to yourself." Presumably, any manufacturer who understands women this well will know exactly what they want in a pair of sneakers.

Sneakers and sports clothes and jeans have the advantage of being familiar and user-friendly. They constitute the uniform we wear when we're off duty, and if we've now invested them with the sort of aura that we used to bring to a Chanel suit, maybe it's because we're looking beyond our work to other areas of our lives for fulfillment. We tend to think of clothes like this as being outside— or maybe even above—fashion, although that obviously isn't the case. (In denim alone, we've been through stone-washed, acid-washed, black, white, and now colors; button fly, Silver Tab, and "relaxed fit.") But in our minds they signify not the death of fashion but its absence, and by wearing them we purge ourselves of the glut of the eighties. Calvin Klein says he believes that despite all the anti-fashion rhetoric in the air, people still want to feel good about themselves when they get dressed; it's just that what makes them feel good about themselves now is different from what made them feel good about themselves during the Reagan years. Ultimately, it seems that most matters of fashion for us Americans come down to moral issues. We may not have invented this complex, but we've perfected it to such an extent that other cultures—the French, for instance, who are more adept at moderation—would surely find it baffling. It occurs to me that in the long run our attitude toward the clothes we wear isn't so different from the mentality that gives rise to binge eating and starvation diets. Fashion isn't dead—we're just swearing off it for the time being.

The Sympathy Vote

There is no question that Gianni Versace's murder was tragic and horrific, that his career was cut short at its height. But in their distress and in sympathy, it seems, many of his colleagues, friends, and admirers have been moved to overstate his place in history. During the past few weeks, it has been claimed that no designer before Versace had mounted fashion shows as large-scale theatrical productions (in fact, Kenzo, Claude Montana, and Thierry Mugler got there before him); that Versace was the first to stock his front row with celebrities (although some fifty years ago, Christian Dior commanded the likes of the Duchess of Windsor, Rita Hayworth, Lauren Bacall, and Humphrey Bogart); that Versace's death is to the nineties what John Lennon's was to the seventies (and yet Lennon embodied the idealism of an entire generation, while Versace stood for the cynicism that is rampant in our culture, for the money and the hype that have become the chief criteria for greatness). In the midst of all this, Versace's true contribution—which is both less sensational and more complicated—has gone largely unremarked. His talent, a gift for innovative cut, was eclipsed by his celebrity: by the time of his death, he was more famous for the company he kept than for the clothes he designed.

And yet when historians look back on our era, Versace will indeed stand as a pivotal figure for a number of other reasons—chief among them that he legitimized vulgarity. The brazen colors and the baroque prints, the hodgepodge of motifs appropriated from antiquity, all smacked of "new money," and he reveled in them, flaunted them, threw them in the face of those who preached understatement. Until Versace came along, new money aspired to the conditions of old money; he reversed the flow, outfitting none other than the Princess of Wales in the clothes of an arriviste and overthrowing the tyranny of elitism—a snobbery based on age-old notions of good taste. In fashion, thanks to Versace, the issue of whether something is in good taste or in bad taste is now moot.

Like Andy Warhol, Versace changed the operative questions in his field. He, too, was preoccupied with wealth and celebrity, though without Warhol's ironic distance. Warhol made those things the subjects of his art, to be held up for scrutiny. In Versace's hands, wealth and celebrity became the twin engines of fashion, the driving force behind our naked dreams.

* * *

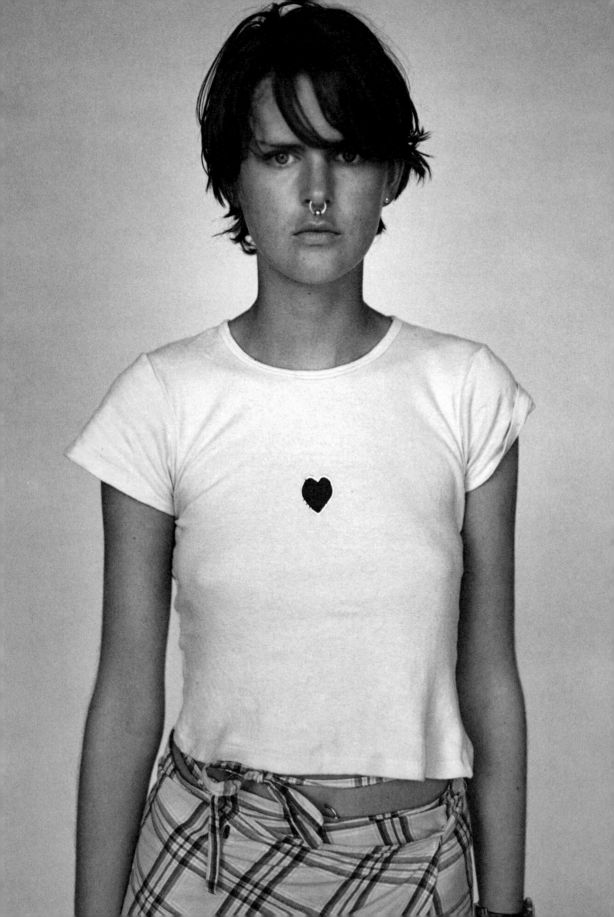

The End of Elegance

WHEN PEOPLE in the fashion business predict the demise of the haute couture, which for years now they've been saying is just around the corner, it is generally because the very concept of exquisite clothes made to order seems so out of date. All that money, all those fittings. All those rows of little gilt chairs with crimson velvet cushions. Even the rules for recognition by the Chambre Syndicale de la Couture Parisienne, the industry's governing body, strike most observers as outmoded: a minimum of twenty workers in the atelier, of seventy-five numbers per collection, of forty-five shows to private clients per season—terms that disqualify many of the designers who have moved fashion forward over the past decade (it is rumored that the Chambre Syndicale is about to relax these requirements; it is also rumored, however, that the changes will be slight). Thierry Mugler challenged the system this season by showing his fall ready-to-wear collection, with roughly a fifth of the numbers made to order, during the five days of haute-couture presentations, even though his house is not accredited as a *maison de haute couture*. Other designers, like Azzedine Alaïa, Claude Montana (whose guest stint as a couturier at the house of Lanvin was distinguished but brief), Jean Paul Gaultier, Vivienne Westwood, Rei Kawakubo, and Romeo Gigli, though they may produce occasional one-of-a-kind pieces on commission or for the runway, send out their message in the ready-to-wear. Meanwhile, the couture has come to rest primarily in the hands of an older generation of more established designers, set in their ways. As for the clients—front-row spectators like Joan Collins and Princess Caroline of Monaco and Ivana Trump—they are not exactly what you would call leadership material, unlike Millicent Rogers and Wallis Simpson and Marlene Dietrich, whom other women looked to in their day as examples. And so, in one of those curious reversals brought on by seemingly inexorable changes in the world, the haute couture, which was once the vanguard of fashion, now finds itself bringing up the rear.

Watching the latest round of shows, for fall, in Paris, I was struck all over again by how quaint they seemed, and by the fact that they're predicated on a notion that most of the rest of fashion has pretty much given up on: elegance. The models walk down the runway enveloped in an aura that is yellowed and fading. When did elegance die? Sometime in the late sixties, evidently, though no one seems to have paid any notice at the time. It may have been a casualty of the sexual revolution, which did away with all restraint, or of women's liberation, which relieved women of the need to work so hard at their appearance, or of the assault on society's established order, which overturned everything that smacked of refinement and sophistication, those instruments of élitism. In any event, when the smoke finally cleared, at the beginning of the seventies, elegance had expired.

My dictionary defines elegance as, first, "refinement and grace" and, second, "tasteful opulence." To judge from the clothes on the runways in recent years, most designers feel that these qualities reside primarily in the past—that elegance is practically extinct, though not, apparently, obsolete, since the yearning for it appears to be so widespread.

Elegant fashion is now, almost by definition, retro fashion. In an interview published in *Discourses: Conversations in Postmodern Art and Culture*, Trinh T. Minh-Ha, a writer, filmmaker, and composer, contends that "Tradition as the Past is a modernist idea," in keeping with the modernist goal: to break with tradition and establish a new and better order. It is in this context, she explains, that postmodernism arises, out of "the reactive impulse to retrieve tradition in its authenticity." This season, Valentino transformed the Palais de Chaillot into a replica of the nightclub on board the *Normandie*, the ocean liner decorated by Jean Dunand, as the setting for a collection—a tribute to Dunand—that looked as if it had walked right out of the pages of forties fashion magazines. "Enter the Era of Elegance," the cover of the current issue of *Harper's Bazaar* (the first under the magazine's new editorship) urges optimistically, alongside a fifties-style photograph of Linda Evangelista. Every so often, a designer like Montana or Gigli or a photographer like Steven Meisel or David Seidner gives us a glimpse of some new breed of elegance, articulated in contemporary terms; but for the most part these are not the images that predominate. The images we find definitive, that crystallize our sense of the present, are arresting, provocative (sexually and intellectually), vivacious, sometimes vulgar; they come on to the viewer. Elegance in this climate is almost always pleasing and somehow reassuring and often striking but finally—oddly—irrelevant.

WHEN "ELEGANT" is used to describe a work of art today, it is sometimes meant pejoratively. In painting and, more recently, in photography, the spell cast by a beautiful image has given way to the impact of an image that acts as the vehicle for an idea. Beauty is no longer the standard to which artists aspire, the ultimate criterion by which a work succeeds or fails. We're beyond that now, artists seem to be saying, and some fashion designers evidently agree.

In a century as secular and materialistic as ours—when God is for many people no longer part of the picture and the self is considered a work of art, when paintings are talked about as "product" and "lifestyle" is a form of self-expression—fashion and art have more in common than meets the eye. Unfortunately, it's the superficial correspondences that spring to mind: Saint Laurent's homages to Braque and Picasso, or his sequinned version of van Gogh's *Sunflowers* as an evening jacket; Perry Ellis's coats patterned after the paintings of Sonia Delaunay; Emanuel Ungaro's haute-couture collection this fall, in which otherwise unremarkable clothes were festooned with appliqués of eyes and lips—token Surrealist motifs reduced to logos and used as decals. For the most part, examples like these serve to confirm the suspicion that designers are out to trade on artists' loftier reputations, that fashion's only relationship to fine art is a derivative one.

As for the legitimate parallels, the most obvious are the ones identified with some familiar movement. Elsa Schiaparelli's inkpot hat topped by a quill pen, her "desk" suit, with drawer pulls on the pocket flaps, were ingenious extensions of the Surrealists' fascination with mannequins and clothing. Halston and Zoran and Calvin Klein in the seventies exercised the principles of minimalism in basic shapes in which the interest was confined to the play of color or texture. That fashion designers have been dealing with many of the same ideas as artists is perhaps not so surprising, though fashion lacks the sort of discourse that takes place around painting and sculpture. The "found" object has come to play an increasingly important role in fashion, in the flea-market chic of Martin Margiela and other designers for whom the act of choice is every bit as noble as the act of creation. It's the context of the runway that confers on these clothes the status of fashion, just as much of the sculpture of our century relies on the context of the museum to be understood as art. Designers now quote each other and the styles of the past as a matter of course, just as artists refer to other paintings, in what amounts to a kind of intramural crosstalk. As in art, a lot of the ridicule aimed at designers and their work these days comes from within the field. Franco Moschino, with his plays on words ("Fashion/Fashioff") and his disdain for the sanctimonious, has become the Marcel Duchamp of the style set.

In recent years, both fashion and art have come to be considered worlds unto themselves—worlds that revolve around marketplaces—and both have begun to seem overpopulated. Meanwhile, the authority of the designer and of the artist has been severely undermined; the designer is no longer in a position to tell people how to present themselves, and the artist, similarly, can no longer tell people how to organize their experience. What is missing now in both worlds is an avant-garde. The notion of a small band of innovators, two steps ahead of the rest of us, capable of scandalizing the establishment and legislating the look of things to come presumes a herd instinct that we seem to have lost. There are still artists and fashion designers whose work shocks certain people, but to no apparent avail. Besides, even if there were some sort of public consensus on matters of art and fashion, we have no reason to believe that the cutting edge of that consensus would be the most innovative place for an artist or a designer to be.

In 1983, the Metropolitan Museum of Art mounted a retrospective exhibition of Yves Saint Laurent's work—the first tribute to a living designer at such a high-profile institution—and it was hailed by people in and around the industry as a sign that finally the rest of the world was giving fashion the serious consideration they had always known it deserved. This, along with the celebrity-journalism treatment that has lately documented every last aspect of the life of the person behind the name on a label, has convinced many a designer that though he may not have the right to call himself an artist, he deserves to be treated like one.

But the problem with thinking about fashion in the way we think about art is, of course, that fashion is not so disinterested; it's a business, and in the end, more often than not, the commercial concerns win out over the aesthetic ones. For all that designers would like to be treated as artists and given the respect that they believe to be their due, the majority of them are unwilling to subject themselves to the sort of thoughtful examination of their work that could qualify as criticism, unless, of course, it comes down in their favor. These issues get especially confused in the case of someone like Saint Laurent, who has for years now been the most obvious candidate for promotion from the category of fashion to the rank of art, not only on account of the quality of his work but also because he appears to be so introspective and tortured. And yet the house of Saint Laurent routinely "decides not to invite" to its shows journalists (like this one) who voice opinions that aren't in keeping with the management's party line—a practice left over from the days when the fashion press's mission was to help boost sales.

THE FEW attempts at elegance that remain these days are not confined to the haute couture, but there are more of them there than anywhere else, if only because, despite the publicity stunts and photo-ops, the audience for the haute couture is, finally, the customers themselves. The ready-to-wear, by comparison, relies much more on theater, playing to jaded retailers and magazine editors who act as intermediaries, interpreting for their constituencies the clothes they see in the shows. Women—most women, at any rate—still consider fashion a service industry, whose job it is to make them look attractive, and if they are often disappointed, not to say appalled, by what they see presented on the runways, perhaps it's because many designers feel that making women look attractive is no longer their duty, or that it's just one of their many duties, and not the most interesting one. Here is where fashion, the clothes that people wear to make them feel good about themselves, and Fashion, the clothes that designers present in order to make some sort of statement about the times in which we live, part company.

The haute-couture clients who had gone to Paris in search of clothes that would make them look pretty this fall surely found them. At Givenchy, there was a becoming black one-shoulder cocktail dress with a velvet bodice and a full faille skirt; at Nina Ricci, a smart beige-black-and-white checked wool pants suit; at Dior, a graceful evening gown of taupe chiffon, twisted at the bodice, worn with one long gold leather glove, like a sleeve; at Christian Lacroix, a ravishing steel-gray draped silk-faille wrap dress, tied off the shoulder with a giant asymmetrical bow. Give or take a few inches at the hemline, plus or minus a little width at the shoulder, these are clothes that exist outside time, in a tradition that is classical; and the type of woman they imply is fairly unchanging, as well.

Some designers—Gaultier, Margiela, Kawakubo, Helmut Lang, and Yohji Yamamoto, to name only a few—seem to be saying that a woman's feeling good about herself these days doesn't come down to looking beautiful. Or, rather, what's beautiful to them isn't beauty itself, with its perfect proportions—the small, even features, the long, slender body—but anything that is interesting and particular, even peculiar. The models who work their runway shows (many of them not models at all but so-called "personalities" and "real people") aren't icons; they're an assortment of characters who look as if they might be worth getting to know. They have lines in their faces, or long waists, or short arms, or big noses. They look engaged, as if they cared about the issues that confront us all. The women on the runway at Yves Saint Laurent or Givenchy, by comparison, seem glamorous and somewhat detached, as if they inhabited a world in which the sky is not about to fall. And so dissonant are these times that there is something unsettling, even jarring, about the harmony that the haute couture projects: the hat, the coordinating belt and gloves, the earrings, the shoes dyed to match.

In painting and in sculpture, women's bodies—naked and clothed—have been a vehicle for high moral principles and for urgent desires, for fascination and for contempt, for philosophies about perception and for techniques of applying paint. Women have been placed at the center of sylvan landscapes or on divans in cluttered studios or on pedestals that elevate them to the plane of ideals. Like a riddle to be solved, Woman has been for millennia one of the main recurring themes in art, and she has yet to be displaced. In fashion, too, she is the subject, the central premise, even if the terms in which she is portrayed today are not as rhapsodic as they used to be. What gave rise to elegance was essentially an elegiac impulse, but we have since discovered the limitations of elegy, and the way it precludes both designers and the women who wear their clothes from participating in any larger cultural debate.

The New World Order

First of all, I just want to say that seeing the movie *Clueless* has made me realize that this class is, like, relevant to my life? That this could be, like, a vehicle? I mean, Alicia Silverstone was the most popular girl in her school, and I think that's because when she stood up there in front of her public-speaking class and took her turn, everybody got a good, long look at what she was wearing. She had the coolest wardrobe! Anyway.

O.K. "The New World Order." So. In Russia, you have the czars running the country, and they're overthrown by the peasants. And in France, it's, like, the same story: the king is out. And in a lot of other countries, too, the people take over and do away with the royalty. "Off with their heads!" That kind of thing. I mean, monarchy is *over*—the whole concept is, like, *finished*—and the aristocracy isn't doing too well, either, since they're, like, part of the same system.

So. Democracy replaces monarchy. As if everybody were created equal, which is, like, a nice idea but, I mean, totally hopeless. And then for class structure you have the whole idea of meritocracy replacing aristocracy. At least, that was the plan. As if the intellectuals were going to take control (hel-*lo?!*), or the artists, or the businessmen. Right.

O.K. So the world *has* turned out to be a meritocracy but not the kind those guys that somebody called "the architects of social change" predicted. I mean, this is a *fashion* meritocracy we're living in! In the immortal words of Coco Chanel, one of my personal heroines: "Adornment, what a science! Beauty, what a weapon!" *She* knew what an impact the right accessories can have. If you, like, read the papers or watch the news, you could get confused and think that the world was being run by politicians and the army generals and the Walt Disney Company. But these are, like, puppet regimes, and the only reason they exist is because the people with the *real* power—looking fabulous—have endorsed them. So you have the people in control, behind the scenes—the ones with fashion charisma—and the ones without it in, like, public office. A place for everyone! "The New World Order"—I'm proud to be a part of it.

Thank you.

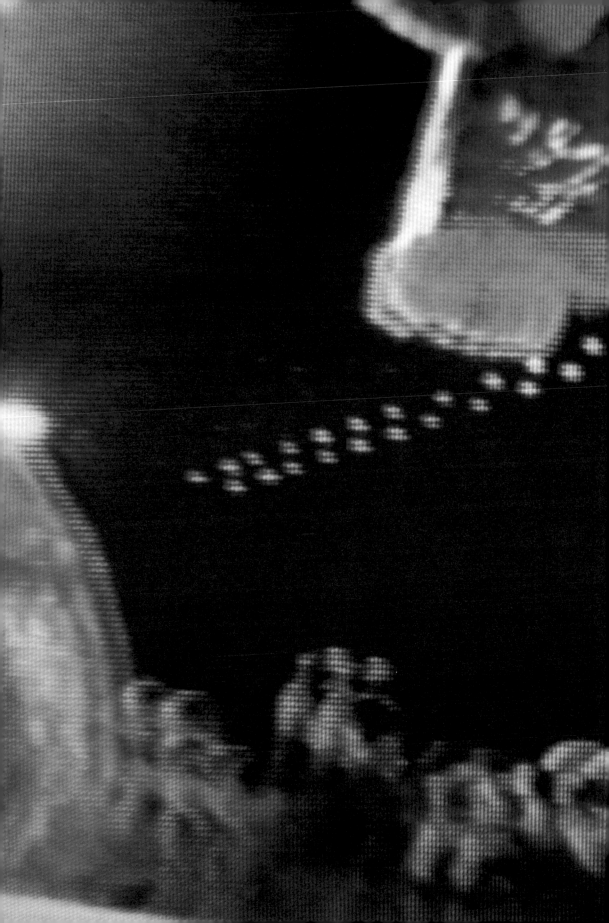

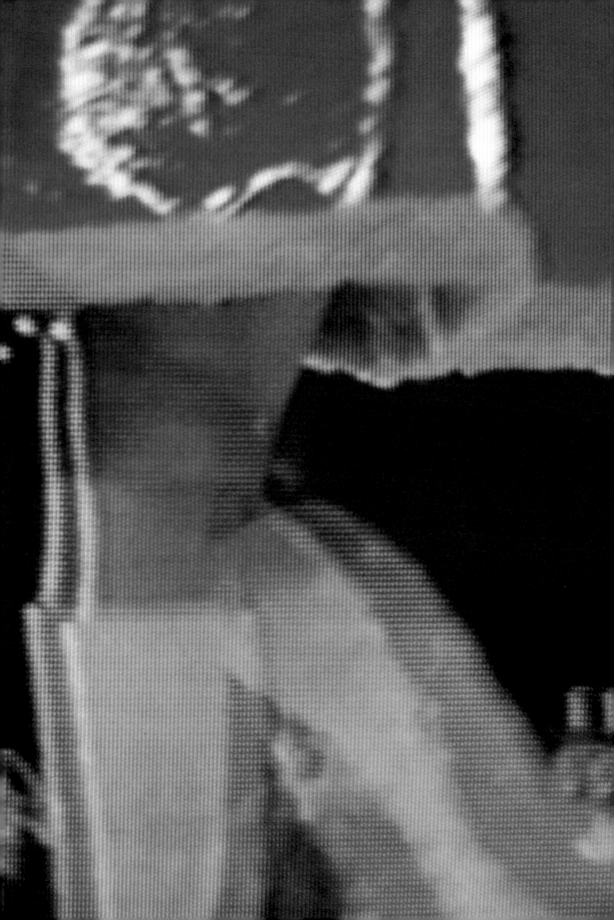

Acknowledgments

My FOND and continuing gratitude goes out to the following people:

Alexander Liberman and the late Leo Lerman, at *Vogue*, for giving me a chance; Bill Whitworth, at *The Atlantic*, who believed in me before I believed in myself; Bob Gottlieb, who made a home for me at *The New Yorker*; and Joe Lelyveld, Max Frankel, Jack Rosenthal, and Adam Moss, who granted me a place within the pages of *The New York Times*.

My editors, Jack Beatty, Alison Humes, and Corby Kummer, at *The Atlantic*; Chip McGrath, at *The New Yorker*; and Andy Port, at the *Times*, for their unstinting efforts and invaluable suggestions.

The various copy editors and fact checkers who over the years cleaned me up and set me straight, among them, Eleanor Gould, Elizabeth Pearson-Griffith, Meredith Davis, Anne Mortimer-Maddox, Rob Hoerburger, Kit Combes, Jaimie Epstein, Linda Magyar, Renée Michael.

My assistants, Justine Cook, at *The New Yorker*, and Lizzie Gottlieb and Melissa Bellinelli, at the *Times*, for coming to the rescue on a daily basis.

Richard Schlagman and Karen Stein, at Phaidon Press, who saw fit to collect these essays in a book; Liza Walworth and Sarah Chalfant, at the Wylie Agency, who fought for it; Megan McFarland, at Phaidon, who painstakingly saw it to press; and Michael Rock, of 2x4, who designed it.

Also, David Seidner, Peter Lindbergh, Mats Gustafson, Paolo Roversi, Martin Parr, Ellen von Unwerth, Carlton Davis, Niall McInerney, the Mattel corporation, and Douglas Keeve and Isaac Mizrahi, who have so generously allowed their images to be reproduced in these pages.

H.B.

Credits

THE ESSAYS in this work are reprinted by permission of the author and were first published in the following magazines:

The Atlantic: "Shoe Crazy," "Quoting Chanel," "Men Will Be Men," "Ralph Lauren's Achievement," "Fat Pride"

The New Yorker: "Life's a Beach" (originally published as "On the Beach"), "Visionaries," "The Eye of the Beholder," "The Religion of Woman," "For Better or for Worse?," "Landscape with Figures," "Fanfare in a Minor Key," "Survivors," "Camelot," "Musclebound," "Sackcloth and Ashes," "The End of Elegance"

The New York Times Magazine: "Serial Dresser," "A Model Bride," "Witness for the Defense," "Shirt Wars," "Natural Settings," "Wrap Star," "Designer Genes," "The Spirit is Willing," "The Sympathy Vote," "The New World Order"

Index